ONE HUNDR

IN

HAMPSTEAD

THE WATHEN DYNASTY

R T Gladstone, nephew;
Headmaster 1920-1929

T H Willes Chitty, nephew;
Headmaster 1920-1922

G A Wathen
Headmaster 1924-1955

Miss K Gladstone, niece;
Principal of Junior School
1928-1960

J P G Wathen, son;
Pupil 1929-1937
Chairman of Governors 1972-

ONE HUNDRED YEARS
IN
HAMPSTEAD

The Story of The Hall School
1889 – 1989

Told by its Staff and Old Boys

Researched by James Earle

Edited by Paddy Heazell

Hampstead · London
1989

The front cover illustration of The Hall is by Paul Hogarth
The back cover, showing the Junior School, is from 'A street scene in Belsize Park' painted in 1917 by R P Bevan (1865-1925) and reproduced by kind permission of the Museum of London

ISBN 0 9514384 0 9 One Hundred Years in Hampstead (pbk)

Printed in England by Cheney & Sons Limited, Banbury, Oxfordshire
and bound by W. H. Ware & Sons Limited, Clevedon, Avon

Contents

*'Notanda Quaedam' was the title given to what might more prosaically be termed 'School Notes', in the earliest magazines of the Marshall era.

Dedication

This history of the boys and staff of the first hundred years of The Hall is dedicated to the 5,000 boys – and perhaps, who knows, girls – who may confidently be expected to enter the school during the next hundred years, and to all staff, teaching and non-teaching, who will 'slave' to support them.

Preface

by Julian Wathen, Chairman of Governors

As I have followed the story of The Hall in these pages, I have reflected, not without pride, that my family has been intimately associated with the school for some seventy of the one hundred years of its existence. My father, G A Wathen, always regarded his tenure of the headmastership as something in the nature of a trust. This has made my task of sustaining and developing The Hall all the more important to me, since I assumed the office of Chairman of Governors fifteen years ago.

But this book is not only about GAW, or 'Dub', as he was known. It is about the whole community, the headmasters from Wrottesley to Cooper and Heazell, the teaching staff, the bursars, secretaries, matrons, caretakers and cooks, the parents and of course the boys – indeed it is a picture of a Hampstead community, changing over the years.

This book has been a labour of love on the part of Paddy Heazell. It has required a lot of research and he has shouldered the load without complaint in spite of several other extra demands on his time – designing and overseeing the Centenary Building and the Appeal that accompanied its construction, all at a period when the educational scene has been enduring hectic upheavals.

Looking to the future, the provision of the Centenary Building represents a major development, eagerly awaited. Its completion will take place at much the same time as the appearance of this book. With its emphasis on new facilities for science and technology and its large activity space designed to meet the needs of physical education, drama and music, it will equip The Hall for the decades ahead. The school has committed £1 million to its achievement. In these days of competition only the best will survive, and The Hall remains determined to stay among the best.

It is my hope that this history celebrating The Hall's one hundred years in Hampstead will in fact be of interest to a wider circle than just its boys and staff, past and present. For I believe that The Hall has played a significant role in the whole story of the development of twentieth century private education. Certainly, I can confidently assert that the portrait painted by the many contributors to the headmaster's book is a fitting testament to a great school.

OWLPEN, GLOUCESTERSHIRE

Foreword

by Raymond Cooper, Headmaster 1955-1976

A picture of The Hall's new headmaster in the *Hampstead and Highgate Gazette* of 21st April 1955 carried also the comment that my predecessor reigned for over thirty years. Thinking back over the twenty-one which were to be my lot I realise how intense were the pressures to change and to resist change. Yet, what the editor of the Hall Magazine once called The Hall's 'life noise' survived and I dare guess it would still be recognised by Gerard Wathen could he experience it today.

It is, I think, essential for an independent school that survives in good health to celebrate its centenary to have a recognisable identity. The flood of children flows on, everchanging, but with sparkling shallows and hidden depths recognisable as belonging only to that one river. So, after a decade away from Hampstead, it is tempting to recall some of the sparkle. I go back to a summer's day in 1954 and an incident, so characteristic of The Hall, which I am quite convinced led to my appointment.

Before the major rebuilding at the Senior School (in 1972), the playground wall ran very close to the old squash court and it took most boys all their school days to master the skill of rolling an old tyre through this gap. 'You try it,' said the retiring Headmaster, and behold my tyre, upright and unwobbling, rolled through and carried me with it.

A little later I was left by GAW at his study desk. 'I'm taking it with me but it will give you the feeling of things,' he said. A boy entered the open door. 'Sir,' he began in that tired voice of the young when all adults are to be mistrusted, 'Mr Bathurst went home last night and left me in the corner. I'm Winkleman,' he added as he realised a stranger sat in the chair of destiny. Not liking to ask if he had been there all night nor foreseeing that here was the first evidence of that exciting unpredictability of prep school life that was cheerfully unlike the ways of the ordered public school from which I had come, I promised firmly to deal with it and felt the authoritative bluff of heads and politicians settling on me.

One of the best reasons for the existence of prep schools at all is that they keep children beyond the age of eleven so that they are at the top of an environment they know and not plunged too soon into a world in which teen-age tensions rule. This can be rewarding for all and particularly so for the gifted, who learn most from each other and from having time to know each other and hence from asking questions and not just 'being taught'!

There were always for me decisions to be made and it soon became clear that boys could be as shrewd as adults when our life together had to be discussed: not pupil power but pupil view, which was not always right but at least always to be respected. I soon learned that any changes I proposed resulted in howls of protest from the staff, whoops of joy from the boys and some three hundred different opinions among the parents. Then it was that we decided to do away with the school bells, to abandon that pink cap, ration daily announcements at assembly, treat prefects as advisers and not policemen and to ask questions (if not always find answers), like 'Why does the school supply books, carpentry tools and footballs but not violins and clarinets?'

It is very easy in the prep school world to take routine trivia too seriously and treat injured innocence lightly. For ordinary men, a wife is essential – the right wife.

Ninette gave health to the boarders, noticed the lonely day-boy, picked up the contents of a match tea deposited from an open car door in Fitzjohns Avenue, coped with the boy who had to be taken to hospital attached to the lid of his desk when his thumb stuck in the ink-well hole, knew the domestic staff worries (and only told me when I asked!), and could be relied on to find the right hat to grace the formal occasions of the year.

At the time of the seventy-fifth anniversary, we received an indignant letter from The Hall's only known surviving Old Girl. As guest of honour at the prize day, she described the lonely walk to The Hall across the fields from the other side of the Finchley Road. That was a hundred years ago now.

What can 1989 do to match that, I wonder?

Anyway, the very best of health, hope and happiness to The Hall and all who slave in her as she sets sail into the second century.

Hinc in Altiora? I am not so sure the heights are always to be found later.

Acknowledgements

The authorship of this work has been undertaken in circumstances which may go some way to explaining its apparent shortcomings. But for the patient and painstaking efforts of Mr James Earle, who acted as chief contact with the Old Boy correspondents, who compiled vast portions of the story from the magazines and who served as critic, corrector, advisor and encourager, the project could never have been completed. Other members of the staff have likewise assisted by providing a critical eye for parts of the text; notably here, Mr Terence Wincott and The Reverend Michael Vine, whose reflective analysis of the most recent years has in part prevented the last chapter becoming an uncritical autobiography!

I must express my gratitude to many Old Boys who have provided me with such a rich wealth of material from which to draw for the final section of this book. The very quality of so much of their writing speaks volumes for the standard of the English teaching they clearly received at their prep school. I would like to add a particular word of thanks to Mr Edward Blishen for the gracious enthusiasm with which he greeted my amateur efforts at editing his professional words.

Any book that is undertaken by a part-timer who is unfamiliar with the business of authorship, and that is published privately, without the benefit of commercial expertise and promotional skills, must rely all the more on the guidance of the professionals involved in its production. I could never find a wiser mentor than Mr John Cheney, printer and, for his long and loyal service to The Hall over the years, honorary member of its Common-room.

Finally, I must record my appreciation of the Governors of the school who have permitted this centenary venture to go ahead by underwriting its cost, and of my staff and my family, who have tolerated my periodic disappearances behind a word-processor screen.

P H HAMPSTEAD 1988

An Introduction

The Hall, Hampstead is probably the oldest surviving school for boys in what must surely be one of London's most ancient and affluent boroughs. For this, if for no other reason, its story ought to be told. A hundred years ago, the establishment of small private schools to prepare the children of the swelling ranks of the middle classes for entry to the increasingly prestigious public schools was commonplace.

The first claim to distinction therefore for The Hall is the very fact that from just such origins it did not wither, but grew strong roots, expanded, and unlike so many of its contemporaries and rivals, survived to celebrate its centenary.

The Hall's location, in a highly prosperous, vital area of the metropolis gives it a second claim to individuality, to justify this history. Over the past ten decades, it has been chosen as the preparatory school for their sons by an astonishing string of peculiarly interesting people. This is no sycophancy or snobbism that seeks to claim by association some special distinction through such links with so-called celebrities. The fact is that Hampstead families, spiced and leavened by a totally exceptional number of immigrants from, in particular, central Europe and the New World, have been independent-minded, inspiring and original. Hall boys have come from as interesting and stimulating a variety of homes as it is possible to imagine. Whether or not they have in their turn become celebrities (and who is to decide what these are, or whether it is to their credit to be so judged?), they have seldom been dull.

A further reason for claiming a peculiar distinction for The Hall has been the stream of significant personalities associated with its establishment and expansion.

For the very scale of its operations (it was to grow by the 1950s into a school unusually large for its day), for the uniqueness of its founding fathers, for the progressive thinking that pervaded its walls and above all, for the long procession of supreme individualists who have filled its classrooms, on both sides of the teachers' desks, this story is well worth the telling.

'School histories are usually bread and butter affairs, the aim of which is to provide a plain chronicle of events which offends no one. Such histories are not inaccurate but they can be dull.' So wrote Dr John Rae, formerly a governor of The Hall. He was commenting on a recently published account of the story of Westminster, one of The Hall's most admired 'feed' schools. Neither Westminster, nor in its more modest way The Hall, has ever been in serious danger of sliding towards that safe mediocrity or complacent conformity that leads to dullness. Without ever succumbing to the sensational extravagances of the greater public schools, The Hall has a history of intrinsic importance, interest and amusement. It is the author's hope that it will prove headier fare than mere bread and butter.

PART I: THE FIRST FORTY YEARS

Chapter 1
An Outline History

In 1964, The Hall celebrated its 75th anniversary. A number of pleasant events were arranged to mark the occasion, but the historian is chiefly grateful for the special edition of The Hall Magazine which provides us with a wealth of detail about the preceding decades. The principal author was Mr P G Drury-Lowe, the Senior English master at the time. A number of other articles were included. This chapter is largely, but not entirely, an edited compilation of these various contributions.

The first recorded headmaster of the school which was to evolve into The Hall was Francis John Wrottesley, who was born in 1848, the son of the then Rural Dean of Brewood, in Staffordshire. He went to school at Marlborough, then as now a great school for the sons of clergy, and thence to Worcester College, Oxford, where he took a degree in classics. He was afterwards ordained and held a curacy at Chichester, where he met and married a Miss Agnes Mabel Freeman. He was next curate to his father at Bishop's Wood, near Brewood, and close to Boscobel of 'Royal Oak' fame, and then came to Hampstead.

He lived at 18 Buckland Crescent and acted as an assistant clergyman at nearby churches. By now, however, he was the father of a growing family of boys, and the problem of educating them prompted him to set up his own school, taking in some fee-paying pupils to help make ends meet. The year in which he formalised this school was 1889, some eight years after his first arrival in Hampstead. There is some evidence that a private school, called the Belsize School, existed in Belsize Park prior to this date, but the institution which gave birth to The Hall as we know it was F J Wrottesley's small school in Buckland Crescent. His three growing sons provided the nucleus – and impressive boys they must have been. One became a Captain RN, the second a director of the biscuit makers, Huntley & Palmers, while the third ended as a Lord Justice. Moreover, he had, for his day, the right sort of scholastic background, and his wife had drive and organising ability, so they made a good pair to start a school. They both professed high ideals and accordingly acted within strict rules. Wrottesley was a good teacher in many subjects but was probably best at making classics interesting to the young. No doubt he was assisted by books like Church's *Stories from Homer* and *Stories from Virgil.* A copy of the latter, awarded as a prize in 1891 is still in the possession of his grandson, A J F Wrottesley, who came to The Hall and became the first Chairman of Governors in 1952. F J Wrottesley was keen on teaching and enjoyed his spell as headmaster.

As his sons grew, so the urgency to maintain a school disappeared but not the problems of keeping up the numbers to sustain it financially. In 1898, these numbers had in fact dwindled to an ominous thirteen. At this juncture, Wrottesley was offered the living at Denstone in his native Staffordshire. He was fortunate to find a purchaser for his school, and armed with his presentation gift, a silver teapot still in the hands of the family, he moved north, to make every bit as good a country parson as he had been headmaster. He retained his link with the educational world, being an honorary chaplain of Denstone College, and he never ceased to deny his pride and pleasure at having been a schoolmaster.

He was not a very fit man, and in view of the energy he devoted to his various tasks, including his commitment to local history – he was a founder member of the Staffordshire Historical Society – it was rather a wonder that he lived on to 1922.

His successor as Headmaster of Belsize School was also a clergyman, but one rather more committed to the profession of teaching, and aware of the particular challenges involved in running a school.

The Reverend Douglas Hamilton Marshall was born on 25th June 1866 and was educated at Fettes and Worcester College, Oxford, where he was ordained. He was a considerable classical scholar and had a deep knowledge of Shakespeare, whose plays he could bring alive for boys without difficulty.

Marshall, or 'DHM' as a generation of small boys affectionately knew him, was a Victorian parson in an age when parsons were not in short supply. He had much of the narrowness of that age, and in any gathering of people – apart from small boys – was reserved and shy. He had been strictly brought up in a Victorian household. He disciplined his own manner of life and expected the same from others. He found anything false or shallow intolerable, and it did not take him long to find out that to be a parson in a country town with its compulsory Victorian tea-fights would be no life for him. He may have been encouraged in this also by his own shortcomings as a preacher.

The only outlet for his talents was schoolmastering, and he set about it by taking over Belsize School. Just before becoming Headmaster he had married a Miss Jane Harding, who had a London University degree in mathematics, which she was to teach throughout their partnership.

Marshall's arrival fairly quickly inspired the important increase in numbers of pupils which was essential if the school was to survive. It seems that besides being a forceful teacher whose successes included Winchester scholarships, he had a way with him, for one of the pupils of his later years at The Hall, Robert Bevan*, records that it was obvious to him even then that he was extremely highly thought of by parents. Apart from his own entrance exam, which consisted in reading from a very solid *Times* leader, he remembers Mr Marshall's 'grey tweeds and very straightforward look' – a look which was sometimes perhaps a sight too straightforward for small boys.

As numbers neared the fifty mark larger premises became necessary and Mr Marshall did not have to look far for them.

One of Marshall's pupils at this time was H W Dallas, who entered Belsize School in 1904 and left the same term as Marshall, in 1909. His description of the events that followed and of the personality of the man who shaped them is taken from the 1964 account of the development of The Hall:

> When I went to Belsize School in September, 1904, there were then less than 45 boys, but so fast growing was Marshall's reputation in the neighbourhood that expansion was by then a matter of urgency. He arranged to exchange the Belsize building for that of a girls' school at The Hall, Crossfield Road. The exchange was carried out in the summer holidays of 1905 and Belsize School re-opened at The Hall in September of that year. There he remained until April 1909 by which time there were over 100 boys in the school. About 40 of these finally went with him to Ovingdean, Brighton, where his ambition to run a preparatory school of boarders only was realised.
>
> DHM was, then, a strict disciplinarian and a stern master, but this was no more than in tune with the standards of those days. Corporal punishment was rare and then only administered with a light cane across the hand – one or two cuts. A small boy I remember received a cut or two from Marshall on the hand for what nowadays would I expect be regarded as the trifling offence of shouting 'Hell', and his plea that he had in fact uttered 'help' was not accepted! Indeed what was regarded as an attempt to wriggle, so far from improving his prospects, only served to make matters worse.

*R A P Bevan, Head Boy, Scholar to Westminster and subsequently to Christ Church, Oxford, and son of the noted artist, Robert Polhill Bevan, whose portrait of the Junior School appears on the back cover.

The punishment was not in public, though the tears which followed were.

He was more inclined to keep a boy in, and give him extra work or a punishment task, and the punishment was generally selected to fit the crime. Mrs Marshall, however, I recall keeping *me* in, whilst others played, to write out 20 times or so the word 'renunciation' because my handwriting had not been up to standard. I had no idea what the word meant, and I did not see the need to ask. There perhaps was the basic difference between his methods and hers. He would have told me, and probably have given me its derivation.

DHM's capacity for teaching both classics (Latin and Greek) and the English language, all of which came easily to him, was immense, and he had a natural ability to hold a class interested and attentive. He was, in short, a born teacher.

That he had this ability and could inspire others too, was indicated by the Honours Boards*, and the variety of schools, both great and small, named upon them. I remember as an old boy of my public school, where many of us had gone, talking to a master there about him. That master told me that any boy from DHM was welcome, because of the soundness of the grounding he gave.

We all had a great respect for him, and if we held him in awe, it was largely because we had not done all that we were capable of doing, at any rate in his opinion. Laziness was anathema to him, and he would shout and bellow at his culprit. He had an unfortunate disability in having a tongue too large for his mouth, which caused him in his wrath to splutter, at times excessively. In his abuse however he remained classical and would bark at a delinquent such lines as 'You BLOCK, you STONE, you WORSE than senseless thing.' The sibilant exuberance of this not infrequent outburst gave rise to many a shower bath, not necessarily involving the offender only, or, for that matter, at all, for whoever was nearest got it! But as soon as out, it was all over, and boy and book mopped up.

He never lost the interest of those he taught. He had a strong sense of humour and would interlard his teaching with anecdotes, often against himself.

At The Hall, Marshall inaugurated Sunday afternoon services, and there we learnt, twelve at a time, to dress ourselves in cassock and surplice, to the admiration of our doting parents, and the disgust of our less doting sisters, who were wont to attend in fair

*The Honours Boards no longer exist, which is perhaps in line with The Hall's proclaimed attitude towards them. A less ostentatious and certainly more dignified substitute is the very handsome Honours Book, with inscribed leaves of vellum, listing the names of every award winner since 1900. No record exists before this date. See Appendix 5 on page 239.

numbers. We also learnt to read the Lessons, and what it felt like for an hour or more beforehand. It was his gentle and kindly words of encouragement while giving us a trial run as we shivered in our shoes, and his words afterwards, that softened the ordeal.

If, however, in school he was a stern disciplinarian, in the hours of play he would continually contrive things for our amusement. Of those times, Sunday evenings remain clear in memory. He himself was a beautiful reader, notwithstanding the impediment mentioned above, and on those evenings all boarders would assemble in the boarders' sitting room for about an hour before supper. There, having dished out a sweet or two to each of us, he would engage us in an intelligence test of some sort for a short time, and then read such books as *Sherlock Holmes*, then very popular with the young, and *Tom Sawyer* and *Huckleberry Finn.*

No words about DHM would be complete without mention of his wife, who was called 'Janie' behind her back, to whom he was devoted, and to whom he had been married by the time he died for about 50 years. I never knew if they celebrated their golden wedding, but if not, it must have been a near thing. They shared to the full their joys, their sorrows, their successes and their disappointments.

She lived indeed a full life. She taught mathematics and to a lesser extent modern languages. She also did most of the housekeeping, and acted generally as DHM's secretary. Looking back, one wonders when she ever had a moment off. She was a vital person and played a vital role in the school, and was responsible in a large measure for its success. But for all her knowledge of mathematics, her teaching was less sound than that of DHM, and it was to the clever boy only that she appealed.

They were in fact exact opposites which was no doubt the reason why their partnership was what it became. If *he* had the untidiest writing imaginable, *hers* was of the neatest and a thing of beauty.

He regarded classics and the English language as all important; mathematics, which he did not understand, he had no time for, looking upon them as a necessity for examination purposes only. *She* was never happier than when explaining an abstruse problem to us on the blackboard.

He could grip a class by the interest he inspired, a gift *she* did not really possess.

She walked with short, quick, decisive steps. If, as sometimes happened, we went out with her to fetch and carry, it was known as 'going for a run with Janie'. *He* had an ungainly splay-footed walk.

After his death, Mrs Marshall said to me, 'Mr Marshall was, I think, the most untidy man ever, but on the whole I think I like an untidy man'. And there perhaps she spoke for many women.

Both were upright and honourable, both abhorred an untruth, deceit or hypocrisy. Had one been asked to find an epitaph for DHM no better choice could perhaps be made than a verse from a favourite Lesson of his, read, at his behest, by countless small boys both at The Hall and after at Ovingdean:

> 'Let us hear the conclusion of the whole matter;
> Fear God and keep His commandments, for this is the whole duty of man.'

As for so many schoolmasters of that age the First World War was also a personal tragedy. He and Mrs Marshall, like all their kind, were deeply affected by the constantly increasing number of deaths of those they had taught.

Settled in Crossfield Road, the school had prospered fast and was clearly very soundly based. By 1909, its number had exceeded the 100 mark. When Marshall sold the school to Mr E H Montauban, he moved south to the boarding school he always wanted to run and became Headmaster of Ovingdean Hall, Brighton. He took almost 40 boys from The Hall with him, a blood-letting which Montauban's school survived with only a mild shudder. That the pied-piper charms of Marshall could woo so many was a tribute to his capabilities; equally, that Montauban survived the skimming off of the cream so quickly demonstrated the strength of The Hall by the third decade of its existence. Academically, the pre-war years were lean. By 1915, things had fully recovered, and the records show that no less than eight major scholarships or exhibitions were won (in a school with a top year of less than 20). Among them was one destined to become a noted scholar of distinction, W A H Rushton, who was elected a Fellow of the Royal Society in 1948.

Curiously little is known of the man who, for some 15 years not merely sparkled, but established the scale of The Hall as it is now recognised. He arrived as an experienced headmaster, having spent several years as Headmaster of the Junior School of St Lawrence, Ramsgate. He left to set up yet another school, and covered in the glory of being the prime mover in creating a major public school. Research fails to reveal much about his background, nor about his subsequent career. Yet, while he was at The Hall, he was undoubtedly a remarkable man. One of his old boys was K R A Hart, who wrote of his recollections of the Montauban era as follows:

> A humorist, Montauban was also a consummate quick-change artist, and the twinkle in his eye could yield in a split second to an ominous frown for the terror of juvenile malefactors. All, however, soon understood this, and had great affection for the tall,

> slightly stooping figure, who sported a dark moustache and had a mole just beneath one eye.
>
> He is said to have declared at the outset of his headmastership that he would never have more than seventy boys in the school – 'otherwise I can't possibly get to know them all as well as I want to.' One way at least of getting to know them all he certainly had – by refusing to allow any master to teach scripture. This he taught himself, to every form in the school, and he had a way of doing it that was all his own. Boys were taught, for example, to remember that Hiram was king of Tyre by remembering that Hyams – a firm of children's outfitters – sold attire, a dubious mnemonic seeing that it was quite easy to forget both facts!
>
> Parental vagaries held no terrors for 'Monty', as we called him. The mother of a boy more noted for brawn than brain waxed indignant with him for some real or fancied slight to her son and told him that he, as a headmaster, 'had favourites'. 'Well, at any rate', rejoined Montauban smiling, 'you can be proud of his carcass'.
>
> There was, too, yet another aspect of his headmastership which deserves mention. On occasion he would accept into the school the physically* and even the mentally handicapped. He went to great lengths to be sure that the former took every part in games that was possible to them, and to see him instructing and helping the latter was an object lesson in boundless tolerance and sheer, uplifting faith. One memorable instance was his explanation to a deaf-and-dumb boy on the cricket pitch of when a batsmen was 'out' and 'not out'; another, his quiet but firm insistence to a mentally extremely backward boy that certain matters usually coped with in private must not be dealt with in public.
>
> General knowledge he taught with 'general knowledge cards' – a self-explanatory system of question and answer, from which it is highly probable that he learned as much as his pupils. Sometimes he could be downright naughty.
>
> 'Caviare', I remember he once boomed, 'is the stur of the roegeon'. Then to a supposedly not very bright boy, 'What is it?'
>
> 'The roe of the sturgeon, Sir,' said the boy wearily as the humorist laughed against himself.
>
> Boxing was another thing in which he was particularly interested and we used to have to bring benches down the stairs into the hall itself to form 'rings' in which we boxed under Montauban's severe eye.

That Montauban was a dedicated and devoted teacher who could hardly have done other than schoolmaster is clear merely from the

*The writer of this reminiscence was himself a severely handicapped spastic. See Appendix 3 on page 233.

record of his time at The Hall but he was a fish well able to swim in other and often bigger ponds. He gave up The Hall to Mr R T Gladstone in 1919 but continued with his wife to run the Junior School★ for boys under eight, by then in the stately building at the junction of Buckland Crescent and Belsize Park, which he had bought in 1916 as providing additional accommodation to house three forms of the younger boys. In 1923 this Junior School was gathered in under the aegis of the new regime at The Hall (Senior), as it is now called, and Mr and Mrs Montauban moved off from their residence at 11 Belsize Avenue to 60 Avenue Road, where this time they set up a girls' school called Selwyn House. It seems they were a pair who could not help setting up, or being in at the birth of new schools. Stowe would probably never have come into existence but for his driving efforts and determination.†

The reader may wonder what fate befell The Hall during the 1914–18 World War. To be truthful the answer, if one is speaking in terms of upheaval as it came to be understood during the Second World War, is that 'business was much as usual'. In fact rather better, for in 1918 there is mention in the magazine of the school being 'positively bloated with prosperity' and of buildings 'bulging' with boys. The war seems to have intruded little, though in the magazines for these years there are some poignant reminders of what was happening to men so many of whom were little more than boys. As late as 1916 a close description in one issue of frightful wounds suffered by an airman Old Boy can be followed by '"Dulce et decorum est pro patria."' – thus truncated – and then, 'it was hard luck to be put out of action in such a way, and if we know anything of British grit, it is this that he will regret most.' The next paragraph begins blithely, . . . 'Swimming (we hear) has been very useful to M at Uppingham.' Indeed delight at the acquisition of new playing fields at Preston Road beyond Wembley, in 1917, seems to have occupied the minds of staff and boys quite as much as the war.

So far, the Great War seemed to be affecting the life of the school remarkably little. Then, from out of the blue, the quite unimaginable thing happened. W H Copinger, the master who was already the linchpin of the teaching staff and was to become the veritable Mr Chips of The Hall, was called up for service in the Army, in early 1917. In fact he never made it! The Board of Education intervened and classified his work at The Hall as being of higher priority. Perhaps the most interesting aspect of this episode was the school's reaction to the temerity of the military authorities, as voiced in the pages of the magazine. It adopted a tone of near apoplexy: ' . . . it is no part of a

★See below on page 32
†See below on pages 10–14

man like Mr Copinger's job to clean up the horrible mess into which the country has been plunged . . . Training boys who are the future soldiers and builders of our Empire is of national importance . . . .' If the sentiments that ring out from the editorial are to be taken at face value, then it clearly goes to show how little the war impinged on an intelligent adult civilian in the capital city, and hence, on the school itself. Later that same year, the editor reflected on a Government request to all schools to break up for Christmas by a given date: did this apply to schools like The Hall, he wondered, as if such prestigious institutions were quite above any such forms of restriction. He had the grace to conclude however that there must be good cause for the 'very reasonable request – in the circumstances . . .'

This ostrich-like but, at that time, not uncommon attitude in certain circles seems to contrast oddly with Montauban's next decision. Although in the event it was no more than a mild hiccup in the evolution of the school, it could have had quite dramatic consequences. In the story of so many prep schools, wartime evacuations proved fatal to the continuity of their pre-war pattern of development. Often, the school never returned to its original home. In 1918, Montauban took the risk of allowing the school to become split into two sections when he sent about half of the boys to his own big house in the country, Balmore, at Caversham, which was in those days an unspoilt village on the Thames, near Reading.

The timing of the move, the early summer of 1918, was slightly odd, for the major threats of impending disaster at sea and on the western front were by now past.

Having stuck things out for nearly four years one begins to wonder why Montauban decided so late in the day, and with the school seemingly in perfectly good spirits, to risk breaking it up. The air raids were trifling and considered so even then, and if the Germans had overrun England, Balmore would have been no safer than London. As the magazine records, 'it was a move fraught with peril. It might succeed or it might endanger the whole future of the school.' One is rather driven to feeling that Montauban himself was either tired and needed a change of air but could not bear to take one without his boys around him – or was simply trying a little experiment of his own on a sound pretext!

But now read the magazine editorial covering the school's splitting up:

> The majority of the boys seemed anxious to go down to Caversham for the idea sounded . . . attractive. It had one great draw-back, however, which was that the fellows down at Caversham would see nothing of any air raids that might occur . . . We want to be in it

> . . . and while the fellows left behind in Hampstead will be in the middle of all the excitement, those down at Caversham may not even hear the guns . . .

At all events there remained at Hampstead only about thirty boys, with Mr Carpenter in charge, whilst forty or so found grass under their feet with Squire Montauban. It seems too the Balmorians, soon grown bucolically uncommunicative, came to be regarded with some slight resentment by 'the old school', as those at Hampstead for a time styled themselves. By March 1919 however, everybody was back at Hampstead and at the end of the same year Montauban announced, in rather veiled terms, what amounted to a change of headmastership. Mr R T Gladstone and Mr T H Willes Chitty, masters from prep schools at Elstree and Haslemere and 'genuine public school men', as Montauban pointed out in a kind of farewell note, came in to run the Senior School, whilst the old Headmaster continued at the Junior, till 1923, presumably watching for a time to see how the Senior fared.

Undoubtedly, the chief reason for Montauban's waning interest in The Hall was his deep involvement in the foundation of Stowe School. Because of The Hall's connection with this remarkable event, it is not out of place to include a brief explanation of the role played by The Hall's Headmaster.

In 1975, R A Harrison wrote a Memoir of the Preparatory Schools entitled *How Was That, Sir?*. With all the authority of his 45 years in school-mastering, latterly as Vice-President of the IAPS*, he was so mindful of the significance of E H Montauban's role in helping to found Stowe that he devoted a whole chapter to this momentous episode in the history of prep schools – when IAPS initiative was instrumental in the creation of a major public school. A relevant passage from this chapter follows:

> To the great majority of our members E H Montauban is just a name, a rather unusual one that they have seen somewhere but cannot remember where. Some may be able to locate him as one of the seven Headmasters who put their signatures, on our behalf, to our Memorandum and Articles of Association. This was in 1923 and his address was given as Belsize Junior School, Hampstead, better known to us today as The Hall.
>
> Edward Montauban had another reason for remembering 1923, for it was on 23 May of that year that Stowe School, under the Headmastership of J F Roxburgh, opened its doors to its first pupils.
>
> The end of the Great War had come more quickly than many had expected. Among the other problems that followed in its wake was

*Incorporated Association of Preparatory Schools

the tremendous pressure upon the public schools which found themselves quite unable to cope with the unprecedented demand for places which suddenly confronted them. It was impossible to find a vacancy at any of the better-known schools for a boy who had already reached his ninth birthday.

The Council of the IAPS was naturally alarmed, but few among them had the courage or vision of Edward Montauban, who was convinced that the only possible answer was to found a new public school. Right from the beginning he was determined that it was to be a great school which in time would take its place among the first half dozen in the country; nothing less would do. He began his campaign among his own parents and then enlisted the support of his fellow-members of the London District of the IAPS. Eventually he persuaded Council to set up a small committee of four who were asked especially to investigate his scheme for financing the project.

This was in 1921. Next year came the news that Stowe House, the historic home of the last Duke of Buckingham and Chandos, was to be auctioned. Montauban lost no time in taking himself off to Buckingham, together with as many of his friends as he could muster. The house was sold for £35,000 to a Mr Shaw, who was planning to pull down what he regarded as his white elephant of a house and turn the whole concern into a vast building estate. Eventually Montauban was able to announce that he had persuaded Shaw to hand over, as a free gift to the IAPS, the house and 280 acres on the understanding that, within a limited time, they could find the necessary money for conversion and endowment; the figure named was £200,000. In addition it was reckoned that a further £25,000 would be required for the immediate purchase of equipment.

This represented a formidable sum fifty years ago, but Montauban was not daunted. He was planning to go into action in a big way. Meetings were called in Hampstead and he was quickly assured of a large measure of support from parents both from his own school and from other schools in the neighbourhood; many of them were becoming increasingly alarmed at the prospect of no public school places for their sons. He took a house in Buckingham and made himself readily available to show off the beauties of Stowe to any parent, or possible subscriber, who might be even faintly interested. He was delighted with one part of the architect's report which he had commissioned: 'The buildings would lend themselves to adaptation to school purposes.'

Montauban's next step was to sell his idea to the public schools. Here he met with much less success, many headmasters feeling that they might well be cutting their own throats if they were to support the founding of a new school, which in less prosperous years could well turn out to be a rival to themselves. Dr Lyttelton (Eton) immediately wrote to *The Times*: 'Can anyone reckon on this congestion lasting? For if it does not, the expenditure, at this time, of many thousands – most of which will be drawn from other charities – will be a flagitious waste. It will be worse than a waste, for it will deal a serious blow to many public schools, day schools and grammar schools.

'Headmasters tell me that they expect the congestion to come to an end at any moment. If this view should prove to be erroneous, the right way to deal with it would be to ask the public for £100,000 for the subsidising of existing schools, especially the Cathedral Schools.' Montauban was not impressed and his answer appeared in *The Times* the next day.

Fortunately, support was obtained from a small but by no means insignificant section of the Head Masters' Conference. Norwood (Marlborough) was enthusiastic and so was Fletcher (Charterhouse) and David (Rugby). A new Committee for Stowe was formed. Every aspect of the new Stowe was thrashed out, but time was against them, as the money had to be found within a few months. Clearly there must be a real danger that, unless some miracle occurred, the demolition squads would soon move in. Publicity had made the scheme widely known, and fortunately attracted the attention of another committee which, under the chairmanship of Lord Gisborough, was already examining the possibility of starting up other schools, for girls as well as for boys. As they had the necessary money to take over the Stowe scheme, the two projects were merged and a new committee was formed which included Montauban.

Their first action was to appoint Roxburgh as headmaster and to invite Montauban to become a governor of the new school. On 12 May 1923 Stowe opened with 99 boys and 12 masters. At a special dinner of celebration the Chairman of the Governors said: 'I have been described as one of the persons who helped in the foundation of this very considerable enterprise; but anything I did I did merely on the inspiration of our good friend Montauban. I did so because that great driving force of his, animating his own great ideals about Stowe and the necessity for a new public school in England, urged him forward and compelled me and others to join him in trying to attain his ambition. We could not hold a candle to him, with his clear foresight. Two or three years ago he was ploughing a lonely furrow but the little candle Montauban then lighted has started a great conflagration in the world of modern England.'

Not surprisingly, many Hall boys entered Stowe during its early years. Among them were the two sons of Stowe's first historian, The Hon. Sir Reginald Croom-Johnson, whose definitive *The Origins of Stowe School* provided Arthur Harrison with much of his material. The family were further involved in establishing a handsome memorial to E H Montauban, which at the same time was his leaving present from The Hall and his lasting monument to his labours at Stowe. David Croom-Johnson recalls the events. As a memorial of Montauban's part in the founding of Stowe, many of his friends decided to put on record in the School Library what he had done. It took this form. The parents of the boys whom he had taught at The Hall, after a suggestion from Lord Gisborough about the empty shelves in the great library, set up a small committee. By subscription, a collection of standard books was purchased to form a complete English section of the library of some hundreds of volumes as a gift to Montauban in recognition of his work. Great care was taken to buy only volumes printed in beautiful and plain type and well bound. David Croom-Johnson remembers that these books were purchased from the Army and Navy Stores and his mother took a leading part in their selection.

On 18th July 1923 Montauban received this testimonial at a meeting of parents and on the next day he handed it over to the Headmaster of Stowe, J F Roxburgh, MA, B ès L, with the following letter:

My dear Headmaster,

Most kind and generous action on the part of a number of parents of my boys has placed me in a position to ask the acceptance by Stowe School of a collection of books for the School Library.

These have been specially selected and will be delivered to you tomorrow. I shall be indeed proud and happy if they may be retained and used by the boys and the masters as you shall find convenient.

If this gift may be taken as a small token of my interest in and zeal for Stowe School, I shall be more than gratified.

Yours sincerely,

(Signed) E H MONTAUBAN

The volumes appeared in the English section of the Library marked with a suitable brass plate, 'Montauban Presentation'. A special book-plate in each volume said this:

Presented for the use of the Library
by
Edward Henry Montauban, MA
who first imagined a School at Stowe
and became a member of its original
Governing Body

Very shortly after this, Montbauban fell out with a faction of his fellow Governors who forced his resignation and then all but bankrupted the school he had helped to create. He disappears from sight thereafter. He died in June 1954; his funeral at Golders Green was attended by the Headmaster of The Hall.

Between 1920 and 1923, the administration of The Hall went through a somewhat confusing stage. Montauban relinquished control of the Senior School in Crossfield Road, but remained firmly in charge at the Junior. For a brief while, the school was simultaneously one school and two. This explains why Montauban's membership of IAPS already referred to was in respect of 'Belsize Junior School', rather than The Hall. His successor at Crossfield Road was Robin Gladstone, who proved in his nine short years to be the first 'modern' Headmaster of The Hall.

Gladstone brought a partner with him. Such arrangements were almost inevitable in the days of proprietary schools when the availability of ready capital was even more important than capability in the varied tasks of running the institution. T H Willes Chitty joined Gladstone for little more than a year. The reasons for this brief partnership, and the significance of this period is vividly recounted by his son, Thomas Chitty, better known as the novelist, Thomas Hinde:

> Throughout my childhood I knew that my aunt, Kitty Gladstone, ran The Hall Junior School. I was more distantly aware that my great uncle, Gerard Wathen, was the school's Headmaster. Though he was in age more like an uncle than a great uncle (he was the last of twelve children) he seemed a distant, respected figure and I only remember visiting him once, when we went to his school study to collect tickets for the zoo.
>
> Gradually I learned that another uncle, Robin Gladstone, Kitty Gladstone's brother, had preceded Uncle Gerard as a Headmaster of The Hall, but it wasn't till much later that I realised that my father, Henry Chitty, was taken into partnership by Uncle Robin and had also briefly been a Headmaster.
>
> My father never mentioned this to me. He was usually silent about episodes in his past which didn't entirely please him, and I suppose this was one of them. Certainly he had been recruited by Uncle Robin for personal rather than scholastic reasons. He was in love with my mother, but because he was divorced she had been forbidden by her father to see him. She could not, however, be prevented from visiting her own brother and meeting his new

partner. My parents' courting must in part have occurred in my father's attic rooms at The Hall Senior School.

There is my father's photograph, pasted into the front of The Hall Magazine for May 1921, looking just as I first remember him (I wasn't born till five years later), his hair brushed straight back and plastered down with grease in the fashion of the time. I am sure that the unsigned editorial which follows is also his. It not only quotes from his favourite poet (and uncle) Henry Newbolt, but is full of his right-wing sentiments and military imagery. After congratulating the people of Britain as a whole for surviving the threat of Bolshevism, it tells the boys of The Hall that school is their training ground where they learn to tilt with 'blunt-tipped lances.' 'In a few years', it ends, 'you must go forth into the world to take your part in the battle that is fought with sharpened points, when no quarter is given, and victory is to the brave.' I strongly suspect he also wrote the account of Prize Giving, which reports his own speech, with its give-away phrase, 'plucky struggles on the football field'.

Later come descriptions of some of his other activities at the school which show that, although he had qualities which should have disqualified him from ever becoming a headmaster, he had others which made him a good teacher. The chief of these were enthusiasm, and an instinctive understanding of how to create this. He knew, for instance, how to use the more spectacular effects of science, and the previous term had given three lectures on the subject. In one, 'motors were driven . . . from a large wet battery of the Leclanché type,' in another 'a variety of experiments were performed with oxygen gas which was manufactured during the lecture,' and for the third 'Mr Robertson had kindly lent a model vertical, standing [steam] engine which was successfully set in motion.' It was at The Hall that my father learned that he enjoyed teaching, and as soon as he found a suitable house – a derelict, war-damaged one at Felixstowe – he moved there, taking two Hall boys with him to start a school of his own.

After Chitty's departure, Gladstone soldiered on for a short while on his own, but in 1923, his uncle, Gerard Wathen, destined to become the most significant of all the men in this story, paid his first visit to The Hall. The following year, he entered into full partnership, and remained Headmaster of The Hall for 31 years. Gladstone retired from the school in 1929, initially to travel round the world (although he continued teaching almost up to his death in 1962). Wathen's only other partner was Major R S Williams, who, like Gladstone before him, was more the administrator, bursar and games coach than the academic inspiration, which was Gerard Wathen's essential role.

Gerard Anstruther Wathen was the youngest of twelve children. His father was, by all accounts, a not wildly successful city tea merchant, but 'Dub', as he was affectionately called (an abbreviated version of the intitial letter of his surname), was sent to St Paul's, a school for which he had a lasting affection and which he was proud to govern in his capacity as a member of the Mercers' Company. His experience there, of unremitting academic pressures and too little opportunity for wider activity, coloured his approach to the style of the curriculum at The Hall.

He won a very fine classical scholarship to Cambridge, and shortly after completing his degree course, he trifled with the idea of being an archaeologist, working in Anatolia. 'There didn't seem to be a living in it,' he later explained, 'and when I was offered a teaching post at Tonbridge School (in his native Kent) I took it. I first thought schoolmastering a very moth-eaten profession!' His elder son, The Reverend Mark Wathen takes up the story of his earlier career:

> When my father was at Peterhouse, Cambridge, his father, was made bankrupt due to the failure of the bankers, Overend Gurney. He, therefore, had to tutor others in order to earn the resources to keep himself at Cambridge. He finally gained his degree in Classics and, spent a year or two doing historical research in Anatolia. He then passed into the Indian Educational Service, one of the stiffest of all Civil Service examinations at that time. This took him to India in the early years of this century and, shortly before the First World War, he was appointed Principal of the Khalsa College, Amritsar, a college to which all the Sikhs went. He was much loved by the Sikhs and played an important part in bringing to an end the riots of Amritsar in 1919. He was a man of liberal ideas and pressed the Government at home to give the Indians a greater say and more responsibility in the running of their education. These pleas fell on deaf ears and finally he felt it difficult to continue working under a Government who would not accept his views, so he resigned. It is interesting to note that within a few years of his resignation his recommendations were acted upon. He was however made Commander of the Order of the Indian Empire.

The Hall was seemingly 'taken over' by the Wathen-Gladstone family from 1920. As heads, pupils or governors, they have been deeply involved ever since. It is therefore especially interesting to have the recollections of three members of the Wathen family, to provide an intimate portrait of their father's regime.

Mark Wathen, who was a pupil under his father until he left for Gresham's in 1926, continues the account from the family viewpoint:

> It so happened that my father's nephew, Robin Gladstone, was

Headmaster of The Hall Senior School at the time of his resignation from the Indian Civil Service in 1924. Mr Montauban was in charge of the Junior School. Montauban was anxious to retire and the obvious solution was for Gladstone to take a partner and run both schools as one.

Here was the very job for Wathen to take on. He would have to find £20,000 to buy out Montauban and the Junior School buildings and No 3 Buckland Crescent, Montauban's house. Wathen had no capital. He had married into a family whose members had built up Barclays Bank. He, therefore, rather naturally sought help from that source. He was somewhat taken aback when the bank refused to lend him the money on the grounds that his father had been a bankrupt. The reason for his bankruptcy had been the failure of the Overend Gurney Bank which had been part of Barclays! However, all was not lost for he appealed to the Westminster Bank in Finchley Road who were happy to help. The £20,000 was paid off within four years.

So the scene was set and Gerard Wathen went into partnership with his nephew, Robin Gladstone. Considerable reorganisation was necessary and Robin Gladstone's sister, Kitty, was appointed to run the Junior School. This triumvirate worked smoothly for a time but Gladstone became ill and had to retire, so Wathen took on another partner, a retired regular soldier, Major Ronald Williams who became the bursar.

Shortly afterwards the lease of No 2 Buckland Crescent became available and this was bought for the school and No 3 was sold. I shall always remember the move across the road which was accomplished without the help of professional removal men. One of my many jobs, aged twelve, was to carry a heavy Minimax fire-extinguisher across the road. I dumped it, with relief, at the top of the steps leading up to the front door of No 2, only to set it off. The terrific pressure was enough to water all the top windows of the house opposite with a solution that left them all in a state of white-wash. No power on earth could stop the machine!

I was at the school as a pupil before my father took it over. I remember little about the preliminaries but all seemed to go smoothly. There was a certain entertainment for me being the son of a Headmaster. My recollection is that discipline fell on me more strongly for that reason. I was only at the school from the age of twelve until I was nearly fourteen, having been previously at another preparatory school in Kent.

I look back on those two years with the greatest happiness. The masters and mistresses stand out vividly. Morton, who seemed to be extremely aged, taught us Latin and Greek and to this day I can remember so much of what he taught. He had written a small book *Gods and Heroes* and this was our text-book, full of all the old Roman and Greek fables. Then there was Miss Bolton, a tall upright Victorian lady who taught us all to respect discipline and to respect her! Madame d'Ouffet taught us English. She was married to a Belgian. But the greatest character of all was W H Copinger who taught us mathematics in a way that made a wonderful grounding for the rest of one's life. He was an enormously strong personality and we all admired him. Millard ran the Scouts and we had many happy Saturdays on Hampstead Heath with our long poles marked off in feet and inches. That training was a splendid foundation for enterprise in later life. Finally I must not forget Miss Large, my father's secretary, a splendid lady with white hair and an extremely efficient manner. She must have shouldered a great many of the administrative burdens.

My mother never really liked the atmosphere of a preparatory school with lots of noisy and tiresome little boys. She was wonderfully loyal to my father and always made the best of things, running the commissariat with a smooth and quiet efficiency. On many occasions the parents complained that the food at school was so much better than it was at home! She was blessed with domestic servants whom she had found in her native county, Norfolk, and whom she trained to a high standard.

For sport we used to go on the Metropolitan Railway to Preston Road near Wembley, where we had the use of lovely grounds. I can remember a cricket match when one of the boys hit the ball so high into the air that it came down on the groundsman's head as he was carrying two large cans of paint. The mark left by the paint on the ground was there for weeks afterwards.

I only have one vivid recollection of going back to the school as an Old Boy, at about the age of eighteen. There was a crisis in the French department and I was asked if I would fill in and teach for a few days. The subject did not daunt me as much as the boys. I had no conception of how to keep order; in fact I found that my feelings were all on the side of the boys. It came to a sticky end when a plot was hatched to entice me into a large cupboard where books were stored. Having got me in, the door was locked behind me and my class disappeared. It seemed a long time before I was rescued. I decided that school-mastering was not for me.

My father built up the school considerably in numbers and he was, of course, the owner of what had became an enormously valuable property, The Hall itself, 69 Belsize Park (the Junior School) and 2 Buckland Crescent. When he came to retire it was obvious that it would be difficult to find a person to take on the

> school and, at the same time, raise so large an amount of capital so he gave the buildings to the school and turned the school into a Charitable Trust, hoping that it would in consequence go on in perpetuity.

The Reverend Mark Wathen now lives on the Island of Skye. He was briefly a governor of The Hall, and a trustee of the GAW Memorial Fund until it was wound up in the late 1970s. A much more lasting family link was maintained by his younger brother, Julian. He was a pupil at his father's school for eight years, before going on to Harrow as a scholar in 1937. The war prevented him from taking his place at Cambridge, and after his army service, he joined Barclays Bank. Julian preserved the intimate family link with the school by becoming chairman of the Governing Body in 1972. He thus was able to continue his father's work for The Hall, becoming responsible for the major developments in the fabric of the buildings which The Hall School Trust has undertaken during the years preceding the centenary. He continues the family recollections:

> Many people used to say that I must find it very difficult to be at my father's school, but I do not recall finding it so. I certainly have no recollection of being bullied because I was Dub's son! In fact GAW kept the relationship very much at arm's length; indeed I was sent to board at Crossfield Road as soon as I moved across to the Senior School. The only problem I can recall is when I broke the rules by buying fireworks on the way from gym at the Hampstead Baths (in those days in Finchley Road, opposite the bottom of College Crescent).
>
> GAW seemed to his family over-committed to the school, and home life was not allowed to impinge on his routine. He would arrive at Buckland Crescent for tea (very strong, dark, Indian) at 16.45, eat a large piece of chocolate cake (the same recipe all the time that Florence Roberts was at the school), do *The Times* crossword and depart at 17.30, returning again just in time for dinner.
>
> He hardly ever fully completed the crossword. Woe betide the setter if an answer next day was felt not to 'click'. My mother was absolutely hopeless at the crossword, claiming, I think, that she only ever solved one clue.
>
> Perhaps someone else can recall the significance of the summons to the presence, outstretched arm, fingers down for bad news, fingers up for good (or was it vice versa?).
>
> There were weekly boarders and full boarders. The ritual for those at the school on Sundays was unvaried. Walk to the zoo after lunch, where GAW as a fellow seemed to be able to sign everyone in free, and to go by tube to Mercers Chapel in the City for evensong.

There was 6d (or was it 1d?) for anyone able to run up the down escalator at Bank Station. A great excitement at Mercers Hall was watching the spits in the kitchen which turned magically when you lit newspapers under them.

My mother gave lunch to the newest boys, in Lower 1, at Buckland Crescent every day, and was always voluble on the subject of how lacking in table manners (and often also appetite) were the very young on arrival.

I used to sit at the front of every class once I got to the Senior School because I could not read the masters' writing on the blackboards; I assumed that others, prepared to sit further back, lacked keenness. My short-sightedness was only discovered when walking along Buckland Crescent my mother realised I could not read the Guinness advertisement on the hoardings on College Crescent, with letters several feet high! Nowadays I imagine this problem would show up in regular medical checks.

I have mostly happy memories of the staff. Miss Bolton, tall and thin and ascetic. Mrs Baker, warm and comfortable and jolly. Mr Castle, professing I think some naval connection, giving us a tantalising introduction to science, just 2 periods a week and only for one year. Mr Dodd, small and rather cruel, once refused to believe me when I said I was in pain from having jabbed myself on my desk; when I got home I had a 3-inch splinter in my behind! Everyone surely remembers Mr Copinger, with his pipe and chess; and Mr Rotherham who inspired all on the geography front; and Mr Fyson, classics, whose link with his (and GAW's) Indian past was mysterious. He suffered enforced irregular disappearances due to malaria.

We should not forget the domestic staff. Mr and Mrs (Ellen) Fox at 69, for whom nothing was ever too much trouble. Mr and Mrs (Florence) Roberts at the Senior; he 'fixed' everything. And Florence's sister, Agnes.

We always ate well, in spite of all the rationing. My mother would bring up eggs from Norfolk and salt them away in tanks of waterglass in the Junior School or Buckland Crescent store cupboard. I remember also barrels of sugar. Catering for boarders and resident staff was all concentrated at Crossfield Road, and these arrangements persisted long after the war, and my mother was not always best pleased that the Buckland Crescent contingent had to turn out in all weathers to walk round to Crossfield Road to join 'Sir' for dinner.

The dining hall in the basement at 69 was strengthened to make it bomb-proof, and the boarders and family and matron (Miss Monro) all slept there in bunks. It looked a flimsy arrangement and it all used to shudder when the mobile anti-aircraft guns fired now from this side, now from that. One night a bomb fell 50 yards away just east of the Lancaster Grove junction; GAW went out into the thick dust with his warden's helmet to help how he could.

A firm taboo with GAW was the word 'parents', the correct phrase was 'people who have a boy at the school'. He was aghast at petty crime, and most upset when it was proved that one mean little red-headed boy was stealing – but I seem to remember he was not sacked. Our English essays were corrected with symbols developed by GAW at the Khalsa College, Amritsar. It was an important tenet that no one could possibly be successful in life unless he wrote good English. French was taught firmly by the direct method. Experiments were made with yellow boards and green chalk.

One wonders what GAW would have made of the visual aids of the 1980s – of the video recording machine, the overhead projector, the word processor or even that most precious of innovations, the white-board with the 'dry-wipe' marker-pen!

GAW's daughter, Diane Hargrave-Wilson completes the family contribution to the picture of the school:

Both my father and mother were inclined to be vague. On one occasion my father was sitting in the pavilion at Lord's when a man came and sat next to him. He began to talk to him as if my father should have known him well. After some time my father plucked up courage and said, 'I'm very sorry, I seem to know your face but I cannot remember who you are.' The man looked slightly astonished and said, 'I used to be your son-in-law, for nine years.'

My mother was equally vague. One evening they were going to a smart dinner-party with the Headmaster of Westminster, Mr Costley-White. It was a bitterly cold night and the bedrooms at Buckland Crescent had no form of heating. My mother went up to dress. Evening dress was normal wear before the 1939–45 war. Rather than freeze to death she tore off her jersey and, as quickly as she could, she put on her evening dress over her thick tweed skirt, fully intending to remove the latter but at that moment the telephone rang and she hastened to answer it.

During dinner she felt very hot and uncomfortable and it suddenly dawned on her, with horror, that she was still wearing her thick tweed skirt under her velvet gown!

Father had two loves – cricket and The Hall. After he retired he went to live in St John's Wood to be nearer Lord's. If there was no cricket he would walk up to The Hall and just stand and gaze at it – really rather sad. The school was his whole life.

The pages that follow will contain countless further glimpses of this remarkable man. It is impossible to imagine that so powerful and original a personality could not inspire volumes of anecdotal reminiscence. At this juncture, the recollections of one Old Boy, H St J B Howe may suffice to provide a sample:

> After a hymn and a prayer at morning assembly the Headmaster read out the notices for the day and made any observations he felt necessary for the smooth running and the discipline of the school.
>
> On one occasion, when he came to his observations, 'Dub' was heard to say, 'I'm furious . . .' There was a pause and then, turning to his secretary, he asked in a still audible voice, 'What am I furious about?'
>
> ⋆ ⋆ ⋆
>
> On the occasion of his wedding anniversary he would say, 'To-day is my wedding anniversary. We shall sing the hymn "Fight the good fight".'
>
> ⋆ ⋆ ⋆
>
> 'Dub' taught French. One morning he entered a beginners' class. He was wearing his gown and from its voluminous folds he produced first one, then another and then another tennis-ball. Bouncing one ball at a time in such a way that it returned to an awaiting opening in the sleeve of his gown, he then asked 'Qu'est-ce que je fais? Que fais-je?' No one answered, knowing a reply in French was required. After the fourth ball had bounced back into his sleeve 'Dub' said, 'Je joue avec une balle. . . .', and he laughed. His false teeth, never very well anchored in his mouth, fell with that ball into his waiting sleeve!
>
> Everyone started tittering. 'Dub', a very good sport, just retrieved his false teeth, put them back in his mouth and went on, this time in English. 'I expected you to say: "Vous jouez avec une balle."'
>
> 'Dub', never one to give in, then went through the whole process again, this time without shedding his teeth. And this time everyone gave the answer expected of him.
>
> ⋆ ⋆ ⋆
>
> Seeing me pass the open door of his study 'Dub' called me in. 'Did you know,' he asked, 'that down the road there's a nursery school where they have far too many children of both sexes? Well, each time HM Inspectors are due the 'extras' are taken to the greenhouse, put on pots and kept there until the inspectors have gone! A greenhouse converted into a potting-shed, that's what it is!'
>
> ⋆ ⋆ ⋆
>
> On leaving the Senior School for Buckland Crescent at the end of

the school day with another master, the latter said, 'It must be awful in town in the rush hour.' 'Russia! Never been there.'

'Dub' was conveniently deaf at times and he used this pseudo-deafness to advantage when he wanted to!

★ ★ ★

The Junior School was totally incorporated into the Senior with Montauban's departure, and from 1924 to 1928, one of the existing staff, Mrs Mason, was in charge. She was succeeded by Gladstone's sister, Kitty, whose long reign as Head of the Junior was no less significant than her uncle's in the Senior. She retired after 33 years in office, in 1960, and was followed by another long-term servant of the school, Miss V C Bearman.

Returning to the first period of partnership, with Gladstone and Wathen together, one easily senses that as the broader outlook of these two energetic men prevailed a good deal more daylight was let into the lives of everybody at The Hall. A ferment seems to have started: after only one term, Wathen had so made his mark that people were already saying it was hard to remember the school without him. He was noted as 'certainly progressive' and quickly introduced new notions such as the Dalton System, which took care, for instance, of what happened on a wet school-day afternoon.

If GAW had ideas about wet afternoons, Gladstone had plenty about finer ones for it was he who saw to it that sport and other outdoor activities were allowed a larger share of the curriculum.

In the Easter term of 1921, early in his time as Headmaster, he had introduced Rugby football, seeing that so many boys were leaving for rugger-playing public schools having learnt to play soccer only. Then by the summer of the same year he had persuaded the parents of that day to subscribe two thirds of the cost of a court in which both squash and fives could be played. (He may well have wondered what sort of a pass things had come to when later this court was converted into a room for art!) Next, in May 1923, he very much encouraged the formation of a Scout Troop within the school under Mr Millard. But perhaps the finest service that was ever done for sport at The Hall was Gladstone's and Wathen's successful efforts to ensure the saving of the Hampstead Cricket Club's ground.

Gladstone's other forte was as an organiser. The school during his nine years of partnership with GAW becomes recognisably the school we still know today. Until this era (1920-30) the flavour of The Hall was somewhat different and is naturally faded and therefore hard to catch as one reads back amongst surviving records.

The opening chapter in The Hall's history ends on a note of new confidence. Numbers rose steadily and demand for places was by now constant. By 1926, there were over 240 boys. No less than five new classrooms were added to the two buildings during Gladstone's time, and of course the teaching staff grew to match these numbers. The size of classes remained relatively modest – about 15. The style of the school advanced too with the major cosmetic 'improvements' to the main hall, in the words of a previous writer, 'to be more in keeping with the somewhat grander air of a solidly-established foundation'.

The fortieth anniversary year, 1929, was to see the departure of Gladstone, but the reassurance of a most favourable Board of Education Inspectors' Report. The school's 'forward policy' was noted enthusiastically as auguring a 'great future'. The Inspectors approved the good discipline and marked courtesy of the boys. The short-comings in the curriculum, especially with regard to geography and the creative arts were noted, and were quickly acted upon. Thus it was that The Hall was set to embark on its fifth decade of existence in very good heart, notwithstanding the chill breath of depression with which the year 1929 may be more readily associated.

PART I: THE FIRST FORTY YEARS

Chapter 2
Quod Bene Vertat

The growth of The Hall's buildings

While a school must have teachers and pupils, it is an inescapable fact that its growth and ultimate consolidation frequently hinge on the buildings it is fortunate enough to secure, especially during the fragile formative years. Many a school has collapsed because it could not sustain its impetus in accommodation that was ill-suited to its needs. Indeed, a glance at The Hall's fixture list of the early decades of this century demonstrates the point. How many of its rivals have either moved out of London to more spacious premises or have disappeared altogether. They may have suffered from inadequate leadership from their head; this was certainly never a problem for The Hall. More probably it was the inappropriate accommodation which crushed them.

The Belsize School is first recorded as occupying the detached white stucco three-story house at 18 Buckland Crescent. This was the home of the first accepted Headmaster in the tradition of The Hall, The Reverend F J Wrottesley. It was clearly far too cramped and restricted, and this explains why the school was so precariously reduced to the mere handful of boys which Marshall inherited at the turn of the century. The move to 23 Crossfield Road in 1905 was mentioned with a surprising lack of fervour, although the implication of its significance is evident, in a passing comment – one of several *Notanda Quaedam*, in the fourth issue of the Magazine.

> Since the issue of our last number the School has removed to The Hall, Crossfield Road, Eton Avenue. Owing to a steady increase in our numbers, the need of larger premises has been felt for some time. The new home of Belsize School admirably meets all wants, as The Hall, built specially for a school, is both beautiful and spacious. We have now room for more than a hundred boys, a number which we hope will shortly be reached. *Quod bene vertat.*

Let us put the clock back to the same period as Belsize School was founded, for this will explain how the school came to find its ultimate and permanent home.

In 1889 two sisters, the Misses Sarah and Rita Allen-Olney, had opened what an advertisement in the *Hampstead and Highgate Express* that year called 'a select school and classes for the general and higher education of girls', at 41 Belsize Park Gardens. The establishment must have prospered, for on 7th May 1891 we find it opening for term in a brand new building in Crossfield Road, NW3. It lay on land leased to Mr William Willet by Eton College. The lease, dated 25th February 1891, runs for 90 years from 29th September 1890, at a ground rent of £2 per annum.

Contrary to what many people have supposed, and indeed surprisingly when one considers the hall itself, with its pseudo-baronial air and the curious layout in general, this building was not planned as a school, though there was a clause in the lease allowing use as a school. E R Robson, the architect, was of some note as a designer of schools. It was adapted for that purpose, according to the following note on the subject published in *The Builder* magazine for 28th January 1893:

> *'THE HALL', HAMPSTEAD*
>
> *This building, planned for the purpose of a residential mansion, but adapted to the uses of a ladies' high school, has been erected by Mr Watson, builder, of Ascot, from plans and designs by Mr E R Robson, FSA.*
>
> *The building possesses a fine central hall from which it derives its name.*
>
> *The illustration shows the front towards Crossfield Road, near Eton Avenue.**
>
> *Owing to the levels of the land in relation to the street, the school entrance, the central hall, and the lower classrooms are placed on what is termed the basement, but which is, in reality, a ground floor. The central hall – lighted principally from the top – extends through the two storeys, and has a gallery on one side, giving access to three classrooms. There are also rooms for piano practice, ample cloakrooms, lavatories, and a large tennis court. The classrooms and hall floors are laid with oak parquetry. The whole is warmed by means of low pressure radiators in conjunction with open fires.*

At this point it is interesting, and even at this distance in time slightly spine chilling, to recall that as the building neared completion during the autumn of 1890 it found brief notoriety as being very close to the spot where was discovered the body of a woman who had been

**See plate 26*

savagely murdered. The Camden or Crossfield Road Murder is to this day commemorated in The Chamber of Horrors at Madame Tussaud's. And we have it on clear authority of Mrs Rosemary de Fonblanque who, as Miss Fenwick, was a pupil of the Misses Allen-Olney at the time, that this association of Crossfield Road with murder so horrified the good pair that they made sure that their school was known thereafter simply as 'The Hall, Hampstead'.

Mrs de Fonblanque well remembers making her way to Crossfield Road for the first day of school there, on 7th May 1891. She walked from her home in Hempstall Road, West Hampstead, by way of Aberdare Gardens, then a path embanked between fields worked by bird snarers, using decoy birds in cages. (Later, when it rained she took a steam train from West Hampstead to Swiss Cottage, paying a fare of one half-penny!). Her recollection of Miss Sarah as 'very upright' and 'seeming to wear kid gloves day and night,' and of Miss Rita as 'small, precise and greyhaired' and once asking of a girl who related some incident, 'And did it fill you with much *awe*, my dear?' adds dimension a little to the following rather prim advertisement, typical of many of its day, of the Allen-Olney establishment, as it appeared in *The Hampstead and Highgate Express* of January 14th, 1893:

THE HALL, CROSSFIELD ROAD,
HAMPSTEAD
Select School & Classes.
(Removed from 41, Belsize Park Gardens)

Conducted by the Misses ALLEN-OLNEY, formerly Headmistresses respectively of Blackheath and South Hampstead High Schools. Assisted by qualified English, French & German Teachers, holding University Degrees or Certificates.

Large playground and full-sized Tennis-court. Pupils taken from 6 years old. Boarders & Weekly Boarders received.

The Classes for Physical Exercises are on Wednesdays from 9.30 to 11.30 am. Painting, Dancing and Singing Classes are held in the afternoon.

A Literature Class for Ladies on Chaucer given by Professor HALES, MA (Clark Lecturer at Trinity College, Cambridge), will begin on Jan 18th at Three pm. Applications to join can be made to the Principals.

EASTER TERM BEGINS Jan 17th.

By 1893 it seems that the taint of the murder had weathered off Crossfield Road, for here we have it writ large as part of the address on the copy the Misses must themselves have sent to the newspaper office.

The eye of the energetic and successful Mr Marshall, then, with his numbers fast rising, inevitably fell on The Hall as the place he needed to accommodate his school. Conveniently enough for him, things there, with the Misses Allen-Olney ageing and thinking of retirement, were on the decline. Mr Marshall proposed that he take over the lease and after long and difficult negotiations he persuaded the ladies to agree, one of the conditions being that when the boys moved out, Mrs Marshall should continue the girls' school, at 18 Buckland Crescent, for at least a year. This she certainly did and one of Mr Marshall's boys of that time, H W Dallas, recalls that whilst he was of 'Belsize and The Hall', his sisters were of 'The Hall and Belsize', the double move having taken place in 1905. There was, incidentally, no deliberate change of name for the boys' school at a given date – it seems that the name of 'Belsize' just faded out.

No reference at all is made to the nature of these new premises in the pages of subsequent numbers of the magazine. To obtain even the sketchiest picture of what the school offered its Edwardian pupils, we must turn to the prospectus of Belsize School, a copy of which, produced for the move to the new buildings, survives in the school archives. The prospective parent was given the reassurance of some twenty distinguished persons to whom reference might be made as to the quality of the school. These ranged from the Bishops of Ripon and Hereford, the Provost and two Fellows of Worcester College, Oxford (the Headmaster's former college), an MP, two public school headmasters, several of the local clergy and a string of past and present parents. The opening pages of this lavishly produced booklet describe the building:

> The school house, which stands detached and in its own grounds, was built for the purpose by E R Robson Esq, FSA, Consulting Architect to the Board of Education.
>
> It is divided into three blocks. The central one consists of a lofty hall, running the whole length and height of the building. This is used for lectures, drill, dancing and generally whenever the boys are all required to meet together.
>
> The school block contains five large classrooms, each 21 ft square, and two smaller ones, each about 20 ft by 14 ft. There are also a boarders' sitting room, carpenter's shop, senior and junior cloak rooms, and changing rooms, lavatories etc.
>
> These blocks are heated throughout with hot water. They have the maximum of window area, and a complete system of through ventilation.

> The private house has a large dining hall, drawing room, study, bed-rooms, and excellent dormitory accommodation. All classrooms and dormitories face south or west, and are in consequence very bright and sunny.
>
> The sick room is in a separate wing, and can be completely isolated from the rest of the house.
>
> The sanitation throughout is on the most approved modern plan. All drains are thoroughly cleansed, water tested, and certified before the beginning of each term.

The modern reader familiar with the current layout of the school, cannot but be fascinated to wonder just how and where all these facilities were located. The very serious attention paid to health is, too, a telling reflection on the considerable impact sickness made on the life of the boys in those early days. A whole page of this 12-page booklet is devoted to Health Regulations. Infectious diseases were a constant source of anxiety, and boys could find themselves missing weeks of school through the rigorous application of quarantine regulations.

This, the first intimate picture of The Hall and its routine, amply explains the reasons why it was about to embark on a long history of development. The daily timetable is described in detail. The day opens with prayers at 9.10, and the morning allotted a rather leisurely 3 hours of lessons, with half-hour break. 'Dinner' (and a footnote advises 'If a boy is to gain the fullest advantage from the corporate life and discipline of his school, it is essential that he should dine there') was at 1 pm, and an hour (only) given to games. Lessons resumed for 1½ hours at 3.00, except on half holidays, which were on Wednesdays and Saturdays. A break was followed by tea at 5.00, and 1¼ hours of prep ended the day at 7.00. This latter was not necessarily done at school, but another footnote suggests: 'Experience also shows that preparation is much more thoroughly done, when performed at school under the supervision of a master'. Here was started The Hall tradition that prep, not home-work, is set, and time is given at school for its completion.

The prospectus explains in detail the school's provision for games.

> Great attention is paid to physical development. There is a large playground attached to the school house. In addition to this the School also has a small playfield at Swiss Cottage (the so-called Strathray), and a large one (about three acres) in the Finchley Road (at Lyndale, Child's Hill). The small field is chiefly for the use of the little boys. The elder boys also practise there daily, but use the large one on half-holidays, for matches etc.
>
> All boys attend the Hampstead Gymnasium twice a week. They form a special class for instruction by the fully-qualified staff of the Institution, under Sergeant-Major Biggs.

During the summer term swimming is substituted for gymnastics.

There is a carpenter's shop, where lessons are given during the winter months.

The final picture drawn of the school at the turn of the century relates to the uniform. School colours ('black and cerise') were obligatory, and travelling to and from school, boys were obliged to wear school cap or straw hat with school band. At cricket, players had to wear school tie and belt, with white flannel trousers or knickerbockers and white flannel or canvas *(sic)* shirt. Likewise, football necessitated black serge knickerbockers with school jersey, belt and stockings. The uniform had to be obtained from Messrs Hyam of Oxford Street.

And what did all this cost the long-suffering parent in 1905? The termly boarder's fee was just 30 guineas (£31.50) and weekly boarding was £5.25 less. Laundry was a compulsory extra. The day-boy fee was £9.45 per term, reduced by one third for boys under nine. Music and games were charged as extras, and the day-boy attending lunch and tea would have to pay a further £6.30 for this privilege.

As for other facilities, no other details are provided for our illumination in the earliest magazines. The library and museum, described elsewhere, were functions rather than locations. The numbers of pupils clearly began to rise, and the target of 100, which the new premises made possible, must have been commonly discussed. An Old Boy, E G Drysdale, concludes a long letter describing his adventures in Argentina (prior to going on to Tonbridge School) with an off-hand postscript: 'I suppose you have got over one hundred boys now at the school'. The attractions of the building were obvious, but there is a regular note of anxiety about sustaining the numbers, especially of boarders. This is detected in the style of the Valete notices for the senior leavers, that so-and-so's departure represents a loss not readily replaced. More than once the editor inserts a comment, congratulating the Headmaster for recruiting new entries, thus ensuring that the school was full for the forthcoming year. The Great War must have affected matters too and the target of 100 seems to have been revised. The school photograph of 1914 shows just over 70 pupils.

Success breeds success, and the lists slowly grew. Indeed, Montauban formally announced that he was going to raise the maximum number of boys as a conscious part of the war effort, and by 1916, the 100 figure was passed. The acquisition of a separate Junior School at 69 Belsize Park effectively guaranteed that numbers would always be sustained.

Montauban was a remarkable empire builder, with a talent for inspiring the development of schools as well as for acquiring property. During his time in Hampstead, he owned the lease of The Hall and from 1917, of the Junior School. He had his own house in Belsize Park and property in the country. Just how much is not altogether easy to deduce from the clues provided by the magazine. In the summer issue of 1915 E W Lindeck describes, with a somewhat bland indifference to the reality of war raging across the channel, his summer holiday as a guest of the Montaubans at their farm, Layfords, between Brookwood and Bisley, in Surrey. After expressing his dismay at being denied his expected, customary summer holiday abroad he goes on to describe with vivid enthusiasm the variety of delights the six fortunate guests were to enjoy during their three-week stay. Besides the novelties of the farm and wild animals all around, there were the period go-carts, called 'Tommiemobiles', with one-boy-power engines, dams in the river, and fishing and boating and riding the local 'Dobbin'. But only a few months later, the Montaubans' country farm is at Burghfield, just outside Theale in Berkshire, and a no less evocative piece by another lucky guest, C Harris, describes attempts at blowing up the moles that threatened the lawns. The Tommiemobiles were there too, and one must suppose that Montauban had swapped properties.

Not long after this, he must have exchanged the Burghfield farm for yet another, Balmore, at Caversham, a property destined shortly to play a significant role in the story of The Hall. Meanwhile, with his seemingly compulsive instinct to acquire ever more buildings, he bought Woodcote, a large house in Belsize Park. On the final page of the Christmas 1916 number of the Magazine appeared a very formal if somewhat clumsily expressed and type-set notice:

THE HALL

I have to announce a further step in the development of the School.

It is common knowledge that some years ago I stated that the policy of The Hall would be to limit the number of pupils to 75 and to establish a waiting list of applicants should that number be exceeded. For two years or so we have kept to this arrangement; but presently, in consequence of the changed conditions involved by the war, it was found necessary to relax the regulation and to admit more boys.

The number has now grown to 99 pupils, and there is a teaching staff of 5 masters and 4 ladies, apart from the assistance that we get for singing, music, gymnastics, boxing etc. There seems to be every probability that by next May we shall need accommodation for even greater numbers.

> We are most anxious that neither the health of the School nor the work shall suffer in any way in consequence of overcrowding, therefore we have now purchased further premises as extension of and addition to The Hall.
>
> We have been so fortunate as to secure for this purpose the building which stands at the junction of Buckland Crescent and Belsize Park and which has hitherto been known as 'Woodcote'.
>
> This was formally *(sic)* used as a school and is eminently suitable; for its rooms are very large and lofty, the site, which is only 200 yards away from The Hall, is very accessible and the general arrangements render it just what we want for our Junior Boys.
>
> It will be known in future as the 'Junior School of The Hall', and we propose to transfer, next May, to this building, the teaching of our junior boys. . . .
>
> The games, drill and swimming will be carried on just as present under my own personal supervision; the work, the discipline and the general tone will also be personally directed by me; our teachers will continue just as before; the only change will be that there will be greater space and larger accomodation *(sic)* for both Seniors and Juniors.
>
> I am anxious to emphasise the fact that there is not the slightest breaking apart between Senior and Junior School. . . .'

Clearly, this major development in the school won widespread approval. The editor referred to the splendid expansion in the scope and scale of The Hall in the opening pages of the next magazine. 'It is an undertaking of which we may all be proud, and no one can fail to recognise and be pleased at this sign of success. It is one, too, in which we all have a share; for if the School generally had not responded to Mr Montauban's influence, it would never have won for itself the high reputation which it now enjoys.'

That spring, the Junior School duly opened with 30 boys; the editor mused:

> This term promises to be interesting in many ways. The Junior School at 'Woodcote' will be in full swing, and proud should these juniors be of their new premises, especially of those nice airy class-rooms and the big hall with its French style of decoration. All this means that the seniors at The Hall will now have room in which to stretch themselves without running the risk of doing injury to stray infants. . . .

This was wartime, and while external events clearly had their impact, life for a long while seemed only slightly affected. Certain activities were curtailed, notably games. A melancholy term was endured in

1917, with no formal Easter term games because of the rotten weather, but transport to the fields was growing yearly more difficult; only five 1st XI matches were played the following term. The threat of zeppelin raids overtook all other considerations.

That autumn, the motion at a school debate was on 'The Advantages and Disadvantages of enlarging the School'. The editor tells us that somehow the speakers drifted off the narrow line of discussion and came to decide that 'some gigantic institution was to be erected in the country'. Within weeks, the fantasy became, in part anyway, reality. In December Montauban explained to the parents that the succession of air raids which had taken place earlier in the season had raised a problem which he was bound to recognise and face, and he had felt it his duty to present parents with a scheme which would provide for the safety of their children, should any be desirous of removing them out of the danger zone of London. This decision had exposed him to some criticism, as was only natural; and though there were just one or two parents who, probably through some misunderstanding, had disapproved of the course he had taken, results had only proved the widespread loyalty and sympathy of the parents and staff. At that time some twenty-eight names stood on the list as certain boarders at Caversham, whilst another thirteen were still undecided; the remainder having definitely determined to continue as they were in London.

The effect on The Hall was of course quite considerable. Boys and staff were split. The Montaubans travelled to and fro between Caversham and Hampstead but they regarded their prime responsibility as lying with the boarding party in Berkshire. We learn almost nothing about the school's brief excursion to the country. Indeed, there seems almost a sense of resentment at the lack of communication between town and country branches. The Londoners felt undoubtedly that they were braving it out in the battle zone, while their comrades enjoyed fun and games away from danger and privation. The editor reported in March 1918:

> As we write the notes, the school at Balmore has settled down and is now in full swing, and the 'die-hards' at The Hall and Woodcote are carrying on with vigour, keeping the colours flying in Hampstead. It seemed all rather strange at first, having only thirty-one boys present instead of about seventy, but we have all knuckled to with a will. . . . The Junior is flourishing, some twenty boys remaining on. . . . The current number of the magazine will be found to be shorter than usual, but of this we must be held blameless. Apart from extra work involved (the editor was the senior master in charge at Crossfield Road), up to the time of going to press the

contingent at Balmore has totally failed to supply us with any news, in spite of earnest entreaties. . . .

There follows a long thinly-veiled moan at the attitude evidently emanating from Caversham.

The evacuation lasted less than a year. The boys at Balmore suffered a very serious 'flu epidemic, which led to the term ending prematurely. This was not before one of the Hamilton brothers had felt obliged to offer the following description of life at Balmore:

Gardening and Farming at Balmore

The Balmorians, like the little nigger boys – this is not a comment on to the colour of their skins – diminished considerably towards the end of the present term; but this has not stopped their outdoors labours, such as wood-cutting and gardening, in the slightest degree. . . .

There is always plenty to do. Carpentry is one of our pastimes; also sawing wood into suitable lengths for logs.

. . . Another spirited animal, a horse named Prince, trampled down all the bunkers on our golf-course one night; but we cannot blame him, as we all have probably made mistakes when on the golf-course for the first time. Though it has nothing to do with gardening, or farming, golf is one of our health-giving exercises – it is we who get the exercise; the ball takes a back seat and remains on the tee.

The clock, which has commenced to strike since the armistice, is also an asset to Balmore, to which we bid farewell for the present, and which we hope to see once more.

If the writer did, it was not as his school. The evacuation was over that Christmas, and in January 1919, the whole school was reunited in Hampstead. There was slight reference to all this in the magazine. 'What a treat it is to find ourselves all back again at The Hall under such happy circumstances and with renewed forces and vigour!' This was the sum of editorial comment, apart from references to the fact that numbers were swelling in a post-war boom. Morale was high, and activities resumed, so far as were possible, the 'flu epidemics being the chief threat. Steadily, numbers of boys in each half of the school rose to top the 200 total, and significantly, references in the magazine to the worries over recruiting pupils disappear.

It was at about this point that rather more detail about the lay-out of the facilities in the building are included in the magazine. In 1917, mention is made of 'handsome oak tables' which were acquired to turn what it refers to as 'the large open space', the main hall, into the refectory. 'With the large increase in the number of boarders and day-boys staying to dinner and tea, the old dining-room (the front-of-building room which in 1983 was made the staff common-room) has become far too small for meals and there was nothing for it but to make use of the hall. Though we miss the open space to which we are so accustomed, there is no doubt that the hall looks much more imposing now, with its polished oak tables, its chair of state, and the great sideboard at the far end adorned with a handsome array of silver challenge-cups. And when in the years to come that long desired panelling is on the walls, the hall will look handsome indeed.' A photograph of the hall as it then looked was reproduced in the 1920 prospectus.

War-time travel problems clearly caused this shift towards a more residential character. The feature of the assembly/dining hall as seen in the illustration of it is the splendid furniture, which still, over 60 years later, is happily adorning the school. The prefects' bench is surely one of the more remarkable pieces in this collection. It is first referred to in 1917, and although the names of Hall prefects dating back to 1915 are to be found on it, it was clearly acquired somewhat later. The probability is that it was S V Dickens, himself a prefect, who was instrumental in the school's obtaining the most unusual four-seater carved oak settle which now graces the entry hallway into the school. For some years it languished somewhat uncared for, but repairs and restoration have since made it the object of universal admiration.

There was a burst of development in the early 1920s which saw the restoration of confidence in the school's future. This rings out from the pages of the magazines, with the new Gladstone/Chitty regime, which began in 1920. The squash court, built at the south-eastern end of the Senior School was a notable and remarkably imaginative novelty. How many prep schools can boast having one as early as 1921, many years before squash had become the popular sport of later days? Sadly, the pressure on precious space meant that the court could not survive, but throughout the 1920s and '30s, squash was an immensely popular school sport at The Hall. Two-thirds of the cost of the construction of the court was met by parents, a generous gesture on behalf of what was still a proprietary school. Simultaneously, Montauban's part of the school at 69 Belsize Park was also witnessing improvement. Now over 100 boys strong, a classroom extension and changing room facilities were provided. Montauban at the same time added to the playing fields by hiring a three-quarter acre field in Antrim Road, a ten-minute walk down Eton Avenue and England's Lane.

Chitty's stay at The Hall was brief, and on his departure, the residential accommodation at the western end of the Senior School was converted to classroom use. The school was growing and needed the space. These pressures continued. Montauban in the Junior School section of the 1923 issue of the magazine announced:

> We have to chronicle a further extension of the School which has become necessary owing to the growth of our numbers, and owing also to the fact that boys have been coming to us of such tender years that we have found it desirable to open a special department. This extension of the Junior will be known as the 'Minimi', and will be housed for work and games at 60 Avenue Road.
>
> It is to be in no sense a new or separate school; the same teachers and the same methods will be found in the 'Minimi' as have been in the Junior, the hours, however, and the programme will be lighter, but our aim will be, as it has been at the Junior, to turn out little men.'(!)

Sadly and curiously, virtually no further reference appears in the pages of the magazine to this Kindergarten venture. The Minimi class-list appeared at the end of the Junior School lists just twice, in December 1923 and the following term. It was never referred to again. Clearly therefore the Minimi was a very short-term experiment. Montauban's energies rapidly switched elsewhere; Selwyn House girls' school was the outcome. The Minimi boys were absorbed into the Junior School. It was typical Montauban 'empire building' and it foreshadows the development of a 5+ department some 60 years later. Avenue Road was a long way from the rest of the school, and the following year there was another major development. As Montauban's interest in The Hall was waning his commitment to the founding of Stowe School grew. In 1924, Gladstone was joined by his uncle, G A Wathen, and simultaneously, the pair bought out Montauban's Junior School. As Gladstone announced to parents in July 1924:

> . . . in future there will not be two schools but one school; moreover, a boy will come up from the Junior to the Senior when he is ready and when he has completed his syllabus regardless of age. By this means, more attention can be given to backward boys and the scholarship boys can get on faster.

Thus ended the curious arrangement whereby Junior and Senior were clearly the two halves of the same school, yet endowed with separate identities and separate headmasters.

The story of expansion and widening facilities received a sad and distinct reverse in 1926 with the loss of the Strathray field, and Eton Court reared its unhandsome back-view to the school. 'The top flats will get a fine view of Upper VI at work, and this privilege will enable the agent to ask high rents,' quipped Gladstone. Nevertheless, the same year, Wathen felt able to comment on what proved to be as dynamic a year as any over the previous decade:

> We number today 128 boys in the Senior and 114 in the Junior, and we do not intend to expand further, for we have now 18 class-rooms always occupied and 19 regular teachers, an increase of three forms and three teachers during the year. But the buildings are not elastic and classes must be kept as small as at present.

Throughout the remainder of the period, this stayed the normal capacity of The Hall. There were even then some 19 classes, the same number as 50 years later, when the numbers had swollen by 80 more. Class sizes were pleasantly small: this was a key to the high academic standards achieved.

Various further improvements are reported in the magazine, the largest of which was the 'Shell' form-room which filled the gap at the southern end of the Senior School, hitherto a small garden, on the site subsequently occupied by the so-called Bandroom. A radio and gramophone were acquired for teaching and recreation. In 1929, the latter was regarded as particularly significant. 'The Hall likes to think of itself, if not in the van, at least in the advance guard of educational method, and any new ideas are given a welcome. . . . It is suggested that we begin to form a library of gramophone records. . . .'

The period of the Gladstone/Wathen partnership ends with The Hall so physically well established that its future was assured, even though immediately ahead loomed the daunting threats of the slump of the '30s and the war in the '40s, which between them put paid to so many prep schools elsewhere.

PART I: THE FIRST FORTY YEARS

Chapter 3
Hall-marks of The Hall

The Hall has long been recognised in North London as the school whose boys wear pink and black: the more discerning will also notice the cross, often mistaken for a teutonic Iron Cross. No written record survives as to the precise reasons for these choices, nor the exact year when they were instituted. We may suppose that pink as the principal colour was inspired by a conscious imitation of one of the school's most admired public schools, Westminster, although, as has been already noted, the colour was described in 1904 as cerise, which is a cherry-red. As to the emblem and motto, the most detailed explanation we have comes from the magazine for 1929, in which was printed a brief notice:

> A correspondent has asked us what is the origin of the use of the Iron Cross as the school badge. The 'Iron Cross' is of course, the Maltese Cross, and was the emblem of the Knights of Malta. It has been from time immemorial the school badge, and was, we presume, chosen to indicate that the school aimed at pursuing the chivalrous ideals of the knights of old.*
>
> The school motto, *Hinc in Altiora*, is a Latinised version of some Dutch words engraved on an old medal won in 1808 *(sic)* at the Academy of Amsterdam by the great-grandfather of Mr E H Montauban, headmaster of The Hall for many years.

Reference to an earlier number of the magazine, 1914 in fact, will yield further evidence of the origins of the motto. Montauban instituted four medal prizes, in memory of five *(sic)* inspirational figures in his life: and the magazine editor most usefully prints a long extract from the local newspaper report of Montauban's Prize Giving speech of 1911, the year the medals were first presented and the motto introduced to the school. He is quoted as follows:

*The Editor of 1929 was alas not strictly correct. The Hall's emblem is, in correct heraldic terms, a Cross Paty, and not a Maltese Cross at all, although it has invariably been so described. One can only speculate as to the true reason for its adoption by The Hall.

> I want the form of the medal to serve the purpose of a memento, and at the same time I want the thing itself to be of practical value to the recipient. Thus instead of presenting a boy with a solid gold medal, beautiful and possibly expensive, but of utility nil – I have designed these cases. Inside you will find an embossed token, a copy I have purposely had made of a gold medal gained by my father's grandfather in the year 1801 in the Dutch Academy. It bears the inspiring words, *Hinc in Altiora* – Rise from this to something higher. Thus far, the sentiment; underneath comes solid utility, for the token covers a gold sovereign, and this gold sovereign it is my desire that the boy should use. . . .

The four medals were presented for the next few years, but regular reports of their existence ceased the year Montauban finally left the Junior School in 1924. The last recorded winners this time were G A Weiss (Ashbee Medal), H J C Stuart (Browne Medal), A E K Salvi (Suffern Medal) and J N Eagleston (Astley Medal). The medals were irregularly awarded in the '30s.

Another Hall institution, the Reading Over, was likewise a creation of the resourceful Montauban. The first formal reference, in 1915, suggests that the system had its origins before that year, but by 1917 it was clearly established and part of the vocabulary of the school. Originally Reading Over seems to have been a weekly recital of the school in form order, accompanied by a comment from the Headmaster – a fairly daunting experience but of course quite unexceptional in those harsher days. Yet, as in so many cases, The Hall was conspicuously ahead of its time, at least in its thinking and aspiration. The insensitivity of the purely marks-based form order, which subjects the slower boy to a constant reaffirmation of his inadequacy, was recognised by the Gladstone/Chitty regime. The magazine in 1923 reports:

> At half-term two innovations were introduced. A new system of marking was adopted, the alpha, beta, gamma, system being substituted for that of ordinary marks. This gives the boy who may not be clever, but really tries, an equal chance against the more gifted boy. Secondly, the last hour of work on Saturday morning has been made into a Detention Hour, when the careless or idle boy is kept in, whereas those who have worked well throughout the week are rewarded.

The radical nature of the change in the whole philosophy of the teaching at The Hall implied by this is nicely encapsulated in this somewhat corny sonnet, written by Mrs d'Ouffet, the then Head of English:

The Mark Grub
(Then and Now)

I grubbed for marks, it was my sole intent
To get the topmost place by hook or crook
And to this end my energies I bent,
Nor blotted carelessly my inky book.
I minded not to what I turned my brain –
To Chaucer, Latin, French or Mathematics,
It mattered not, so long as I could gain
An extra mark for scansion or for Classics.
Now – all is altered: he who works the best
Is he who to the top at last must win,
Count with the quickest, if he bring real zest
To learning – pep is the important thing!
Henceforth 'Work for Work's sake,' I'll have to hammer!
Lest losing Alpha's joy I drop to Gamma.

This approach to 'stick and carrot' in appraising boys' work led shortly to another Hall tradition – the Over and Under as a grade for work. The first reference to them appeared in 1925. Was it coincidence that Gladstone, in his Junior School final Reading Over address, coupled his pleasure at the high scores of Overs awarded with the keenness and enthusiasm of the staff and the happy spirit that permeated the whole school? Overs for good effort, and dreaded Unders for lack of it, have been with us ever since.

Speech Day is, of course, the archetypal school high-day. The earliest major event for which we have documentary evidence from the pages of the magazine is the Speech Day and Prize Giving which took place in Hampstead Town Hall on December 22nd 1903. The pattern for these occasions was generally the same: a dramatic and musical presentation, followed by an address on the school's year from the Headmaster, and then the presentation of prizes by a notable. In 1903, the boys performed scenes from *A Midsummer Night's Dream* and this was followed by 'two selections from Mendelssohn' (exactly what this comprised, we are not told!), recitations in French and English and part-songs by the school (all of it?). The Headmaster reported on the high success of the year in both sport and academics. The guest of honour, the Vicar of Hampstead, made some suitably uplifting observations, suggesting that the century ahead would provide great opportunities for the young which were not to be missed through over-great reverence for the achievements of the past. After singing the National Anthem, the report continues,

> everyone adjourned to the tea-room. Here, a chosen body of boys hastened to look after the needs of the visitors, by running

to-and-fro with cups of tea, scattering sweets right and left about the floor, and stepping on the toes of any who chanced to be within reach. Many of the junior boys were observed to take up a position as near to the supper table as circumstances would permit: we might also add that some of the said juniors failed to answer the roll-call next day.

In 1915, as a contribution to the war effort (or perhaps as forced by circumstances), there was no Speech Day, and the prize winners were presented with 'scraps of paper', as tokens of their success.

'Every boy was the happier for it,' comments our correspondent somewhat self-righteously, 'conscious that he was doing something towards helping a fellow creature to receive that which he would otherwise have lost . . . through the war.'

Montauban never revived the Speech Day. It was his successors, Gladstone and Chitty who, in July 1920, reintroduced it, transferred to the Summer Term. This annual jamboree continued throughout the period, usually incorporated into the final Reading Over of the academic year, and in essence a combined school play, concert, annual report to parents and distribution of cups and prizes. The guest of honour tended to be the expected important public school headmaster: in 1930, the current Chairman of HMC, the notable Headmaster of Charterhouse, Frank Fletcher, filled the role. Four years earlier, an even more distinguished figure presided over the proceedings: Lord Chelmsford was a former Viceroy of India.

The Hall had prefects during the first decade of the century. Their identity was not made evident before 1906, and it may be concluded that their appointment was deemed appropriate with the move to Crossfield Road and the expansion of the school. With Marshall's departure, the institution seems to have lapsed, until Montauban felt confident that his school was established soundly enough to confer such responsibility on boys. In the summer of 1914, we read: 'Hitherto we have not had four boys with sufficient strength of personality to maintain order in the school and to take any prominent part in its government, but at last our Head has been able to appoint four boys to this post of honour. . . . Theirs is not an easy task, in spite of the powers with which they have been invested, and we look to the whole school to assist them to the best of its ability. . . .' This sounds something of a pious hope, even in more conformist and submissive days; one also wonders just what these powers were.

In 1917, the standing of Hall prefects was such as to warrant the provision of a special chair or bench for them at assemblies. Reference has already been made in the last chapter to this remarkable piece. An insight into contemporary attitudes at The Hall towards the prefects is provided by a 1922 article, 'The Diary of a New Prefect':

> *May 15th.* Today I was made a prefect. I am glad, as I can now give lines and have none myself and bully to my heart's content. . . .
> *May 16th* . . . today I put a drawing pin on the master's chair, but did not get punished for it as he was afraid I would give him lines.
> *May 18th* . . . Whenever I see anybody with anything I like I always confiscate it. Today, I took Smith's gold stud and silk tie just before chapel. . . .
> *May 19th* . . . I heard rumours today that people were saying that I was not a good prefect. I can see no faults. Today I caught Johnson fooling so I gave him a million lines to write. . . .

This not altogether serious piece highlights some of the dilemmas surrounding the elevation of small boys to positions of authority over their peers, a dilemma which by the 1980s was to inspire the thought that a school could operate and boys be taught the disciplines of responsibility and leadership without a prefectorial system at all.

It was in the Gladstone period that another familiar institution is first mentioned. In 1922, we read: 'The division of the school into Houses has been, as had been anticipated, a great success. . . . We have not yet found any inner meanings why particular colours have been allotted to particular Houses: blue for Mr Copinger's House, green for Mr Singleton's, purple for Mr Fawcus'; there does seem a fitness in orange for Mr Williams' House.' The idea for this new system seems to have sprung not from the Headmaster but from Mr Singleton and was intended to introduce a means of rewarding boys in every aspect of school life, a form of 'Good Citizenship'.

The house system was immediately applied to the internal sporting competitions, for major and minor games, and by 1927, House Colours and the attachment of other members of the staff than just the housemasters to the four houses, demonstrates that the arrangements familiar six decades later had been fully established.

Of all The Hall institutions which were products of the 1920s, none perhaps has been more significant than scouting. The very earliest reference to scouting in the pages of the magazine was in 1913, in an article on the then relatively novel movement, by a leaving boy, Dick Hart*, perhaps significantly one who suffered the misfortune of being crippled. His interpretation of the exact *raison d'être* of the scouts may be judged a shade confused. No-one should imagine, he insists, 'that it is merely playing at soldiers. . . . Constant drill will do them no good whatever, but in all probability make them sulky. . . . However, the boy who can only play games well, but cannot shoot, would be of no earthly use if England was suddenly attacked.' This was written just a

*See above, pages 6-7.

year before war did break out. Hart went on: 'Scouting's principal aim and object is just this: by a course of training, to make boys honest, useful and loyal citizens, so that they may "be prepared" for anything and everything.'

Exactly ten years later, his advocacy bore fruit. This hinged on the positive enthusiasm and commitment of the Headmaster. Gladstone and his successors believed in the idea. The Hall became the very first school in London to have its own troop. The story of Hall scouting thereafter is told elsewhere.*

Two other Hall institutions given regular mention in the pages of the magazine were the museum and the library. Because of the ever-abiding shortage of space, neither could be allocated a specific room. Both were merely treasured collections. The museum is the more curious to modern eyes, not least because it was evidently the most eclectic and random of assemblages! First set up in 1905, the magazine proudly announced:

> The Museum is an accomplished fact. In two handsome cases at the lower end of the Great Hall, repose some of the wonders of nature and art, from a neolithic axe-head to an extract from the latest Twopenny Tube.

This latter was clearly an item of significant spoil from the diggings of the currently building Piccadilly Line. Bits of bone, stuffed birds and animals, moths and butterflies, birds' eggs and such miscellanea rapidly filled and overflowed these cases.

> A School Museum should be but a means to an end, namely an intelligent understanding and appreciation of the perfect wisdom and beauty of nature.

It must be remembered that this was the era of a narrower curriculum than eighty years later with very limited opportunities to view a wider world. With no formal science taught in the classroom, somewhat austere textbooks and no television 'eye' able to reveal the wonders of the world, this modest undertaking was necessary and laudable. The museum remained a feature of the school through the Montauban regime. In 1917, it is recorded that he had suggested that a collection of relics of the air raids, suitably mounted, might be added to it. Thereafter, references to the museum dry up. At the same time, science as an organised activity, even if not yet the academic discipline it later became, began to feature in the boys' timetable. The need for a museum declined.

The Hall had a library, or rather a collection of treasured books, from the earliest days. Not until the 1970s in the Junior School, and the

*See Appendix 3, pages 233-236.

'80s in the Senior, were rooms provided solely for the housing of these books. The first confirmation of this collection came in 1907, with an acknowledgement of a gift by the author/parent, Talbot Kelly*, of his books on Egypt and Burma. Nine years later, we read that matters had taken a major step forward. The remnants of the original collection, 'some seventy-odd books were collected, placed in brown paper covers, and duly numbered. But with the passing of the founders, the library fell into disuse, and the books became scattered.' The good news was that the Headmaster had tidied all this up, added many more, asked for gifts, provided suitable handsome bookcases, and set the whole thing up in the Great Hall. 'We now have a Library of over 250 volumes, and in such condition, . . .' A year later, the editor noted with pride the popularity of the Library: 80 out of the 98 boys in the school had taken books out. The levy of a termly subscription of 6d (2½p) is recorded, to fund covering and repairing.

The provision of new titles for the Library relied entirely on gifts. There was no idea in those days that a school should budget for any allocation of funds for such a purpose. Instead, a degree of educational profit was made out of the entrepreneurial nature of the Library. A boys' committee was appointed to attend to the finances as well as the maintenance of books and the registration of 'subscribers'. In 1916, the year when it can be safely stated The Hall School Library in a formal sense was founded, a long, rapturous article was published, including an acknowledgement of a single gift of 137 new additions, and a giddily generous sub of 2/6 (12½p) entitling the reckless A B Steinheim to 'life membership' of the Library.

Some ten years on, another library article provides a vivid picture of the situation in the 1920s. New additions to the shelves came solely from donations and presentations, often from distinguished academic or literary parents. Boys were playing an active role in the organisation. The total numbers of books topped 1,000 (with a further 400 in the Junior School). The titles mentioned strike a modern eye as being somewhat daunting, but then the inspirational generation of specialist children's writers had scarcely emerged, and the literature of the age was either 'classical' and semi-adult, or highly period, racy, 'derring-do', or morally improving. However, The Hall Library in those days boasted sections headed: Art, Adventure, Boys' School Tales, Biography, Classics (novels, fables and short stories), Fairy Tales, History, Plays, Poetry, Humour, Detective Stories, Annuals and Books of Reference. Sixty years later, it is a bigger list, but not much!

It is often suspected that reluctance on the part of boys to read books

*His son became art master at Rugby School, in whose name its Art Scholarships are now awarded.

arose with the intrusion of TV. The impression given in the pages of the magazines is that the young of the '20s were little less reluctant, and they needed chivvying too. The National Book Council offered the school prizes for the best essay on reading books from the Library. It does seem that this encouragement/bribe was necessary. One concludes that for all the pride and pleasure noted in the building up and running of the Library it can scarcely have been a prime feature in the education The Hall provided. Boys were not very eager to absorb themselves in books. The Headmasters were far from lavish in the Library's financial support.

A notable characteristic of The Hall over the years has been the number of competitions the school has arranged, not as a means of fostering a competitive spirit so much as stimulating the boys' interest and exercising their skills and talents. In a curious way, it seems never to have promoted unhealthy elitism. The very first mention of some embryonic form of what would later have constituted a major school competition occurs in 1916, when veiled reference is made to a spelling quiz which clearly dismayed some seniors! Later, in the 1920s, The Hall took part in regular inter-school spelling championships. Membership of the team was a matter of obvious pride.

In the 1920s competitions comparable with those familiar to later generations began to be instituted, invariably as the result of a parental donation. In 1924, there was a poetry recitation competition, adjudicated by Professor H V Routh of Bedford College. Another parent provided the prizes for hobbies competitions, which by the end of the decade, were well established Easter Term traditions. One section of this particular competition catches the eye; the Meccano Model prize was particularly keenly contested. Meccano's attraction for small boys has subsequently died almost totally, until, reborn out of curricular revolutions of the '80s, it has been brought back, this time in the class-room, as the medium for Design and Technology teaching. Its appeal and popularity have been restored.

In 1930, a peculiarly Hall-style competition was inaugurated, the 'AE' Essay Prize. This was for 'the most original essay on the most original subject'. One must suppose that its inspiration was A H Elt, who left The Hall that April for Highgate. This particular competition has disappeared.* Clearly, the funding for the prizes came solely from outside gifts; the school saw no need to undertake it. Only when the Prize Fund was established on such a scale as to generate an income sufficient to prompt the school to run it more positively were these competitions guaranteed the immortality which ensures their continuation long after the original donor has left the scene.

*See below, page 190.

Chapter 4
'There's joy in mere grass in London'*

Sport at The Hall in the early years

No self-respecting preparatory school of this or any age can hope to avoid being judged by its prowess on the playing fields. The problem with a school located less than 400 metres from Swiss Cottage is a critical one. Just where *are* its playing fields? The lack of nearby grass is a recurring theme throughout the school's history. When in July 1929, the Headmaster announced to the parents the decision to re-surface the playground, he did so in a manner which highlighted the perennial handicap facing Hall boys. Mere grass has always been too remote and in too short supply.

But despite the unending search for more and better playing field facilities, The Hall has, from its earliest years, endeavoured to take a full part in the sporting scene. The first issue of the magazine quotes the Headmaster proudly reporting to parents on the highly successful cricket and football seasons, the latter seeing eight wins and only one defeat in the ten matches played. Add to this the fact that three fixtures for a 2nd XI were arranged – this for a school well short of 100 boys of all ages – and it will be seen that games mattered. It is interesting to note how few of The Hall's rivals of 1904 still survive in Hampstead. Where are Upton, Maida Vale, Kenmure, Cricklewood, Loudon House or the Anglo-German School now?

Sport was as much a subject of boy interest then as ever. No less than two of the sixteen pages of the inaugural magazine were devoted to an anonymous piece, 'Cricket at Little Mudbury', which would have owed much to the famous *England Their England* cricket match had it not pre-dated A G Macdonell. A further two pages were allocated to football reports, and the final page of issue No 1 tells us that the reward for a scholarship to Westminster was an extra half-holiday, enjoyed by many at Lord's, where Middlesex were playing

*Typical remark by GAW, speaking to parents in 1928

Surrey. A few lines below is a report, that 'feverish interest has been displayed in the recent Test Matches, and cheers on 'Ash' Thursday were long and loud.'

Early magazines describe typical school sports days, with races up to 440 yards in distance, high and long jumps, the latter rather nicely and possibly aptly described as the 'broad jump', and the familiar egg and spoon, three-legged, obstacle and tug-of-war events. These sports were held at The Hall's ground at Lyndale, Child's Hill, just off the Hendon Way and now long since covered in prosperous houses.

In 1906, rugby football was first attempted, reflecting the fact that increasing numbers of pupils permitted a 15-a-side game to be organised. The editor of the magazine was enthusiastic in his report on the innovation with words which are the more interesting in the light of the ups and downs of this particular sport at The Hall over the years.

> . . . The institution of rugger has been quite an event. The first game, played on a day more fit for cricket than football, was a huge success. There can be no doubt that Rugby Football is vastly superior to Association, in one most important respect. It keeps the players as a body more on the move, makes it impossible to shiver and shirk and almost impossible to funk. As to the dangers, they have been vastly exaggerated, and were we an insurance firm, we would grant an accident policy much more readily to a devotee of the All Blacks than to the followers of the Association game.

All this seems to over-state the case, for rugger remained a minor activity for another 20 years, until re-introduced and made a major sport, with inter-school matches in the mid-1920s. And if The Hall's constant problem over good, local playing-fields has always affected its level of performance, this has been especially so with rugger, and it is true to say that a strong tradition for the game has never developed.

The search for playing-fields is regularly referred to in the pages of the magazine. A tantalising note in the 1907 issue tells us: 'We have been fortunate in securing an excellent new field for football and cricket. It is situated not far from the old one, and is about 5 acres in extent. This gives ample room for two full-sized football pitches; and, in summer, it will be quite possible to have 3 games of cricket going on at the same time.' The mists of time enshroud the exact location or nature of this facility. One thing however that the move to Crossfield Road did permit was a wider range of sporting activity on, as it were, home ground. From 1906, basket ball in the yard, and boxing in the hall were introduced.

One sporting tradition which developed into a major feature of The Hall's annual calendar seems to pre-date the earliest surviving records. There was a gymnastic display at the turn of the century, but sadly, no report appears in any of the magazines and it may never be known how closely these events matched the elaborate occasions presided over by the redoubtable Sergeant-Major Biggs in the 1920s, a tradition ended only in the 1970s.

A postscript to the school's sporting record in the second decade of its existence: in 1907, The Hall recorded a rare victory over the girls of Wycombe Abbey – at cricket. In 1905, the boys had been thrashed, and, as the editor notes, this triumph 'gave us most satisfaction, as we had smarted somewhat under the overwhelming and humiliating defeats of former years.' How sad this particular fixture has not survived!

There is a four year gap accompanying the change in headmasters, when no magazines were produced and hence the story of The Hall's sport is resumed again in 1912. Are any material changes to be discerned? Certainly games remained an integral part of the school programme, and the trend to ever wider diversification in activity is noted. Inter-school fixtures continued to be arranged, and the number completed varied from season to season; it was clearly the vagaries of the weather and more particularly the ravages of health – illness then clearly being far more prevalent than in later years – that reduced the number. The most melancholy term was clearly the Spring of 1917. Under the expectant heading 'Football', appear four sad lines:

> Not a single game was played throughout the whole term, the field being in a very sloppy state and quite unplayable. A few practice games on Strathray was all that could be done; and as far as football was concerned, the term was distinctly disappointing.

This certainly is something of an understatement. Doubtless they recognised that the troops floundering in the mud of Flanders were suffering too.

The extension of physical activity beyond the basic quintet of soccer, cricket, sports, swimming and gym, seems to have begun before the outbreak of the Great War. Various references to them appear in the pages of the magazine: hare and hounds in 1912, horse-riding in 1913, water polo in 1914, fencing in 1917, shooting in 1921, the first inter-school rugby match in 1921 also, billiards in 1922 and, rather significantly in view of the relative novelty of the sport and the considerable capital outlay involved, squash racquets, introduced with the building of the school court in 1921. Add boxing, gym and the very formal 'drill' of the day, and it is clear that Hall boys could scarcely lack regular physical exercise.

Just how high was the standard reached by Hall teams of those days? This must inevitably be hard to judge, for yard-sticks of excellence were different at all levels of sport, and one suspects that the skills in coaching were undeveloped. Somehow, one senses that The Hall's sports correspondents were a shade partisan at times too. Detailed reports of matches were included in the magazines, occupying an unduly large proportion of each issue. In most seasons, the record of success tended to suggest a fairly even balance between victory and defeat. Was it self-deception or a laudable desire to encourage that caused praise to be lavished where little seemed deserved? The 1931 rugby team is a case in point. At Reading Over on April 1st(!) GAW reported that 'we had had a fine football fifteen last term'. He singled out several players for individual praise and recorded the team's debt to its coaches. He neglected to mention that in three out of its five matches it suffered crushing defeats. Often the school played 'pluckily', were unlucky not to score, and lost soundly.

Rugby football clearly presented problems then as later. There was no lack of enthusiasm or resolution. Boys were regularly taken to watch 'varsity or international matches. In A F Blakiston, on the staff in 1920, and R M Garth, who taught from 1927 to 1930, the boys had England internationals to coach them. But rugger was the Easter term game, and quite apart from the lack of nearby playing facilities (and there is no substitute for grass for rugger coaching) the uncertainties of weather and health tended to wreak greater havoc than on other games. Hall boys suffered from a lack of practice and experience so essential in this most elaborate of team games. In 1931, GAW summed up the school's frustrations when, at the Reading Over referred to above, he asserted that rugger was the finest game for boys to play and wished we had a more convenient ground to play on, but still hoped to hear of one. Thus throughout all the period under survey, few rugby matches were played each season and most were lost. The 1930 rugger team were defeated in all four of the term's matches. The selfsame squad of boys the following term provided a rare feat – an undefeated cricket XI.

Indeed, cricket was probably the school's most successful team sport in those days. Even before the Great War, 3rd XI matches were arranged, and net practice was available in the Strathray field, adjacent to the Senior School. The school boasted special cricket sweaters for its teams too. In June 1919 it inflicted arguably its most crushing defeat on another school. The victims were the hapless Heath Mount XI (then located in central Hampstead). The Hall declared at 214 for 4, with R MacColl* 145 not out. G U Salvi then routed the opposition, taking 7 wickets for 1 run, ensuring Heath Mount's dismissal for a total of 3, and a consequent mammoth margin of victory of 211. The same season saw The Hall's first-ever victory over their most redoubtable rival of the day, Tenterden Hall.

*René MacColl was later a notable journalist, war correspondent and historian.

In general, however, there is some evidence that the standards were not very high, suggested by the relative frequency of extremely low totals. In 1923, for example, the 1st XI failed to total 20 on no less than five occasions. However, from 1924, the close proximity of the school to the 'headquarters' of cricket seems to have been recognised, and from that spring, parties of promising players were regularly taken to Lord's for coaching by MCC professionals. 1924 was the year too when Lymington Road emerged as a future home ground for the school. Over the years, The Hall's association with Hampstead Cricket Club has been of vital importance and nowhere more so than in fostering the standard of cricket.

The problem of appropriate, nearby playing fields is a constant nightmare for inner-city schools not blessed with their own grounds. In 1913, the editor of the magazine reported:

> We have a new and better field for matches at Child's Hill this year, part of the old one having fallen beneath the spade of the speculative builder.

A few months later appears the news that 'the vast improvements which have been affected in our playing fields at Child's Hill must have caused satisfaction to everyone. We now have a proper groundsman who understands the work, the fields look smart, the pitches are properly kept, and, what must delight the hearts of those slackers who look upon cricket days as a sort of picnic for their special benefit, there is a real live tuck-shop within a few yards of the pavilion . . . a paradise of ginger-beer and buns . . .'

That very summer, war broke out, and by 1917, the problems of travel to Child's Hill by public transport prompted a switch to new fields at Preston Road 'with its 13 acres, its great pavilion and perfect cricket pitches'. Though further away, the availability of the Metropolitan rail line and the provision of large changing rooms proved irresistible, and for a decade, this north London venue was the home ground for all The Hall's sporting activity.

The first indication in the pages of the magazine that an even better alternative was on hand appeared in the summer issue of 1925, when proper acknowledgement is given to the extreme generosity of a number of parents whose response to an appeal for £3,000 had already produced nearly half the required target. The objective was 'to help Hampstead Cricket Club to buy its ground and thereby secure for The Hall a long tenancy of the ground for use in the summer term. . . . If every friend of the school does 'his bit', and subscribes through The Hall, the school will solve the most difficult and vital problem of finding a cricket field, and secure for Hampstead an open space for many years to come.' Those who had purchased debentures were reminded that the ground itself was their security. At the Speech Day in July 1926, GAW indicated the stark predicament facing the school. The grass at Child's Hill, to which the school still had access, was diminishing monthly as building was extended. Preston Road was inconvenient for the whole school (by now of course greatly increased in numbers) and almost impossible for use by younger boys. The real crisis arose from the notification from Eton College that the neighbouring field, the Strathray, was to be developed for flats (Eton Court). The Strathray was the principal playing space for the juniors, the venue for their sports day and large enough for their football and cricket. It also offered a space for cricket nets and general exercise, including Scout meetings. Its loss brought matters to a head.

Hampstead Cricket Club had used its ground since 1877 but, by ironic chance, in this same year, 1925, it was faced with an ultimatum from its landlord to buy out its lease or accept the loss of the land for building development. Wathen and Gladstone stepped in, seeing the golden opportunity this afforded the school. Their problem was ready capital, since only recently they had been faced with raising funds to buy the school. Hence, the appeal direct to parents, to save H C C for Hampstead and The Hall. The moral issue was not forgotten. 'The preservation of the ground was a benefit to the community and it was desirable to preserve the amenities of the district to those that lived there. In future the boys would be proud of the school, because the school had done this.' Those were the sentiments of the Prize-giver that July, The Bishop of Kingston.

Thereafter, a string of references to The Hall's valiant effort to secure the ground for the club appears in successive issues of the magazine. An agreement with H C C was signed in the autumn of 1925, with Gladstone joining the club's management committee. From the summer of 1926, the school had the use of the Lymington Road ground, a link that has continued unbroken ever since.

The school's initial commitment was for £3,000, a sum all but achieved by the Christmas of 1925, largely by means of the sale of debentures, as well as by straight donations. A donor giving more than £50 became entitled to Honorary Life Membership of the club. Happily, the inaugural season of school cricket at Lymington Road was pretty successful, and the magazine editorial speaks of 'the delights of cricket at Hampstead'. The club's overall appeal was also successful, but a crucial shortfall of £4,000 still remained, and the threat to the survival of the ground continued to lurk ominously. It was a crisis which the school agreed to play its part in resolving. It offered to find half the outstanding figure in return for the use of the ground by the younger boys during the winter terms. This prompt response by the school, although undoubtedly in its own best interests too, proved crucial in guaranteeing the preservation of cricket at Lymington Road, for there was clearly an ultimatum and the money was needed without delay; the threat of a major building development on the site was very real. Its rescue was, in GAW's Speech Day words, 'the outstanding historic event of the year'. Debentures and gifts continued to trickle in: this total figure, £5,000, was a very substantial one and its achievement remarkable especially in the days before appeals by educational charities had become the common occurrence of more recent years. The last few hundred pounds took some getting, and the whole operation was alike a triumph of foresight and resolve on Wathen's and Gladstone's part (both making substantial personal contributions) and of parental generosity.

One significant outcome of all this was the decision to resurface the main playground at Crossfield Road. GAW was apparently told by at least one parent that perhaps this was an even greater priority than the saving of the cricket ground. The consequence was that the draining and asphalting was undertaken, at a cost of £600, an improvement greeted with acclaim. By 1930, a pattern of facilities which is recognisable 50 years later had been established. This did not alter the fact that anxiety over fields for games remained. GAW appealed to parents at Reading Over in December 1929: 'We do need another permanent ground, especially for rugby football next term. We hear much of the crying needs of playing fields for the poor, but the need seems just as great and quite as insurmountable for the rich, and if anyone knows of any land within reasonable distance which we could acquire or rent . . .' he would be grateful for the information.

What clues may be drawn from the pages of the magazines over the attitude to sport and physical education in those days? It would be surprising if the picture we gain of The Hall's games activities failed to reflect widely held contemporary thinking. Sport was essentially for the development of character, and the promotion of masculine qualities of strength, courage and 'pluck'. In this context rugby football had an irresistible attraction, and boxing could be seen as useful and important. It is therefore reassuring to reflect that neither seems to have been of a compulsory nature; the less hardy were spared, although it is hard to guess whether they suffered as a result from the gibes of their fellows. Nevertheless, the display by the 1914 boxing class included a contest which inspired the following remarks: 'This bout presented in a nutshell the whole moral object of learning boxing, for to act manfully and generously is what we want the boxing club to teach, and one only had to watch the various contests to see that the proper spirit was employed by all. Why, to see our tiniest boxer – little Pidgeon – taking hard blows without a flinch was in itself a sight worth a great deal to those who are interested in the boys! And one had only to note the generous handshake at the end of each bout to see no vindictive feelings had been aroused. Long may this fine spirit last!' One wonders what Mrs Pidgeon thought of the proceedings.

Boy participation in the administration of games was introduced in 1914, possibly a product of new attitudes to service arising from the outbreak of the war. No record survives of the permanence of the system which saw a committee of boys given responsibility for the running of the games. The magazine reported: 'There are many small duties, connected with the games, besides assisting in the selection of teams, to be done by the committee, which greatly help the masters. . . . In the old days it was quite a common thing to arrive at the field without the full complement of balls, and often, without a ball at all! Thank goodness, this state of things is now only a grim memory!'

If this shows a commendable approach to training boys in social responsibility, the tone of the editorial a year later is hard to comprehend. Was it meant to be humorous, or did it contain sentiments which genuinely reflected commonly felt contempt for those who preferred not to try hard enough at sport? Having expressed hearty satisfaction at the discomfiture of a hapless swimmer whose concentration was diverted to the spectators on the gallery, the editor goes on: 'We have to confess to the same feelings of malicious enjoyment when we observe one of our football slackers, wandering about the field, hands in pockets, get the ball hard in his bread-basket or some equally tender portion of his anatomy. It compensates one much for having to try to teach these unspeakable bipeds a game which they have neither the sense to understand nor the brain to appreciate.' This passage betrays surely a singularly unattractive attitude to the child for whom organised team games involving the striking or kicking of a ball were an agony; and if written in part jest, it is in singularly bad taste. Unhappily, such references to slackers and idle worms, who preferred sitting indoors to vigorous playground fun, were so regular as to suggest that the editorial was to be taken at face value. Perhaps the stiff upper lip spirit of war-torn Europe had infected even the gentler climes of Hampstead.

While suspecting that pluck counted for quite as much as expertise, it would be an injustice to generations of games coaches to suggest that the teaching of skills was ignored. A long, perhaps rather simplistic editoral article in 1920 explains the degree to which standards at cricket had been reduced by the Great War, and then provides a lengthy summary of the techniques future aspirants to Hall 1st XI teams should seek to perfect. The same issue contains a detailed report of what may well have been a remarkable contest, the 1st XI football v six members of the staff. Clearly, the staff pulled no punches, and were forced to do so by the courage and skill of their schoolboy opponents. The masters won 6–1, but the report suggests a sensitivity to the skills of the 1st XI and the inevitably uneven contest when men (including a current England rugby international) played boys.

Perhaps no activity more encapsulated current attitudes to physical education than gym and drill, a tradition for which had existed from the very earliest days. It is unfortunate that we have to wait until 1913 for the first detailed account of the annual display, referred to by the Headmaster as 'a most important and memorial *(sic)* event in the annals of The Hall.' It cannot be doubted that a starkly militaristic tone characterised these occasions. To begin with, the instructors were retired soldiers, led by the redoubtable Sergeant-Major Biggs. The display, which was the focal point of the year's training, was reviewed by a distinguished military notable, usually in full uniform. The keynotes smacked of Aldershot. 'The new recruits' or 'raw material' had been 'knocked into shape', the reader was informed. 'Evolutions' were carried out with due emphasis on 'smartness'. Boxing and club swinging, dumb bells and tug of war, were followed by gymnastics. Marching and Swedish Drill added to the military flavour. In 1914, General Nicolls was given a formal march past, and he and his ADC inspected the 'parade'. The occasion tended to provide opportunity for the Headmaster or guest of honour – or both – to utter improving sentiments. 'Anything that is worth doing is difficult', the General reminded the boys in that war-threatened summer of 1914, 'and anything that is worth doing is worth doing well.' A patriotic note was evident during the war, and to this, a touch of imperialist fervour was added in the 1920s.

Much of this is understandable. Sometimes another motive for insisting on the virtues of the *mens sana in corpore sano* policy is stated. The editorial in the summer of 1916 explained: 'We have never been so free of coughs and colds, influenza and measles during an Easter term before. We had to work so hard and so often that we left no impurities in our bodies for these nasty little germs to feed on; they were simply starved out of hearth and home, and had to seek lodgings elsewhere. Which is just the thing physical drill was intended for.' The editor goes on to refer to 'our sloppy weary willies and indoor maggots' being made respectable and beautiful to behold, like many another ugly maggot by the beneficial influence of drilling. The implications in this are clear: moral and physical improvement and purification were as important as exercise for exercise's sake or training in co-ordination and control. This is not to deny that an enormous amount of hard work must have gone into what were clearly most elaborate and unquestionably admirable events.

One activity where lack of playing fields created no handicap was swimming. 'Come wet, come fine, come heat, come cold,' declared

GAW, 'every Tuesday and Friday there is a large contingent at the Baths.' From the earliest days, the policy of The Hall has been to regard swimming as an essential skill which every boy should acquire before he leaves. In the late '20s however, an annual inter-school competition did exist for four North London prep schools, Arnold House, York House, Peterborough Lodge and The Hall. Between 1928 and 1931, The Hall won every competition for the Priory Club Shield. Thus, the opening period in the school's sporting history seems to have ended on a rather powerful note.

Let the last word in this section rest with the editor of the magazine in the dim and distant, war-stricken era of the Great War. His tongue was not in his cheek when he proclaimed the ideals to be looked for in Hall School footballers in 1915: 'To sum up, once again, we look forward to seeing our XIs acquitting themselves with credit against other schools, and above all else we hope we shall be able to feel of each individual before the end of the season that he has grasped the meaning of those fine old British phrases of ours, 'to be a sportsman' and 'to play the game'; for bear in mind, now more than ever, that no greater praise can be given to a man than to be told that "he has played the game in the good old British style".' This was after all wartime, in an age when noble heroism in the face of the savage Hun on the fields of Flanders was much in the minds of all. The sullied face of British sportsmanship, evident on football terraces and elsewhere in more recent times was then unimaginable.

PART I: THE FIRST FORTY YEARS

Chapter 5
Fear God . . .★

The Hall's style in the earlier years

Was The Hall notably different from the other schools of the period? From the fragmentary and not always entirely reliable clues to be drawn from editorials, reports on Speech Days and the like, a pattern may be discerned from which a significant understanding of The Hall's style and approach to education is evident, especially in the formative decades between 1910 and 1930. Marshall was a pretty conventional headmaster of a pretty formal school; his successors were far from such. What will prove of particular interest to the general reader is the mounting evidence of progressive attitudes and ideas, well ahead of the times, which spill from the pages of the magazines.

A measure of the calibre of The Hall and the esteem in which it must have been held even from the earliest days, is the number of distinguished parents who have chosen it for their sons. Of course, this is somewhat two-edged: inevitable pressures on school and pupils alike have resulted. In 1916, the editor refers pointedly to the perennial problem of form promotions and the anxious and unpredictable response of ambitious parents. *Plus ca change* . . .! By 1916, however, The Hall seemed both confident and proud, and we read:

> Our success is due to the fact that there has been fostered in the school a more than usually strong desire to get on, to do well, to learn, to excel . . . we have learnt that we do well because we enjoy ourselves and enjoy ourselves because we do well . . .

The personalities of the three Headmasters, Montauban, Gladstone and Wathen, ensured that from the top, there was never that daunting, overbearing atmosphere which inspires learnir g by fear. There was, in tune with the spirit of the age, a greater degree of imposed discipline

★'Fear God, honour the King – and don't be afraid to kiss your mother in public . . .' Advice given to Hall boys in the 1920s.

and formality than would be acceptable fifty years later. The Drill Display with its regimented discipline, inevitably meant that boys were used to military-style instruction. It was the custom in those days, too, to hold a roll-call each morning with backs straight, arms folded and heads held rigidly erect. Interestingly enough, a parent is reported to have complained about this 'Germanic', rather mindless routine. The school protested that it was no more than a useful exercise in self-control.

In one significant respect, The Hall may have been rather different from many of its contemporaries: in the relationship between boys and staff. It is evident that several of the latter were pretty formidable characters. The boys seem remarkably uncowed however, and the atmosphere generated by the Headmasters of the school must have been unusual. GAW, for example, liked to regard boys as human beings. Adults might have their faults, and he even conceived of boys writing reports on their teachers. He could summon the humility to say thankyou in public to the boys for their contribution to the welfare of the staff. And while many of the attitudes to the curriculum current at the time were strongly represented, it is remarkable to read of a prep school headmaster in 1926 suggesting that there was more to education than proficiency in the Common Entrance examination. 'We are always fighting against anything', declared GAW, 'that tends to make education narrow, and in this the day-school has a natural advantage, for boys are brought into closer contact with adults. Home-life gives them many interests and ideas, more to talk about and more to write about . . .' (It was about this time that GAW admitted to parents that he had hoped to run a boarding school, and was disappointed initially to have found himself with only day-boys. He hastened to emphasise how welcome he had discovered the experience of the day-school, not least, one suspects, because it gave him ample scope to put into practice his educational ideas.)*

There was another facet to GAW's approach. It must have been rather unusual in those days to encounter a schoolmaster openly suggesting that parents had any worthwhile role in education. The year he arrived, GAW demonstrated his capacity to introduce positively revolutionary thinking, by establishing a heavily modified and very limited Dalton System for wet games afternoons. Within a very few years, it was possible for a visiting public school headmaster to declare himself 'convinced that The Hall is liberal and refreshing . . . in contrast to many schools otherwise worthily and admirably conducted. . . .' Its two Headmasters were, he went on, 'in the vanguard of educational reform'. About the same time, teachers

*The Hall always had a small group of weekly boarders from the 1910s, up to 1972. This in fact ensured that some of the characteristics of the boarding school prevailed.

trained in the PNEU method were brought into the Junior School, because, so GAW believed, they 'developed a capacity for expression and a facility in English'.

The teaching of English as a positive academic discipline was a feature of GAW's thinking on the curriculum. This was an age when the emphasis in prep schools remained heavily in the abstract realms of the classics and mathematics. GAW's championing of English was but one example of the way The Hall was encouraged to look beyond the conventional. His predecessors, for all their strength and imagination, seem to have given little thought to questioning what, or even how, boys were taught. Admittedly GAW was clearly for the values of intellectual discipline and he frequently recognised that the requirements of the public schools ultimately dictated the style and content of the prep school curriculum. Yet it is very evident from repeated outspoken remarks that he was far from content to accept the received and almost universally unchallenged attitudes. The Hall parents of the 1920s must have been amazed, and one hopes, excited by some of his views.

These were the days when the more academic public schools spurned English as an academic subject in itself. For GAW, English was a subject of particular importance. At a Reading Over in December 1924, Gladstone referred to this. 'Special attention is now paid to English, under Mr Wathen's direction. The improvement in this subject has been remarkable.' Two years later, it was GAW himself who spoke, further revealing the philosophy which was inspiring the school. '. . . English – to my mind, the most important subject of all. Ideas and the expression of ideas are the basis of education and the basis of English lessons. For this there is scope when for one period a week the class ceases to be a class and becomes a club; the master ceases to be a teacher and becomes an interested listener, while a boy takes the chair and calls on members to talk of hobbies they have pursued, experiences they have had or information they have gathered.'

Both Gladstone and Wathen seem to have been decades ahead of the field in their attitude to the teaching of science and of practical skills. This in turn inspired mounting concern over the undue burden created by the classics. Latin and Greek were the keys then to winning scholarships, and this meant an early start and a heavy load: upwards of a quarter of the week's work for five full years was the norm. Yet it was 1925 when formal science teaching was introduced into the Senior School, albeit in a modest fashion and, of course, with very limited facilities. In establishing the balance between this new subject and the heavy bias given to Latin, Gladstone explained 'our hands are to a large extent tied.' By the end of the decade, 5th and 6th forms were studying some science – a syllabus heavily weighted towards biology and by more modern standards little more than 'nature study', supported by 'practical work in the garage'! No such luxury as a laboratory for them. In 1931, GAW told his parental audience that science was 'a subject of great educational value with a big future.' How right he was, yet one suspects that few readily believed him at the time.

No less forward thinking was the encouragement given to practical work. 'It must be our purpose', Gladstone stated in 1924, 'to inspire the boys to learn to use their hands as well as their heads,' and hence his positive encouragement of hobby pursuits years before this was seen as a proper role for school.

In 1930, GAW took the opportunity of the presence of the Chairman of HMC as guest of honour at Speech Day to suggest publicly that geometry be replaced by biology as a required subject for Common Entrance. The idea was sympathetically received, but it was not for another 40 years that a positive move in this direction was to occur.

GAW's attitude to Latin was sometimes hard to interpret. He admitted 'an old-fashioned prejudice in favour of a classical education'. But he did so for a characteristically eccentric reason: 'It makes men seem better than they are and tends to prevent their becoming bores.'! His oft and loudly proclaimed answer to the mounting pressure on the timetable, a problem then as ever afterwards, was a later start. 'My belief is that the intelligent boy learning later will learn more quickly, and for the unintelligent boy Latin is so difficult, and the amount learnt in five years is so small and learnt at so heavy a cost that a gain will accrue by spending the time on English. . . . I feel sure that in a few years' time no one will begin Latin until he is 9.' These words were spoken in 1930. So overwhelming were the conservative forces of inertia that it was not until the 1980s that action was taken in line with these eminently realistic and sensible sentiments.

One of GAW's views, supported by His Majesty's Inspectorate, was that, in the Senior School, specialist teachers should always be appointed in preference to 'jacks of all trades'. By 1929, he could assert that this had been achieved. 'We now have specialists in every single subject who are teaching their own subjects almost entirely.' History had always been a strong subject throughout the '20s, and under a new appointment, Mr Quinton Barber, it clearly became a key one. The same year, one of the great figures in the story of the school, Mr C L Rotherham also joined, to establish geography on no less strong a basis.

Wathen did not neglect the so-called major subjects however. He so reinforced the teaching of mathematics, that in 1930, four senior forms were split into 8 divisions for this subject. Given that classes were slightly smaller then than in later years, this does argue remarkable value for money. In French, Wathen was even more notable for a progressive approach. He saw French as a living language, to be taught by direct method. Pictures of him surrounded by boys in the garden would be captioned *Dans La Cour*, and if the proceedings were *al fresco*, they were essentially conducted *à la française*. It was, so we read in the 1927 number of the magazine, the inspiration of the modern language teaching at Rugby School which prompted his belief in this method.

Where, one may wonder, can the curriculum of these early years be faulted, by modern standards if not by contemporary ones? Possibly in the school's provision for the creative arts. This must include imaginative writing. Nothing marks a greater contrast between the magazines of the early years and those of more recent times than the literary offerings of the boys. This is puzzling in view of GAW's oft expressed passion for English, and the evident talents for debating, public speaking and recitation regularly reported in the magazines. Likewise, drama was certainly represented in annual school activities from the earliest years. Indeed, from the very first recorded Speech Day in December 1903 comes evidence of boys acting, on that occasion, scenes from *The Mad-Hatter's Tea Party* and *The Critic*. Over the years, however, there never seems to have been a serious attempt to undertake a major drama production. Was this because the school had no proper theatrical facilities? More probably, the explanation is that, in large part, school drama was never given consideration as anything much more than a fun hobby in the tradition of vaudeville entertainment. After all, George Robey was a prominent Hall parent!

Music and art were alive at The Hall in the early years, but mere shadows of what they have commonly become in this and most other prep schools since. Indeed, Gladstone in December 1928, speaking to parents, had to admit that while the report of the Inspectors (who had visited The Hall the previous year) was 'excellent', they had expressed the hope that 'we would pay more attention to the artistic side of the school life, such as singing, painting and drama.' Of course, as every account of the preparatory schools of those decades would confirm, the emphasis on this side of the curriculum was generally very slight, and it is proper to acknowledge that the pages of The Hall magazine are full of references to activity. It was however largely recreational and scarcely seen as an essential ingredient in a balanced education. Significantly perhaps, when science first established its toe-hold, it was an option only – and offered as an alternative to drawing classes!

Indeed, art seems to have been the greatest 'cinderella' of them all.

The first specific mention of any serious encouragement for the subject is a single-line reference to 'the winning of the drawing prize', by H C Lee*, in 1921, a year in which a number of boys won Royal Drawing Society certificates. The 1928 Inspector's Report clearly stung Gladstone and Wathen into action, and from 1929, things began to happen.

Music clearly fared better. The first concert held at Crossfield Road, on November 11th, 1905, appears somewhat short on boy contributions: only singing was on offer. But it was a start. The chapel choir, very much the inspiration of the ordained Mr Marshall, was inaugurated a month later, and regular Sunday services were held, with growing congregations, throughout the early years of the century.

It was not until November 1914, with a charity concert in aid of the Prince of Wales's Fund, that we can read of any substantial musical enterprise. Here is the first mention of string players, but still, and for many years yet, it is choral and vocal pieces that constitute the bulk of the programme. This particular occasion was a grand patriotic event, with 'Rule Britannia', the National Anthem and 'La Marseillaise' helping to raise a total of £13.13s.6d.

The almost total concentration on singing as a vehicle for musical education was entirely in line with the practice in most schools of the day. In his memoirs of the prep school world†, Arthur Harrison writes of the music of this period:

> There would be the hearty singing classes once a week, a few boys learning the piano and perhaps the occasional violinist, who was really a beastly nuisance; only the larger schools, with teaching facilities near at hand, could aspire to the less obvious instruments or anything that could be called an orchestra. The cause of music was in the doldrums.

The Hall's first recorded orchestra was something of a fraud! In 1918, we read of the boarders' orchestra, under the leadership of the Headmaster: 'the "patent" humming instruments . . . produced quite harmonious effects . . . their performance was distinctly musical.' Combs and tissue paper. Oh dear! War austerity indeed. No school concert is recorded at all thereafter until the Easter term of 1923, by which time, the appropriately named music master, Mr Chanter, had assembled a pianist, violinist and cellist to play a trio, as well as the various solo items. Not a clue is given as to the identity of the pieces. Indeed, the first published concert programme appeared two years later, but once again the boys' contribution was exclusively vocal and the orchestra was entirely adult.

*See memoir, page 174.

†*'How was that, Sir?'* pub. IAPS.

In 1929, the young Leslie Woodgate was appointed to The Hall staff as singing and music master. This, not one suspects a full-time post, was an immediate consequence of the Inspectors' Report, already referred to. Addressing the parents at Speech Day in July 1929, GAW spoke as follows:

> It is a year now since the school was inspected by the Board of Education, and we are grateful to the Board for the thoroughness of their work and quality of their advice. I stated last term that we had taken certain action on that report, notably by the appointment of a geography specialist (referred to above), by engaging Mr Leslie Woodgate* to teach singing and musical appreciation and by slight alterations in the timetable and text books, and by devoting Thursday afternoons in the winter term to music, drawing and drama.

By the end of this opening phase in the school's history, the arts were recognised as having importance and value, though they were still regarded as optional and essentially recreational and in no way an integral part of a balanced curriculum. The Hall was probably ahead of many of its contemporaries. By the standards of 1930, it had little to be ashamed of.

*Leslie Woodgate subsequently became perhaps the best known of all conductors of the BBC Choral Society.

PART II: THE WATHEN YEARS

Chapter 1
'Halcyon Days' 1930-1938

'The term that has passed has been a jovial one in every way. Everyone seemed to enjoy it in all its manifestations and work has gone with a swing; even the murky fogs added interest by their weird darkness and gloom.'

So began the editorial of the magazine recording the events of the autumn of 1930. Those who remembered GAW can believe it, for joviality was part of his nature and there was always a merry twinkle in his eye.

But sadly a dark shadow had fallen over the school, for Captain Dyson had just died. He had only been on the staff for five years. He was a man of unusual kindness and patience and was quite rightly described in the memorial tablet as *magister magnopere dilectus*.

Two new masters joined the staff that term, Mr C F Dodd to strengthen the French department, and Mr D L M Castle to increase the maths staff; GAW had decided to include two periods per week for the teaching of geometry, to the delight of Mr Copinger. In those days of course, geometry was regarded as a subject quite distinct from arithmetic and algebra.

The school 1st XV had an unsuccessful season in 1930, playing only four matches, all lost. No doubt those murky fogs must have made life very difficult. But if games were scarcely possible, there were frequent debates in their place, and a plethora of debating clubs seemed to spring up; there was the Neo-Georgian Club, The Hot Air and Gas, The Little Parliament and the Query Club. Furious, earnest and contentious seem to have been their proceedings. And there was drama too, and a major concert on the final afternoon of term. This event perhaps lent that autumn its air of joviality and it was quite significant how important was the role played by GAW's staff in providing the entertainment. Mr Leslie Woodgate was by now well established as the choir master. The following term, the boarders put on a vaudeville show and again the final week saw a 'perfect orgy of acting', as the magazine somewhat extravagantly had it. The Spring term saw rugger matches, more lost than won, with The Hall as usual grossly under-trained and inexperienced. The traditional gym display was inspected by a general, the school's squash tournaments were keenly contested, and all in all, an air of busy enthusiasm seemed to bubble from the pages of each term's records. Such was to be the routine pattern in the 1930s.

Another annual event was instituted at this time: the Scout Display. The format was not unlike the gym show, for a distinctly military atmosphere seems to have prevailed and as often as not, a general or an admiral reviewed the proceedings. Clearly GAW was never happier than when he could see his fellows on parade, and even more so when they were dressed in scout uniform. He was always a firm champion of the movement, even to the point of being over-persuasive. Some boys clearly felt almost compelled to join, just to please him.

GAW was nevertheless a very shrewd judge and a keen observer of his boys. He gave them all potted biographies as they left. The legacy of this is still available in the pages of the magazines. A rather more pointed judgement can be discovered on the individual record cards each boy was given through his career. Some have survived; GAW's comments could be highly dismissive. He was never unkind, in public at least, although he could be witty. One suspects that some boys may have been more affected than he would have intended. A tradition he established for his senior boys was an annual party for the leavers, given in formal style by Mrs Wathen and himself at 2 Buckland Crescent. An account of such an occasion comes down to us:

> He who would know all the ceremonies of a city dinner, let him attend this annual festivity. Mr Wathen, at the head of the table, in genial, jovial mood, directs the proceedings, and *sotto voce* gives tips to those nearest as to when to sit, to sip, to stand, and how to address the assembly should it fall to their unhappy lot to do so.
>
> First of all, the company, including a large number of staff from Junior and Senior Schools, enjoys the dainty fare – iced cantaloupe melon, fish, chicken, ices and fruits in their season. Then, when the bonbons circulate, Mr Wathen jumps up and proposes the health of the King. This having been heartily received, he cries, 'Gentlemen – and ladies – you may smoke,' and fat cigars appear with a real city expensive aroma.
>
> Everyone now being fed and in excellent humour, Mr Wathen performs his task to admiration. Fun and wit roll down the table from his lips: no one knows what next he will be saying, and each victim awaits with joy and anticipation the jokes at his expense. How well does he know all his boys and how truthful all his jokes are; his humour is kind and full of knowledge and many a boy will

> remember these parting words all his life. After this coruscation of words, the remaining speeches seem somewhat quiet in tone, but they also give pleasure.

How GAW would have enjoyed an occasion such as this, when he could make full use of the language he so much loved. He was constantly urging the boys to read and so increase their vocabulary. How often he referred to 'the noble English tongue.'

And so time rolled on. The Hall continued to win the annual swimming gala for local prep schools. Cricket, GAW's particular love, flourished and coaching was arranged at Lord's for a dozen promising players. Each summer, the final Reading Over became an occasion for GAW to proclaim his views on some educational matter, often views that were far from the conventional ones of the day. He never denied that the academic work must come first, but not at any price. He felt that scholarship-hunting was a dangerous habit and he never wanted The Hall to be judged by its scholarships or by its games record, alone. He defined the objective he sought:

> It is not merely pouring knowledge into willing ears but creating an environment in which boys may come to believe in themselves, to be confident without being conceited, and to be modest without too much reserve.

At the same time GAW never forgot that such a philosophy can only be made to work well if teachers of inspiring quality are provided. In September 1932, another of the 'giants' of The Hall staff arrived. Mr Hugh Fyson, a product of Rossall and Jesus College, Cambridge had, like GAW, been in the Indian Civil Service, spending some time in the Punjab. For some 27 years Fyson was to be a powerful figure in the common-room, responsible for that key scholarship-winning subject, the classics. This appointment was made shortly after the departure of GAW's partner, Major Williams. For reasons of health, Major and Mrs Williams decided that the summer term of 1933 was to be their last. GAW, who had by then completed 25 terms in office, assured the boys and their parents that he had not the slightest intention of retiring for many years and that he was most unlikely to take another partner. He felt entirely confident in running the whole show on his own. Thus began the great period of Wathen rule.

Williams had taught at The Hall since 1925 and clearly made a mark on the school. The games, gym and boxing had come under his active control, and he had been responsible for encouraging debating skills as well as English, all matters close to GAW's heart. Perhaps his most important role lay in relieving GAW of all the worrying work connected with finance, insurance, repairs and commercial administration generally, all matters that were not GAW's prime interest. Hence, a very significant appointment in 1933 was that of Miss J F Large as resident school secretary and bursar. She remained a vital aide to GAW for the rest of her life, dying in office in 1950. Not the least of the reasons for her appointment was the evident increase in demand for places in the school, and the Junior School found itself accepting boys at rather younger than the customary age of 7. Williams's other function, as GAW's deputy, was filled by promoting the senior man in the common-room. From 1933, W H Copinger assumed the official title of Vice-Principal.

The termly diaries are filled with all the routine events, which it would be more than tedious to recite in repetitive detail. Plays, using the nearby *Embassy*, still a commercial theatre then, savage epidemics, catastrophically inept rugger teams, anxious enquiries about alternative games fields, charity fund-raising, lectures and expeditions, all receive due termly mention in the magazines of the day. Some quaint novelties are recorded. The Hall Boat Club appeared, practising its doubtless impressive skills on the lake in Regent's Park. It is rather more curious to discover that regular fire-drills were so unusual as to warrant mention. The arts seemed to flourish, with successes recorded in painting competitions, poetry writing competitions and most particularly, spelling competitions. These latter were avidly supported. A champion member of Hall spelling teams of the period was GAW's younger son, Julian, who, ever after, has been not merely a meticulous speller himself but a stern critic of those younger generations not brought up in his stricter schooling. He recalls that a princely prize of 5s (25p) was awarded to each member of the winning school's team.

Regularly, GAW made his pronouncements to boys and parents, which were duly reported. Such a lover of language, he is found in 1933 speaking much as his successors might fifty years later, complaining about the Common Entrance Examination in French, and the decision to change its character and suit itself not to his favoured direct method but to more traditional styles of teaching.

> This to my mind is a retrograde step, but here we shall not change our methods for we have never pretended to teach boys merely to get them through examinations.

A year later, he was commenting on the boys' successes in a national competition which had been adjudicated by Alfred Noyes:

> What natural advantages we English have in being able to speak and write our noble tongue, to study a history so full of glory, a geography so full of interest, our fine classical Latin tradition leading to the lively language of France, our modernised methods, our libraries . . . what a rich inheritance, so that school life is not a

> dull preparation for life, but life itself and a full and mighty interesting one.

Very quickly the impact of Mr Fyson's teaching of the classics was to be felt. He produced a complete book of common rhymes translated into Latin and these became popular items in the concerts of those days. Greek meanwhile was being taught to potential scholars for at least two years prior to the exam. 'For my part', declared GAW at one final Reading Over, 'I confess that I am an unrepentant conservative in thinking that for the best brains Greek is invaluable.'

We have by now reached the year 1935. The school celebrated the Silver Jubilee of King George V by re-building two 6th form classrooms. The boys marked the occasion by raising funds for the Jubilee Trust, in aid of the nation's youth. GAW seems rather to have stung them into action, and over £28 was raised from their own pocket money. Can the Fund secretary really have meant it when he described The Hall's contribution as 'the best I have had yet'? A few months later, the King was dead. By way of memorial, the magazine reprinted his Jubilee message. Its sentiments are distinctly of the period:

> The King is speaking to you. I ask you to remember that in days to come you will be citizens of a great Empire. As you grow up, always keep this thought before you: and when the times comes be ready and proud to give to your country the service of your work, your mind and your heart.

This moment of national mourning coincided with the presentation to The Hall of its oldest surviving trophy, the Nordon Topics Shield. The study of national and international affairs had for some years been strongly encouraged. It was seen as an important element in The Hall curriculum. Sometimes, the magazine passed less serious comment on current political situation, as when concern was expressed at the situation in Abyssinia. The boys' anxiety over the implications of the imposition of sanctions against Italy was noted: would the supplies of macaroni hold out in this country? These fears proved to be unfounded, and the boys were able to continue to receive invitations to the Wathens' vegetarian lunches at 2 Buckland Crescent. On a rather more serious note, the first winner of the Nordon Topics was J P Johnson for his essay on 'The Death of King George V'.

During the 1930s, the fabric of the school grew only slightly, to match the swelling numbers of pupils, but very real efforts were made by GAW to improve and enhance the existing buildings. The main hall, which he and Gladstone had wished to beautify with panelling, at parents' expense some years before, now began to be adorned in a style which came to be associated with The Hall in its heyday. It was an indication that GAW had succeeded in making the parents feel that the school no longer was his private property and thus that gifts to it were not, effectively, straight donations to him. So the panelling of the hall began, and continued year by year. Once embarked on the scheme, he did not leave its success to chance but fitted new sections before they had actually been presented. The leaving boys' parents were by now generously giving inscribed chairs, pictures and other objects. The panelling policy was pushed ahead, very mindful, as GAW observed, of Dr Johnson's definition of gratitude, as having 'a lively sense of favours to come'!

The new panelling was only a part of the enhancement of the hall, which was to make it so memorable and dignified. The next step arose from the generosity of an anonymous donor who inaugurated a fund with a gift of £5 with the object of decorating the school hall with the coats of arms of the public schools. Those of Westminster and St Paul's had already been obtained in addition to the shield of Harrow, the first received. Arrangements were made with an heraldic artist to supply the design of any school at a flat rate of £1. 11. 6d or one and a half guineas. Each shield was hand-painted on oak and was heraldically correct.

Thus began in 1936 the unique collection of shields which adorned the hall and proved a singularly characteristic feature of the school for many years. Their fate and subsequent replacement is described in a later chapter. The one quite remarkable coincidence here is that, by total chance, the very first shield to be painted by the College of Arms in 1985 was again that of Harrow. The cost of each shield in the 1980s was nearly £50.

During the 1930s GAW was to make plenty of references to the hall, for here was a development of the school of which he was justly proud. A description of it appeared in the 1938 magazine, explaining the third element in the scheme for its embellishment:

> The panelled hall is the pride of the school and rightly so, for few preparatory schools possess such a stately assembly room.
>
> In April 1936 the idea of collecting the arms of the public schools was suggested. It was taken up and the first shield, that of Harrow, quickly made its appearance and companions soon arrived so now the east side of the hall is full of colour and a beginning on the south side has been made.
>
> Between the gallery and the shields there was left a bare strip of yellow distemper. Here Mr Bainbridge Copnall has started work on a series of mural canvases. The general scheme is to have one canvas for each period of English history. In the centre of each is a large medallion depicting a scene of outstanding importance. To the right and left are two more on a smaller scale. Ships, soldiers,

> weapons and buildings form the background. The medallions are beautifully coloured, whilst the background has a sepia finish.

By the beginning of 1938 Copnall had hung two of these canvases. The first took us to the murder of Thomas à Becket, with a Saxon thane making entries for the Domesday Book forming the centre medallion. The background showed the Roman conquest, the Viking ships and the death of Harold. The chief scenes of the second were King John and the Magna Carta and the martyrdom of Joan of Arc at Rouen. English knights and archers were seen in the background. Copnall was unable to complete the frieze before war service took him off on camouflage duty further away, and it was eventually finished by another artist, Miss Phyllis Bray, in 1942. It survived for just 30 years, being removed with the rebuilding of the hall in 1972. One representative panel was left, to be destroyed by the fire of 1982.

Improvements in the building and facilities were not confined to the Senior School alone. A solarium classroom was built at the Junior. The room was constructed chiefly of timber, the internal wall sheathing being in natural pine, and the floor in oak strips. The room contained fourteen windows, folding back completely so as to leave the east and south walls entirely open. This has subsequently been altered to make the room rather more conventional.

The 1930s saw the inception of two very significant bodies within the constitution of The Hall, which were to develop into the Board of Governors on the one hand the Parents' Association on the other.

As early as 1934, GAW made a formal announcement to parents, reported in the magazine.

> 'This term marks the beginning of a new period in the history of The Hall. It has been for fifty years (sic)* a purely proprietary school, the private property of a self-appointed headmaster. That era is over. The school has now a Board of Governors with whom the appointment of future headmasters will lie.'

It was in fact a great act of self-sacrifice for a proprietor to surrender a degree of autonomy for no obvious personal advantage. GAW revealed a remarkable prescience in recognising his own mortality at such long notice, and hence the need to anticipate the future selection of his successor. He was way ahead of his times in seeing that this was best guaranteed by translating The Hall from being a private profit-making business into a Charitable Trust under a Board of Directors, or Governors, whose principal responsibility would be the appointment of his successor. Admittedly, the men he invited to become his governors were personal friends, all with a close

* Fifty years is in fact incorrect. The misapprehension that The Hall was founded in 1884 was still held in 1939, when this date of foundation was quoted in the prospectus.

commitment to the school, and one suspects that the arrangement was initially pretty informal. GAW remained in effective control for a number of years yet, and any formal establishment of The Hall School Trust Ltd had to wait a further 18 years, until 1952. Even so, the step GAW had taken was highly significant and somewhat unusual, being not the least of the many remarkable things he did for The Hall.

Having taken this initiative, the transition of the Board of Governors from having a purely advisory role, which seemed to be even somewhat artificial, into the body with ultimate reponsibility was not achieved without some awkwardness, as will be revealed. Meanwhile another organisation began to take shape.

Over the years, both the school and the parents had grown more and more concerned over the rising volume of traffic and the possibility of serious accidents.

In 1936, it was road safety which so concentrated the minds of parents as to make possible the formation of the Parents' Association.

Under the auspicies of a newly formed body, The Hall Mothers' Association, the school set up a branch of the nation-wide 'Junior Road Fellowship'. Inspired by its slogan, 'Alert today, alive tomorrow', the purpose of the fellowship was to prevent, as far as was humanly possible, the toll of the roads since, as the figures then showed, the greatest number of fatalities occured to boys between the ages of ten and sixteen. This was at a time when there was far less traffic on the roads and it moved much more slowly. In *Scouting for Boys* Lord Baden-Powell wrote: 'Accidents sometimes occur from runaway horses running down people. It is as well that everybody should know how to stop a runaway horse.' This was still the day of the coal-cart, brewer's dray, baker's and milkman's carts, all horse drawn, and it was only after the Second World War that they were replaced by lorries and vans.

This initiative was destined to lead to a wider transfer of partnership to the parental body. It was, after all, fully consistent with GAW's whole philosophy – that the school was no longer his personal property but a shared responsibility. It was in these circumstances that a well-attended meeting took place at The Hall on 25th January 1937 in response to GAW's invitation, to consider the formation of a Parents' Association. GAW outlined the history of the school, explaining that, although private in name, it might be regarded almost as a public institution. As there was already a Mothers' Association for social purposes, he thought that a larger body including the fathers might serve a useful purpose to foster further interest in the school and to increase and formalise co-operation.

Mrs Ormerod, in formally proposing that a Parents' Association of The Hall should be formed, emphasised the importance of retaining their freedom of choice and of maintaining a school such as The Hall. The Association would strengthen the bond between parents and staff.

Mr Lowson, who seconded the proposal, said that the great strength of The Hall was in the character of its boys. The school stood for something special and something important and necessary in London at that time; for it recognised the right of the boys to be happy and he felt it was worthy of any support that the parents could give.

The list of officers and committee appointed at this juncture was interesting perhaps in two respects. Firstly, since he was Chairman, GAW retained the initiative and Mrs Wathen was one of two members of a Mothers' Committee. Secondly, the committee of 1937 included not just two university professors, but the wives of two of the luminaries of the Labour Party, Harold Laski and GDH Cole. The Association's inaugural meeting under the arrangements of *Rule* 7 was well supported, but in retrospect the subject has a distinctly chilling sound to it. Professor Veit Valentin spoke on the German ideals of education. A few months later, the first AGM of the Association was held, and the debate rapidly focused on such issues which have tended to occupy it ever since: German measles rather than German education.

The outbreak of war was by now only two years off. The routines of prep school life continued, scarcely concerned with looming dark clouds. A new agreement with Hampstead Cricket Club secured The Hall's access to the ground until 1956. The Coronation of the new King was celebrated, again with The Hall fund-raising, generously, for charity. Rugger matches continued to be lost by mammoth margins, while the football teams (composed presumably of much the same players) won most of their fixtures. The magazines reported the normal small boys' crazes. The Easter term of 1938 witnessed an outbreak of 'the royal and ancient game of marbles'. Art, music, the writing of poetry, acting, the Scouts, the Hall Old Boys Association, all had their mentions in the pages of the school journals. The Hall's spelling teams did better than ever; the seniors were third and the juniors first in the national prep school competition. GAW continued to pronounce on all manner of educational issues. One matter which seems somewhat puzzling was his suspicion of boys joining local lending libraries, partly because he believed that the school's own library was perfectly equipped for their needs, and partly because he was highly dubious of the quality of their reading:

> There is, however, a deplorable and increasing tendency, recently, on the part of the younger boys to join local libraries and to borrow books dealing with murder and crime of an unhealthy nature. This

> is most disappointing and makes it difficult for us to inculcate the habit and love of reading good books.

Somewhat abruptly, a quite new and sinister note is sounded. This was in 1938. The Scout movement had recommended, so we read, that boys should specialise in fire drills. The dread initials ARP (Air Raid Precautions) were being used. Members of staff were undergoing army training courses. By far the most serious crisis to face The Hall was just months away.

PART II: THE WATHEN YEARS

Chapter 2 War Years 1938-1945

Storm clouds had been gathering in Europe throughout the thirties. Refugees had brought the reality of Hitler's regime home to Britain and in no place was this truer than north-west London.

GAW felt that the crisis was so serious and that war was so imminent that he made plans for the school's evacuation to Wiltshire. At the end of September 1938 about half the school, including around thirty Junior School boys, left for Codford, near Salisbury Plain, where in spite of many adversities, they contrived to survive and even enjoy themselves.

Meanwhile Crossfield Road was closed down and the Junior School became the headquarters of the 'skeleton school', which rapidly put on flesh and acquired the proportion of a respectable body of a hundred and twenty scholars of all ages and sizes. 'Very pleasant it was to work with a combined staff and welcome back old friends from the Senior School who doubtless thought they had shaken the dust of the Junior School from their feet for ever! Crises have their compensations.'

Mr Griffith, then one of the staff, has left us an interesting account of the evacuation to Wiltshire which in the event lasted just four days.

> It was, perhaps, with mixed feelings that we heard that as a precautionary measure we were going to Codford. What kind of a place was it? How long would we stay there? What should we take? Few of us had even heard of the name before and there was a hurried looking up of maps. What was the house like? Was it furnished? Yes, but we were each to take our own bedding. What about school books? Take them in case we might be there for some time. Games? Yes, take plenty of footballs.
>
> Well, after a hectic day and a half spent in preparation we left London on September 29th. A few went by car but the majority travelled by train from Paddington.
>
> The main body arrived at Codford at half-past four and found that an advance party had, under Mr Millard's directions,

transformed a quiet country house into a very possible preparatory school for boarders. Conspicuous notices confronted us – Boys' Entrance, Assembly Hall, Dining-room, Staff-room and so on. We soon learnt our way about.

We found that Ashton Gifford House, which had been so kindly placed at our disposal by Catherine, Lady Headley, stood in its own grounds of some sixty acres. In front of the house there was an extensive park in which we were able to play football when the weather was kind. Round the house were some shrubberies containing numerous paths and hiding-places, and soon found to be ideal for 'gang warfare'.

The weather was disappointing on the whole, but in spite of that we managed to see something of the surrounding country.

On Friday three motor-coaches were chartered to take us on a tour of Salisbury Plain. First we made for Stonehenge and arrived in the middle of a downpour. Fortunately it cleared in a few minutes and we were able to examine at close quarters this colossal relic of our past history.

Saturday was fine and an expedition was made to the White Horse at Westbury. Coaches took the party to the nearest point on the main road and there then followed a glorious ramble over the downs, over springy turf and in air that was in itself a tonic.

Sunday morning was wet and it was not possible to do much. A special service was held for us by the Vicar in the afternoon.

Many boys were able, with Mrs Wathen's help, to pursue their hobby of studying natural history, and made the best of their opportunities in pastures new.

Nor must we forget those hardy ones who, at Sir Sidney Herbert's kind invitation, bathed in the private swimming-pool which he had constructed in the river that bordered the grounds.

And so we came to our last evening at Codford, our relief at the end of the crisis tempered by regret that we had to leave such glorious surroundings and return once more to the smoke-filled town.

No mention has been made of the domestic side of the expedition and the problems which had to be solved. This is through no lack of appreciation of what was accomplished, but rather through inability to find words to express adequately the admiration which we felt for the way in which we were fed and looked after under such exceptional circumstances.

And so while reference to the crisis of 1938 will conjure up some visions of gas-masks and air-raid shelters and all-night digging of trenches, for us it will bring back memories of rolling downs, birds singing and the peace of the countryside, our common heritage and yet an heritage that so many of us have found necessary to abandon.

The school's connection with Codford was not entirely severed for, with Lady Headley's help, some Wiltshire Scouts visited The Hall and joined the school Scouts for games on Hampstead Heath and a sing-song.

Referring to the evacuation to Codford, GAW thanked the parents for their help, and the staff, teaching and domestic, for their co-operation and then spoke of the future.

> 'Plans are ready for next time but I also hope that it will never happen. I have my eyes on places in Yorkshire and Norfolk. It is thought that evacuation will be compulsory and some arrangements will be made to reduce the cost of boarding.'

Compliance with London County Council instructions regarding fire precautions had necessitated the reconstruction of the interior of the Junior School building. Doors had vanished from their accustomed places and reappeared elsewhere with a disconcerting trick of opening at you instead of from you. Glass doors and panels had mysteriously appeared, adding considerably to the feeling of space and pleasantly eliminating the privacy of the classrooms; but above all, the occasion had been seized upon to indulge The Hall's, or GAW's, love of brilliant colour. Eyes were first dazzled by the display of scarlet, green, orange and blue doors and walls, while an abundance of cream paint greatly added to the lightness of the rooms. It was observed that the decorations had remained remarkably undimmed after a term's close acquaintance with over a hundred of The Hall's liveliest members.

It was perhaps in tune with the sober atmosphere of the times that the boys were being encouraged to look to their physical fitness. Certainly, this has not always been a feature of Hall boys over the years, before or since. The magazine reports that the soccer and rugby teams of 1938-39 were notable for being very fit. Increased resistance to illness and hence better attendance at school lay behind the scheme to introduce a series of physical tests, designed to enable any boy to achieve a pass standard if he practised adequately.

There were three grades – for boys under 10, over 10 and over 12. They were tested in running, skipping, throwing a cricket ball, high jump and, for seniors only, rope-climbing. A long jump test was added later. One test was common to all grades. Candidates had to satisfy the authorities that throughout one term they had not been absent from school for reasons of ill-health. By March 1939 eleven boys had qualified for Grade I, fifteen for Grade II and sixteen for Grade III.

Six months or so after the Munich crisis the boys were clearly becoming increasingly aware of the preparations which were being made for another emergency. In the papers and on placards in the street there were advertisements encouraging civilians to become Air Raid Wardens or to join the Services. It was clear that the 'peace in our time' secured by Mr Chamberlain was only temporary, the lull before the storm.

At the end of term assembly at the Junior School in March 1939 GAW asked the boys to leave the room. He then explained to the parents in detail the evacuation scheme, by which he had arranged that the school be transferred to Claydon House, Buckinghamshire.

Three months later at the end of the summer term, he was once more raising this highly emotive issue. He had to express his anxiety for the survival of the school and at the same time convince parents that he was taking the prudent steps to ensure the safety of the boys. 'I hope that a state of emergency will not force the school to evacuate but we are nonetheless fully prepared.'

GAW somewhat incongruously then went on to describe his vision of the truly happy school. It was as if some ugly premonition of an unhappy future haunted him. 'Listen carefully to what I have to say', he seemed to be hinting, 'because this may be the last opportunity I may have of saying it. You never know what may happen.' He went on to air his views on the best means of securing a proper education of the young, with some thoroughly characteristic sentiments:

> 'A sunny kindly nature is a blessing to him who has it and to those whom he meets, and such a nature may be best developed by a happy boyhood or warped by an unhappy environment. It is for this reason that we who educate to-day emphasise the importance of happiness, but we may differ in our views of how to obtain it. To be happy you need not only laughter, affection, confidence and good health, but a purpose in life, an occupation that absorbs you, work that does not bore you, hobbies that interest you, persons who inspire you. Life here has its laughter. Boys, I hope, are not snubbed. Diffidence is diminished, interest is provided, health is improved; the purpose is not a vague ideal, work is not entirely wearisome, hobbies are encouraged, and I hope every member of our community finds somewhere or in somebody a source of inspiration.'

He said that if the year had been happy, and the school had – in spite of Herr Hitler – carried out tolerably well what it undertook to carry out, it was due to the loyal support he received from both the teaching and domestic staff.

GAW concluded his summer remarks with a reminder about the prudent steps he had taken in the event of the ultimate emergency and issued specific instructions to parents. The London County Council had made contingency plans for the evacuation of schools out of urban areas. If the State of Emergency was declared during the holidays, boys already out of London were to remain away and join the school direct at Claydon House; those in London were to assemble at 9 am at school on the first day of formal education. Thus, the summer holidays of 1939 began on 26th July and the Second World War broke out on 3rd September. The magazine editorial at the time sums up events in a single sentence:

> The magazine has been cut to a mere record, owing to the transfer of the school to Claydon House for the duration of the war.

On 1st September 1939 the school marched off to Kilburn Station, with GAW in front, bravely displaying a worked banner for the information of the organisers of the 'Great Evacuation', a veritable Moses leading his people. Their 'exodus' was to last twenty-eight weeks, with a short rest to celebrate Christmas. From Kilburn they travelled to Euston and then on to Northampton where the boys spent some weeks in billets, while Mr Millard and his assistants were getting things ready at Claydon House.

That autumn term was a long one but fortunately the weather was glorious and remained sunny for weeks. The first few games of football were more than warm when a gigantic kick hardly got the ball beyond the next elephantine tussock of grass.

By contrast the spring term was the shortest ever known and wintry conditions so fierce and so prolonged that there was nothing to do out of doors but winter sports for weeks together and no football till March. Skating was good though there were some rough patches on the lakes. Spade and shovel were manfully plied by volunteers and ashes put down so that the approaches became possible for cars, and it was not for some days that any shortage of coal was felt.

It was regarded as a great experience, a major part of which was the two schools joining up under one roof. The staff who had hardly ever met at Hampstead now daily rubbed shoulders and it had been all to the good. The ladies were invited to 'adopt' the bachelor members of the staff and look after their laundry, darning and the sewing on of buttons.

The boys also had the opportunity of going as a school to church where they 'learnt much about our religion from the simple services there and the lively sermons of the Rector'. One Reading Over took place on 19th March 1940 in the library at Claydon House. Only two parents were present. They were Mrs Ross and the Rector of Claydon, the Reverend W S Hazledine. GAW paid tribute to them both; to Mrs Ross for choosing the school for her war work and for giving to parents that confidence in the school from the knowledge that the health of the boys would be well looked after in her experienced and capable hands; to Mr Hazledine for acting as chaplain and looking after the boys' spiritual welfare. His services, his sermons, his innumerable kindnesses had left an impression that would never be forgotten. GAW added:

> If there is one advantage that Claydon possesses over Hampstead it is in the privilege we have had in our own school services and our own honorary chaplain.

After this Reading Over the chronicler records the last hours spent at Claydon.

> Now it is goodbye to the Park with its noble oaks and cedars, the House with its huge rooms and labyrinthine passages and the free country air of Claydon; and to riding not least.
>
> It has been blowing a southerly gale all day, with leaves and branches tearing across the Park; the air is fresh and cold; packing has all been done and the last load of luggage has left for Claydon station. Boys have been doing yeomen's work, lugging huge trunks. Now we are left with nothing much to do, but play football on the lawn or indoor games and wish for the morn, when we can go marching off in squads to the station bound for Euston. What a lot has happened since we left Euston last September .

So writes the chronicler. There is little else. One of the boys, G E Janner, wrote of his impressions in verse:

I'll always remember Claydon,
Because of the massive doors,
The ceilings and the shutters,
And the wide carpeted floors,
I'll aways remember the cedars,
The moat and the lovely lakes,
The skating and the sledging,
And the soft snowflakes.
I'll always remember the paintings,
Which hung in the lofty rooms,
And the frozen central heating,
And the ancient Verney tombs.★

GAW had no such poetic thoughts when he addressed the school at the end of the summer term, 1940.

> 'There is no room today for complacency. We have had a dreadful year and we can only be thankful that we still exist with more than a

★The author was Greville Janner, the MP, whose father, Lord Janner, inaugurated an annual poetry recitation competition.

> hundred boys. We went to Claydon with a hundred and forty boys. We saw a lovely English autumn; we conquered with innumerable conkers; we slid, we tobogganed, we shot on a miniature range; we studied nature, ancestors and ghosts; we rode horses, we sang songs, we burst boilers, we ate enormously and grew ever thinner. We knew each other better and liked each other more, or less; and after two terms we came back, richer in experience but poorer in fortune: and here we are and here we stay.'

It seemed as if, like Churchill himself, he were shouting defiance at the enemy. The summer term had passed normally. It was true that £450 had been spent on air raid shelters but five scholarships were won that term. There had been an enjoyable cricket season, though no inter-school matches had taken place and the swimming baths were closed in Finchley Road so the school had to go to Marylebone. GAW expressed the gratitude that he and Miss Gladstone felt to all their colleagues, both those who had gone with the advance party to Claydon and those who had shared with the boys that curious, almost uncanny, exile in billets at a Northamptonshire village 'deserving of a better name than Boothville'. He was very grateful to his colleagues who had consented to reductions in salary.

Those who recall GAW during the exile in the country tell of his obvious dismay at being separated from The Hall's true home in London. He never gave up dining regularly at the Mercers' Company in the City, and the journey back almost directly past the school prompted his determination to return. The so-called 'phoney war' of these months seemed to argue that the risks were justifiable. Enforced evacuations were placing many schools in a state of crisis. This perhaps was an added incentive to GAW to reverse the process and bring the school back to a potential war zone. The situation was complicated by the offer of hospitality in America and Canada to 200,000 children from urban centres. One of the evacuees to take advantage of this invitation was H K Morgenstern, whose article describing his experiences aboard the *Athenia*, torpedoed by a German submarine on 3rd September 1939, appeared in the magazine.

Despite the withdrawal of pupils, GAW was adamant: 'The Hall belongs in Hampstead and nowhere else.' Ironically, the savagery of the blitz was shortly to burst upon him and his school. An added burden must have been the first reports of casualities. Flight Lieutenant J L Atkinson, RAF, who had left The Hall in 1926, and Tony Debroy Somers, a leaver in 1929, and serving with the RNVR, were both reported killed in action.

By July 1940 the names of five more Old Boys had been added to the Roll of Honour. It became GAW's custom to read out the names of the fallen at the final Reading Over of the term.

Another immediate and obvious consequence of the war was the departure of members of the staff. No less than four were claimed by the armed services, including Mr Castle who had long been a very active reservist with the RNVR. By Christmas 1939, four of the Junior School team had gone too. Among them was Miss Kempster, who had been at The Hall since 1917 and who was thus one of the teachers in at the very start of the Junior School. By way of compensation perhaps, a newcomer, Mr W K C Barron, destined to lend much distinction to the roll of masters at The Hall, joined the staff in April 1940.

The autumn term of 1940 was GAW's fiftieth as the Headmaster. This prompted him to offer to parents something of a retrospective survey of his years in office, years which, until the current crisis, had seen the size of The Hall swell from less than 100 boys to a norm of 250. It might have been supposed that during these years of plenty provision should have been made for possible years of adversity. GAW clearly felt that some sort of explanation was due to his loyal parents. There follows a recital of the various financial commitments which had to be met, and a list of some of the repairs and renewals of equipment, all of which make interesting reading years later, after inflation had worked its havoc on the value of the pound.

Mortgages had been paid off, leaseholds for longer terms acquired, buildings enlarged and equipment improved. Between 1930 and 1939 alone a sum of £10,800 had been spent on repairs and renewals. This sum included £100 on blackboards, £400 on desks, £120 on new windows, £300 on boilers and radiators; two classrooms had been added to the Senior School and a solarium to the Junior; the study was enlarged and the secretary's office built; fire precautions had been installed at a cost of £1,000; new lavatories were made and changing-rooms reconstructed; yards asphalted; attics entirely rebuilt, classrooms provided with a new lighting scheme, the stage constructed and new pianos and a new billiard table purchased.

He then mentioned the debt of gratitude which he owed to so many parents for their own contributions. He thanked them for the panels, the chairs, the pictures, the teak benches, the magnificent library, the canvases and the coats of arms that surrounded the beautiful hall. All of these the school owed to the generosity of the parents.

Then suddenly, in 1939, after all these years of prosperity, came the crash of war. War found the school without air raid shelters and so it had to move out of London. At once the numbers in the school halved while the overhead expenses in Hampstead remained. With the rent for Claydon, the heating and lighting of that huge cold house, the feeding and washing of all the boys and staff, the repair of damage done, the adaptation of a country house to the purposes of a school, the small reserves were soon exhausted. The school returned to Hampstead with numbers much reduced, to buildings now furnished with admirable shelters, but shattered sadly by exposure to the weather and the bursting of pipes.

GAW was suffering from a state of depression and anxiety shared by dozens of headmasters in those difficult, uncertain days. Another headmaster who went through no less worrying times was Arthur Harrison who later wrote: 'There were few of us at that time who did not believe that the Preparatory Schools were finished.'

The summer term 1940 passed fairly easily and the school opened in September in better spirits and with increased numbers. On 7th September the battle over London began, and helter-skelter went more than half the boys. By the end of the year the numbers were below fifty.

Drastic economies had to be made. Certain members of the staff took a term or two off, in the hope of returning to the school in better times. GAW refused to say goodbye to them, being entirely convinced that The Hall would be saved, though he was equally sure that a further evacuation was impracticable in view of the necessarily heavy expenses of upkeep at Hampstead.

Having, as it seemed, defended his actions we find GAW once again in defiant mood.

> 'But, you may say, the blitz may start again in all its fury. I say let it start. It cannot be much worse and, as we have all been through three months of it, we shall probably get through another three. The seas may be rough, the tempest strong, but the old ship of The Hall is a tolerably buoyant vessel.'

In the spring of 1941 the numbers had begun to rise again. The Hall School Ltd. had indeed gone into liquidation* but out of its ashes a new company seemed to be arising and The Hall was far from moribund. The health of the boys had never been better. Smaller classes meant more individual attention. The working day was shorter to enable the boys to get home before it became dark and there was no school on Saturday. Games were played in the playgrounds but there was promise of cricket at the Hampstead Cricket Club ground in the following term.

By the end of the summer of 1941 we find GAW as defiant as ever and much more confident. The Headmaster of Aldenham (Mr G A Riding) had been invited to present the prizes at the end of the term. Sharing the platform with him were Mr C S Walton, the Headmaster of University College School and Mr K S Snell, a

*This information is derived from the magazine and no further details of this financial hiccup have come to light.

housemaster from Harrow. Their attendance gave GAW the opportunity to congratulate them on their refusal to be disturbed by air raids and remaining in or near London. He declared with pride that The Hall was the last purely preparatory school in north-west London and one of the last in the whole metropolis.

At one time the numbers had been as low as forty-five but they were now seventy-five and there were signs that they would increase. Parents believed that the risks run by remaining in London were worth taking to maintain family life and contact with growing children, while the boys seemed to be little affected in health and spirits by the air raids. The promised cricket had indeed been played once again at the Hampstead Cricket Club ground and with considerable success.

Two matches were played, both against University College Junior School. The Hall gained easy victories. The school had two remarkable bowlers at the time; they were H G Kennedy and C W R Marston whose match figures were quite outstanding.

	Overs	Maidens	Runs	Wickets
H G Kennedy	8	2	9	6
	8.3	3	7	7
C W R Marston	8.3	4	7	4
	8	3	7	2

The increase in numbers was not accompanied by an improvement in the quality of work. The interruptions and changes which had been inflicted on the boys by the war had a sad effect on their education. Yet GAW was in no doubt that the few boys who had braved the blitz had gained in knowledge and intelligence more than those who had run away to come again another day.

Mr Rotherham was battling against the earliest and coldest blasts of the Chilterns and still arriving first at school; Mr Fyson, another youthful Victorian, travelled from Elstree. Mr Millard, after seventeen years' association with the school, had been among those who had agreed to wait in the wings until the numbers rose again. He was offered full time employment once again in 1941 but he chose to continue his experiment of building up a new school at Farnham Royal.*

Everything was done to ensure that life was not monotonous in school. There was a lecture by the Chairman of the Governors, a film show by the Ministry of Information, a well-organised football competition among the Houses and a revival of The Hall Magazine after an interval of twelve months; there was cubbing, music, chess and, of course, books to be borrowed from the library which was now being organised by Mrs Wathen.

*This became Long Close School, Slough, See page 197

The school's Savings Group was formed in 1941 and in its first term collected £19 18s 6d but by the end of the year the boys were clearly more aware of the need to save for their country for they raised £61 14s 0d which was enough to buy one tommy-gun, thirty small bombs, one stretcher and one hand-grenade.

The collection of almost any form of salvage was encouraged and many boys and their parents were thanked for their help. There was an Inter-House Competition to encourage the collection of salvage.

In the spring of 1942 the school had thirty-two new boys, a larger number than had ever been admitted at that time of the school year. It seemed that parents were prepared to take more risks and GAW was of course delighted.

An epidemic of chicken-pox struck the school and February turned out to be the coldest in living memory. The school managed to feed satisfactorily a hundred mouths a day at no small strain on the domestic staff and particularly on Miss Tresidder, the matron. In many schools pupils were now helping with the washing up, but this was not so at The Hall in view of the difficulties of replacing broken crockery. Games, boxing and PT increased the robustness of the body. It was noticed that the biggest boys seemed to be the least fit and it was felt that the lack of clothing coupons and the consequent shortage of the official school uniform was having ill effects 'never contemplated by the Government'. The school had set itself a target of £100 in 'Hardship Week'; in fact £500 was raised, sufficient for a twelve-pounder gun, a small mine, an anti-tank rifle and a bomb. With equal and almost embarrassing efficiency Miss Wilkins organised the salvage campaign and at times so much was being collected that her room would hold no more.

If numbers had increased then the standards of attainment had fallen; it was felt that this was due to some boys constantly changing schools. In the top two forms only one boy had been at The Hall right through the war. More staff were appointed and among those who were to remain a long time were Mr D A Prideaux and Mr W D Maclagan. It was in 1938 that some wag dubbed The Hall 'Wathen's International Zoo', and with some justification for in the school by 1942 there were boys from Austria, Poland, Hungary, Czechoslovakia, France, Italy, Prussia, Belgium, Russia, America, Scotland, Wales, and even a few from England!

GAW had often boasted of the international character of the school but he was always at pains to ensure that it was primarily British. Englishmen were reminded every time they walked down the Finchley Road that they were a minority but even foreigners choosing a school expected that it should have a large majority of British boys. The school's policy was to maintain such a majority and not fill up all the vacancies with the first applicants.

By the end of 1942 the numbers had so increased that it was decided that the Junior School should re-open in January 1943. Since some had come from countries and environments widely separated and followed courses of instruction greatly differing from The Hall's, there were initial problems but it was felt that these would be solved in time, providing the boys remained at school.

The daily feeding of one hundred and fifty hungry boys was solved when a British Restaurant opened within walking distance of the school. They were at least prepared to cook the food and with the help of a trolley and some willing boys, meals were brought back to school and served by the staff. Lord Woolton and the Ministry of Food were thanked for the excellent lunches they provided.

A new activity was introduced. This was a Rabbit Club. The Savings and Salvage Clubs continued to thrive and three Salvage Stewards were appointed. Contributions to the non-ferrous drive varied from copper jugs to drain-pipes.

Happily, there were football matches in this dark war year of 1943, one against the Malvern Colts, two against University College Junior School and two against Leas House, the last having also returned to London.

The school was visited in the summer of 1943 by a lady who held a position of great influence in educational journalism. She was clearly delighted and impressed by what she had seen at The Hall but she added, 'I want to have such schools abolished.' On being asked why, she replied that until the snobs and the nobs were compelled to send their children to state elementary schools, those schools would never improve.

Thus for the first time is mention made of that political spectre that has re-emerged regularly ever since. It was a trifle ironic that only a year before GAW had publicly announced that he would welcome at The Hall boys from any social class and he even requested that The Hall should be placed on the list of Secondary Schools where County Council scholarships could be held, a request that was refused.

'So,' said GAW ruefully, 'we should do away with all our best schools in the vague hope that better ones would grow up.'

Since 1939 the history of the school had been one of ups and downs, numbers falling to thirty-five, then rising till flying-bombs and rockets rained, but by the summer of 1945 they were not only rising but more applications were being made than there were vacancies. This seemed to augur well for the future but, although schools such as The Hall seemed to be in great demand, they received little official encouragement.

The Fleming Report was published in 1944; it proposed that the public schools should reserve a quarter of their places for boys who had been educated in state schools. This meant that there would be fewer vacancies for preparatory school boys and the competition for entry would be greater. Some Hall boys might have to enter the State system for their secondary education, a system for which they were quite unprepared.

The sad 'politics of envy' depressed and dismayed GAW, who resisted the notion that it was snobbery that led parents to choose a school like The Hall. That same year, he stated his views once again to the parents:

> 'Surely it is at least possible that parents like to ensure for their sons at their most educable age an environment where they can count on a reasonably good chance of happiness, good health, cleanliness of mind and speech and even of body, though I cannot claim that knees or even hands are always spotless at lunch-time.'

During these last years of the war, the parents were 'voting with their feet'.

Numbers still showed an encouraging increase and would continue to do so for the next year but the school was having problems. Ominous cracks were to be seen in the school building, the paint was sadly soiled, stationery, even pens, were difficult to find and text-books an even greater problem. Clothing was rationed and school uniform well-nigh impossible to buy and the famous cap had to be changed for lack of cording. Footballs, rubber shoes and cricket gear were all short and new desks almost unobtainable.

But the old atmosphere of the school was still the same. GAW, aided by the staff, did his best to see to that. He still held unswervingly to certain principles: that boys should be happy and unafraid; that their lives should be interesting and suitable to their age; that teaching should be stimulating; games taken seriously and yet enjoyed, and that they should have plenty of out-of-school activities in their leisure time; that discipline should mean the right attitude towards lessons and towards one's fellows; that there should be a clear understanding between right and wrong, based ultimately on the Christian ethic.

The Reading Over at the end of the autumn term, 1943, was short and informal. GAW did not even invite the parents to their usual places in the hall, but asked them to stand in the gallery. Roberts, the school caretaker and handyman had joined the Auxiliary Fire Service, labour was hard to get and it was a difficult task to move all the heavy furniture out of the hall, and then back again. The parents clearly did not mind because they stood again in the gallery at the end of the spring term, 1944. This became the standard procedure thereafter, until the gallery disappeared in 1972.

During the Easter holidays the marriage took place between Mr W K C Barron and Miss J L Wilkins. After the ceremony Mr and Mrs Wilkins held a reception at The Hall, where they welcomed a large number of friends including many of the staff and the prefects.

Scouting owed a great deal to Mr Barron in those years of the war and it was fitting that the Scout Troop came of age a month after the celebration of his wedding. The Cubs were also strong in number and owed a debt to the indefatigable Miss Bearman, assisted by Mrs Gregory, in converting some four dozen tireless, rampageous ruffians into disciplined, useful Cubs. The coming of age was celebrated in lovely weather on Empire Day, when all the fifty-four Scouts in eight Patrols and the one hundred and thirty Cubs in three Packs paraded in the school yard, under the eye of the Deputy Chief Scout, Sir Percy Everett. The District Commissioner, V H T Inman, and the founder of the Troop, Mr E V Millard, were also present. GAW told the boys that five hundred and fifty-four boys had become members of the Troop since 1923. On the Roll of Honour by then, there were thirty-six names of men who had died for their country, and of them thirty-three had been Scouts, eighteen of them Patrol Leaders. In response to an appeal for funds from Scout Headquarters, the Scouts and Cubs had collected £33 4s 3d which was handed to Sir Percy who thanked the boys and said that the Movement's target of £20,000 had almost been reached.

By the end of 1944 GAW was beginning to look further into the future and the time when he would have to hand over to a successor. He said he would welcome warmly any public body who would come to him and say: 'We will take on The Hall as a Charitable Trust and continue to let it perform the same services as it has for more than fifty years.'

He also felt keenly the need for more space for movement and so, when the garden of No 12 Strathray Gardens became available, he made a firm offer of £500 to buy the remaining thirty years of the leasehold of the garden alone and issued an appeal to the friends of the school to raise not only that amount but a still larger sum to make the extra space as pleasant and as useful as possible, and have a tablet suitably inscribed with the names of the Old Boys who had been killed on active service.

A meeting of the subscribers to the War Memorial was convened and a committee was elected. With the help of the architect, Alister Macdonald, a most attractive plan was drawn up, envisaging a beautiful memorial stone, a Garden of Remembrance and a covered-in playground. But it was obvious that such a scheme would cost far more than the sum originally put on one side. Then came an entirely unexpected and incredible blow. Firstly, the authorities concerned

THE FOUNDERS

1: **The Rev F J Wrottesley**
Headmaster 1889-1899

2: **The Founding Sons, 1889**
The three sons of Rev. F J Wrottesley: Frederic, Robert and Edward.

THE HALL AS IT WAS

3: View from Crossfield Road: illustration in *The Builder* Magazine, 1893

4: View from playground: school prospectus illustration, 1905

A GROWING SCHOOL

5: School group, shortly after the move to Crossfield Road
(The Rev C H Marshall seated at extreme right)

6: The school during the Great War: E H Montauban is seated at
extreme right of the masters, and W H Copinger, five places to his right

THE 'GREAT' HALL

7: Above: In its heyday, from the drawing by F Lodge, 1947

8: Right: Demolition and reconstruction, 1972

9: Below: Reconstruction damaged by fire 1982

10: Below, right: The upper hall in 1983

WAR AND POST-WAR

11: Evacuation to Claydon, Bucks, September, 1939

THE HALL, HAMPSTEAD

WHEN I took over The Hall in 1924 the tuition fees were 16 guineas a term. They have remained at this figure ever since. Recently the lowest fees at the Junior have been raised, but the increased revenue has proved quite insufficient to pay the Burnham Scale of fees to the academic staff. The two main causes for the greatly increased cost of running the school, apart from the general rise in prices, are: — (i) The increased wage necessary to procure a domestic staff, and (ii) Increase in salaries to the academic staff. My belief is that the Independent Schools will not survive, unless they can compete effectively with the State Schools in the recruiting of teachers.

These considerations have forced the Governors of the School to raise the fees as from the Autumn Term, 1948, and they hope that parents will think their action reasonable. The scale of fees from September 1948, will be as under: —

SENIOR SCHOOL
Tuition and Games ... fees 20 Guineas a term.

JUNIOR SCHOOL
Tuition and Games ... fees 17 Guineas a term.

BOARDERS (WEEKLY ONLY)
45 Guineas a term inclusive.

G. A. WATHEN.
Headmaster.

March, 1948.

12: A notice to parents, 1948

13: Dedication of the War Memorial, 1949

SPORTING VENUES

14: The Hampstead Baths, Finchley Road, in the 1920s

15: Hampstead Cricket Club, Lymington Road, in the 1980s

THE JUNIOR SCHOOL

16: 'Woodcote', the building as it was in 1917

17: The Junior School in the 1980s

Buckland Crescent, the Headmaster's home

18: Coronation 1953: GAW (waving his mortar-board) characteristically surrounded by his boys

turned down the whole scheme on the ground that, as they put it, the plan would adversely affect the amenities of the adjoining residential property. In view of the Building Act the idea of a covered playground was given up and a new plan submitted. This was for an asphalt yard, separated from the Memorial Garden.

Seventy Old Boys and several of the past and present members of the staff attended a re-union party at the school in April 1945. The hall had been beautifully decorated with wistaria and gentians by Mrs Wathen and tea was provided by Mrs Roberts and her husband. Mr Copinger was there to assist in reviving the Old Boys' Club, which was now to be called 'The Hall Old Boys' Association'. A committee was elected and Mr Barron and Mr Fyson agreed to act as Secretary and Treasurer respectively.

Within less than three weeks the war in Europe came to an end. So began the first term, for many years, free from enemy interference, and it was marked by excellent attendance, the effects of which were reflected in both work and sports. The Scouts were able to camp in Gilwell Park and the older Cubs paid a visit to a German submarine when it was on view in the London Docks. Mr – or to give him his correct rank – Lieutenant-Commander – D M Castle visited the school and gave a lecture about his wartime experiences in HMS *Frobisher*. Cricket matches were not possible but perhaps this was just as well for Mr Rotherham said the cricket was not as it had been in pre-war days.

The school bade farewell to Miss Tresidder. 'Tress', a matron of imperturbable good humour, had been at The Hall since London received its first bombing attack. In bidding her farewell GAW said, 'The boarders will much regret her going and I fancy some of their mothers will now realise how much she did to prolong the life of stockings and other 'couponed' garments.'

The rationing of food and clothing was to continue for some years but now, at least, there were to be days and nights undisturbed by sirens, anti-aircraft guns and falling bombs; of the last perhaps the worst were the flying-bombs and the rockets. How thankful everyone was to take down the black-out material from the windows but, above all, to feel that at last there was peace and, when the school met again in the autumn, lessons could continue uninterrupted and games could once again be played in safety.

PART II: THE WATHEN YEARS

Chapter 3
Post-war Reconstruction 1945-1952

Autumn began as usual with conkers and ended with carols, after three months of good weather, very little rain, some fog and thankfully no more worries about war. There was plenty of football, with some interesting unofficial matches, in which teams played each other with zest, as well as the House matches and two against other schools.

We have already learned of the plan to extend the Senior School by the purchase of the derelict garden belonging to No 12 Strathray Gardens, which stretched alongside the existing property right up to Crossfield Road. It was too good a chance to miss, and by the supreme generosity of Miss Gladstone and of GAW it was acquired for The Hall. Daily, by rotation it appears, forms were permitted to explore the wilderness of lopped saplings and bonfires.

The plan was to create a War Memorial at the southern end of the plot and turn the rest into a much needed extension to the playground. Two problems emerged: the cost and planning approval.

Of the two, the first may have seemed the more daunting. The estimated cost of the scheme was £1,500, of which about £780 was to hand. The business of fund-raising, which had been such a seemingly endless feature of the war years, was resumed. A bazaar was held at the end of the term. As a result £252 was added to the Memorial Fund.

Within a year, the original target had all but been reached, and the playground was asphalted and ready for use. As happens, however, the scheme tended to expand and the costs involved rose. Thus, when in 1949, the time came to open the Memorial, not only was there much yet to be done, but the target had risen to £2,300. More fund-raising followed, and a final sale of work in December 1949 raised the £250 to see the job paid for. A description of the official opening follows later in this book*, but before anything was to become of it, there arose an even greater threat to the enterprise.

*See Appendix 2, page 230

Hampstead Borough Council was very reluctant to allow the school to acquire the plot at all. Partial victory was secured as a result of the advocacy of a member of the Council, F C S Gardner, who was an Old Boy of the school. GAW was no less persistent in his appeals to the Council. This inspired a member of the staff to write a poetic tribute to GAW in the style of Longfellow.

Dubgewathen
Stood alone and unattended
Grey and rosy like the north wind,
Sturdily he strode among them,
Laid his noble plan before them,
Argued long and sanely with them,
Till he felt their anger dwindling,
Till he felt resentment fleeing,
Almost touched them, almost seared them,
Till the hot breath of his speeches,
Warmed their senses and their feelings,
As he sketched his plans before them,
Gave them reasons for his war plan
For the future generation.
For the hope of stronger yearlings . . .
Honour be to Dubgewathen!
With a shout exclaimed the Council:
Henceforth he shall have the playground,
And the Memorial Garden,
And shall have supreme dominion
Over all the ground so planned out.
Call him honoured Dubgewathen,
Call him Wathenga the Fearless.

The Council clearly remained both slow-moving and suspicious, for we learn that four years later, final approval for the total conversion of the area was still not forthcoming. This state of affairs provides an interesting contrast with the experiences encountered by the school forty years later when planning approval was obtained from the Borough Council's successors, Camden Council, for a vastly more complex and controversial scheme.

All in all, the first term of peace restored a real sense of well-being, confidence and prosperity. At the end of December 1945 GAW said: 'I suppose that if ever the history of this school were written, the year 1945 would be noted as one of the most eventful, for in no year have so many boys been admitted and, may I add, refused admission; in no other year has the staff been so large. And in 1945 nine boys have been elected to scholarships at St Paul's.'

In many respects, the return to peace also meant to happier times. Some of the arrangements introduced over the previous few years were retained. There had been no school on Saturday mornings during the war and GAW decided to continue this custom, for he thought that both teachers and boys remained all the fresher for a workless week-end. The debates which had taken place on Saturdays before the war now took place on wet afternoons. From 1946, the familiar institutions of the school reappear. In January, The Hall Old Boys' Association held its first post-war 'At Home'. Mr W H Copinger, or as he was known by so many of those present, 'Famous', returned for this very special occasion. 'Famous' had been one of several staff who had agreed to 'retire' during the war and GAW had already paid a glowing tribute to him in the summer of 1942. For nearly thirty years 'Famous' had been the friend, philosopher and guide to all his pupils. His kindly humour, his original methods, his devotion to the school and the interest of its pupils, his enthusiasms endeared him to all, and many were the boys whose first question when they visited the school was: 'How is Famous?' He was almost the founder, and certainly the moving spirit behind the Old Boys' Club and now in 1946 Old Boys had organised this gathering in his honour. A H Sichel, the Chairman of the Association, presented him with a cheque for £154 6s.

Three years later, the HOBA, as it was by now familiarly referred to, honoured both GAW's twenty-fifth year as Headmaster and the Diamond Jubilee of the school itself. 'Famous' Copinger presided over a dinner which entertained as guests several distinguished names from the past, including R T Gladstone, GAW's former partner, and A J F Wrottesley, son of the original founder. Just three months later, in July 1949, came the news that 'Famous' was dead. No master had impressed his personality so thoroughly, none had won more affection from his pupils nor had greater influence on their happiness and character. It is hard to conceive of any prep school master more nearly conforming to the traditions of 'Mr Chips'. James Hilton's original at The Leys School was of the same vintage and the same mould as The Hall's Mr Copinger.

Likewise too, the Parents' Association celebrated its revival by holding a most successful summer party, with some two hundred people present. Parents felt free and willing to enjoy the school cricket. That most symbolic of peace-time events, the Fathers' Match was restored to the fixture list, albeit with the fathers augmented by the masters to make up numbers. They won, by one run. Even the Mothers' Match against the Junior School was revived in 1946. The account that survives of this latter event is highly evocative of the age, when most adults still could not quite bring themselves to take such things seriously and when many retained nagging doubts that other greater priorities might suddenly call them away:

> The captains, Mrs Dare Bryan and Gold, tossed and the Mothers won. They decided to bat as their team was still incomplete, owing no doubt to chores, queueing, bread-rationing and other domestic worries. Both sides seemed to stand in great awe of each other, with the result that very few runs were scored and opportunities for scoring them were missed. The boys were very helpful, one even going so far as to demonstrate what one should do with a ball on the leg, but in spite of all this the ladies only scored eighteen runs.
>
> Waring and Turnbull opened the innings for the school. After a lot of poking and patting, the latter, who had bowled well for his side, was out. Things then brightened up and the necessary runs were scored.
>
> Most of the ladies tried their hands at bowling but a number of balls kept low, some very low. The wicket-keeper made some spectacular saves with her right foot.
>
> However, the sun shone, the atmosphere was warm and very friendly and we all felt better for an hour and a quarter spent in pleasant, if not exciting or energetic exercise.

Although there are no serious grounds for supposing that any thoughts of retirement were in his mind, the restoration of peacetime revived GAW's anxiety about the ultimate future of The Hall. He had expressed concern on this matter back in 1935 at the time of the advisory Governing Body's appointment. With the creation of a Parents' Association, he recognized that it too was a very interested party in the school's fate. In 1937 he had reminded parents that he could only consent to remain at the helm while he retained the parents' confidence. So it was that again in 1946 he told an audience of parents that the school had to be seen as a business, to be bought and sold according to its commercial value. He went on:

> 'I deprecate the idea that The Hall should be dependent for its continued existence on some wealthy capitalist regarding it as a wise and profitable investment. I have said publicly more than once that an institution of this kind should have a Governing Body prepared to relieve the Headmaster of financial responsibility, but prepared to select a man, lay down general principles for his guidance, back him up so long as he succeeded in his task, and dismiss him if he failed. But my voice has fallen on desert air and so I carry on so long as I have the strength and energy for the task.'

The pages of the magazines were once again filled each term with all the busy routines of prep school life. Even totally frivolous anecdotes could find room for inclusion. One day shortly after the war was over, GAW was surprised and amused to receive a poetic letter from a complete stranger. One of the boys, Cutler major, had left his poetry book on a bus and this kindly gentleman returned it to school, with a note:

Now Cutler i he took this book,
But Cutler i forgot to look,
When Cutler i got off the bus –
But let's not have a row or fuss:
For our poetic Cutler i
Is Mrs Cutler's favourite son.
So please don't chastise careless Cutler
But think of something slightly subtler:
Deprive him of his morning bun
Or otherwise curtail his fun –
And then we'll hear no more, I'll wager,
Of carelessness from Cutler major.

The new academic year, destined to be marked by the most awesome arctic weather in living memory, began auspiciously enough, although it was to prove to be as testing a year of austerity as any during the war.

The Junior School had hoped to return for the autumn term to find an extension built on to the dining-hall. The weeks of the long summer holiday had passed and never a brick was laid nor a hammer heard. Ironically the necessary licence arrived on the last day of the holidays, and then began the exhilarating business of achieving the impossible. Any sane person would have doubted the possibility of carrying out a building scheme to include structural alterations to the Junior School while it was in full swing. However, on the first day of term, a large hole was made in the existing dining-room wall, and from then onwards things proceeded apace. Boys romped in the rubble, puddled with cement, built castles in sand, clambered on, over and around lorries and piles of building materials stacked in the yard, and generally did all they could to break the imperturbable good humour of the British workman. Out of the dirt and dust, by the end of the term, emerged a neat little extension to the dining-hall.

The spring term 1947 came to an end, leaving behind it a trail of absences from school. A slough of 'wet time-tables' and memories of snowballing and sliding continued all too long, until in the words of one small boy, we were 'fed up with all this snow'. Staggering through icy streets, knowing that one was late because of the delays in train or bus, was no joke; and there was slush and the joy of dodging cars as a short thaw set in. Then again frost and snow and the whole process was repeated. And then there was chicken-pox which selected its victims at random and without warning, condemning them to enforced idleness at home.

In the Junior School, 'How's the gas?' became the first question every morning, to be answered too often by a pale glimmer in the gas-fires which betokened another low pressure day. Classrooms in the attic were too arctic to be braved but the art of improvisation, learnt in the days of the blitz, came in useful and the school adapted itself to a more communal existence and shared what warmth there was in the assembly hall and lower classrooms.

In common with most schools in the country, no football was possible that term. For exercise there was the use of the gymnasium twice a week, but even that was affected by the illness of the instructors. The annual gym display took place as usual. The cups and medals were presented by Lieutenant-Colonel Frank Byers (later Lord Byers), the Liberal MP and an Old Boy of the school.

After such a term of cold, snow, slush and chicken-pox, it was hardly surprising that the last bell sounded on April 1st!

The summer did in many ways make up for the dreadful spring. It was a happy term in spite of measles. The Cricket XI defeated all their opponents except the Fathers. The Junior School XI were defeated in both their matches, first by the Mothers and then the Staff!

GAW, a keen cricketer himself, has left an interesting account of the match played between the Junior School XI and the Junior Staff on 30th July 1947.

> Miss Gladstone won the toss and led her humble team into the field. 'We shall never get them out,' murmured the Staff; and then proceeded to exhibit the most remarkable talents. They proved indeed to be destructive as well as decorative. Miss Morgan bowled some alarmingly realistic overs and prevented all but Naftalin and Gold, of the opening batsmen, from really settling down; and then, when the score was 39 for 4, Miss Bearman, wheedling, coaxing, enchanting and bowling, all at the same time, reaped the last wickets for a mere additional one run.
>
> If boys imagined that batsladies – or batsteachers – were easy prey, they were soon disillusioned. The first over yielded eight runs and the third no less than sixteen, with Miss Morgan providing the fielders with a secret sports day, Miss Haggett treating the game very successfully as a branch of handicrafts, and Miss Bearman giving the scorer a rapid lesson in arithmetic. By wearing the expression of a demon bowler McFarlane managed to scare some of the later ladies into graceful futility, but not before 67 very firm and scholastic runs were recorded.

The match made a most enchanting and happy end to a term of pleasant cricketing afternoons; let us hope that it can become an annual event.

The return of peace and relative plenty by the end of the 1940s saw sport restored to its pre-war proportions. As we have seen the gym display was quickly revived since access to the Finchley Road Baths continued. The opportunity to play basket-ball each week at the gym was eagerly seized. Likewise, because of the school's contract with Hampstead Cricket Club, cricket and football were soon back with matches against other schools. Then in the spring of 1949, and notwithstanding the school's long record of relative ineptitude at the sport, came the decision to revive rugger. Many years before, GAW had stoutly defended the game, at a Reading Over, as providing an ideal experience for young boys. The constant difficulties posed by discrepancies in physique of boys of prep school age were made more acute by The Hall's habitual lack of good pitches, or the provision of skilled, regular coaching. The record of the school's rugger was not destined to improve. None had been played since before the war. The school had found a ground belonging to the Old Millhillians at Headstone Lane and twice a week the rugger enthusiasts made the pilgrimage there. It was a long journey there and back so GAW appealed (for the umpteenth time) for any information about a suitable ground nearer the school.

Headstone Lane suggested sinister and blood-curdling fiction, deeds of violence, darkling horrors and mysterious corpses. Headstone Lane, or rather the Old Millhillian ground, was anything but sinister, being pleasantly rural, surrounded by plough and boscage, and genially tended by the imperturbable Mr Grantham, who kept the ground in trim, the bathwater hot, the boys' lost property inviolate and his temper at all times. But Headstone Lane was remote and inaccessible; to reach it involved a complicated journey of an hour, with all the perils of irascible bus-conductors, the temptations of Mr Bicard's ices, the lure of Kilburn High Road emporia, and catching the train by the skin of one's teeth after barely recovering from a bolted billiard-room lunch, not to mention the strain of a half-supervised prep in the attics. But it was worth it. After a few practices a feeling for the game began to develop. Those who were leaving would not find themselves relegated to the scrum from sheer lack of knowledge. Those who were staying another year would form an experienced nucleus for the future. The brief but exciting hour of play was over all too soon, and then came the rush for the baths. A process ensued curiously like the cooking of shrimps, when some thirty mud-coloured boys plunged into the steaming baths, and as they bobbed about in the darkening water, turned slowly and beautifully pink, ready for home and tea! Here a word of sympathy for the awaiting mothers with shorts to wash and mend, at the risk of their ultimate coupons, bruises to tend and horrid tales of violence to endure. For them, perhaps, Headstone Lane all but deserved its name.

Not many terms earlier, reports of school crazes had been hedged about with timely admonitions as to needless waste of valuable materials. Paper darts had been definitely 'out'! Old Boys might well put their recollections of crazes near the top of a list of what they valued from their school-days. So, we read a report that a new craze suddenly swept the school about this time. This was a game with cigarette-cards. It was called 'Ciggies' or 'Faggies'. Although it started in the Junior School, the Fourth Forms were the chief fans. The card could be dropped – 'dropsies' – in which case the opponent tried to cover the card as it lay on the ground with his own card, and if successful, took over his victim's, the aim being to acquire sets of cards. But there were also 'flicksies', which were launched with a turn of the wrist and could sometimes travel considerable distances. This form of the game had been known to be played across the hall, from rail to rail of the galleries. The game, however, was usually played in sheltered corners out of the wind and the best place was the upper changing room*, which was often so crowded, particularly on a wet afternoon, that it resembled an opium den.

On a more serious note, debating was translated to those wet afternoons which plague schools unfortunate enough not to be able to decide the fitness of the pitches for play. There was also chess, stamp collecting and hobbies competitions, as well as more familiar crazes. Boxing was revived. The smaller boys were allocated to weights with evocatively novel names: light and extra light mosquitoes, microbes, germs and gnats. We discover that the contest in the microbes section in 1948 produced only two names, a winner – who won, and a runner-up too ill to perform. One concludes that he and all the others were struck down by fellow microbes.

Drama was back with renewed enthusiasm. Mr Barron had kept the flame alive during the war, but younger men were on hand now, notably Mr Blishen. A Dramatic Society had been refounded, and the school produced a genuine film-star. John Howard Davies was chosen to play the title role in *Oliver Twist.* In the Junior School, major productions are reported each term, and in 1948 we may read an extensive review of a documentary film (no less), *A Day at the Junior School*, directed by the Misses Bearman and Prentice and reviewed by

*This area was subsequently converted into an office for the bursar and then into the pottery workshop.

someone destined to become a considerable critic and man of letters, Edward Blishen:

'The film opens with a shot of the Junior entrance, early morning. With the camera we enter the school drive, and immediately, with a simultaneity, a briskness and a brightness which we refuse to attribute to the editing, the staff converges upon the scene. The camera savours, as it were, the personality of each, and then whisks around the corner not to miss the next prompt arrival. (No need of commentary; the audience buzzes with information). The cheer usually reserved for the cowboy hero greets a tall grey-haired gentleman in impeccable black who raises a familiar eyebrow of inquiry as the camera fastens upon him and follows him and a certain attaché-case up the school steps. ('———', cries a certain member of the audience, using Mr Wathen's non-postal name. We dare not print this piece of affectionate *lèse-majesté*).

Indoors: and boys. Now, what, we wonder, is the fascination of the film? The writer is a hardened pedagogue, who has seen the same boys in that same place on many occasions; and the audience are hardened boys, who have seen one another, and the same pedagogues, with an equally unrationed frequency. Yet here we sit, laughing at one another's appearance, trying to look pleased at our own, positively overcome by this glimpse of the familiar. But, of course, it is delightful to look through the window of the film into the room in one's own past, and to see oneself there, gazing solemnly up from one's exercise book, or to see one's friends immortalised at some furious moment in the middle of a conker battle. And how well the directors of the film know, not only who, but what are the characters of the Junior School; not only the photogenic ladies of the staff, and the bewildering pattern of boys' play but the familiar, unforgettable objects; the rows of milk bottles, the bell swinging in Miss Gladstone's hand, the chef's hat on Mr Rothwell's head.

The morning runs away with a fictitious speed, as we see Mrs Thallon bustle into the yard, for all the world like a jolly farmer's wife with the chickens running round her feet; or Mrs Baker look up with severe shyness from her music; while in the sun-shot hall the band soundlessly percusses. Off we fly, then, to the Hampstead ground, for that memorable struggle between the football teams of Black and Tawny. Robert Francis has a whole episode to rush across the field just in time to see Roome guarding his goal with the massiveness of a Beefeater. Familiar figures dash across the screen and are gone, too hot in pursuit of the ball to be bothered with posing; the projector whirrs for the last time and with a little flip the great occasion is over.

Happily, a print of this rare cinematographical masterpiece survives in the school archive.

In his attitude to the need to maintain a broad base to education, GAW remained entirely consistent to the end of his time. Old age never turned him into a cautious reactionary. He had never wanted the school to be judged by the number of scholarships gained by its boys. 'Any success we may claim,' he said in 1947, 'will not be calculated by the number of scholarships won, the number of examinations passed, the number of cricketers, footballers, swimmers, scouts, readers and writers, but by the general effect in after-life of the memory of the years spent here.'

He seldom failed to explain to enquiring parents that if they wanted their sons to win scholarships, they had better send them to schools where hours of instruction were longer, for they could hardly find a school where lessons were fewer and shorter. If they wanted them to learn games, they would find plenty of schools where games were played, not two but six days a week. If they wanted good physique, the country school always had the advantage and was never so cramped or so crammed as The Hall. This philosophy has largely remained unchanged. Nonetheless, academic triumphs were and are never unwelcome.

Early in 1949 news reached the school that three scholarships had been won at Harrow. GAW was justifiably proud of this achievement by three of the boys. 'For one school to gain the second, third and sixth places out of eight awards is a record of which we may feel proud. . . . few events during my long service as Headmaster have given me greater delight.' In that same week came news that another boy had gained fourth place at Malvern.

The pages of the magazines of the 1950s seem joyously filled with news of all the predictable events of school life, as peace-time routines became more firmly established. Apart from match reports – and the fixture list was swelling again – accounts of debates, visits and trips, lectures, hobbies and crazes, and of course, the melancholy recital of epidemics which afflicted the school as recently as the 1950s, there are a number of references to more serious issues which concerned GAW.

Thus, amidst happy reports of the boarders taking advantage of the opportunity of using their leisure time sensibly, with micro-modelling, monopoly, billiards and – most stressed of all – reading, come stern strictures addressed to parents about the dangers of the 'wireless' (the Light Programme, one suspects), and its newly popular and rapidly growing brother, television. They both threatened the worthy habit of reading, a habit which, if not acquired young, might never be acquired at all. GAW had an even greater aversion to and suspicion of the telephone, which was, he feared, destroying the incomparable art of letter-writing.

Another issue that clearly concerned him was the conflict between the pressures for places in London schools and the desirability of keeping the school a manageable size. In 1951, he is quoted as recalling that his predecessor, Edward Montauban, always claimed that the number of boys in a prep school should never be allowed to exceed eighty. Those with memories that stretched back to the early 1930s perhaps were surprised to recognise that The Hall had grown to over 320. Applications still continued to pour in by every post. Some optimists hoped to arrange everything over the telephone, little knowing the disgust with which GAW regarded this instrument!

In a strange way, history was repeating itself. Thirty years earlier, Montauban had feared the consequences of the post-war boom in demand for places at public schools. He suspected that the laws of supply and demand might well prevent even good prep school candidates from securing places. So he set about the founding of Stowe. Exactly similar fears were felt by GAW and he voiced them in the 1950 magazine. Until recent years all boys at a good prep school were almost certain of entry to public school if they reached a tolerably high standard in the Common Entrance examination. Hitherto, the standard had been one which most could achieve quite easily. That had all changed. One of the biggest problems now facing all headmasters in the early 1950s was that of finding suitable places for those who failed Common Entrance.

This time, the Headmaster of The Hall did not respond by setting forth to found a new public school. Curiously, the man invited to investigate the possibilities has already appeared in these pages. Arthur Harrison was despatched to survey potential sites for a new public school to be owned by the IAPS. In the event, the problem was resolved partly by the existing public schools expanding to meet the demand, and partly by the IAPS persuading existing independent schools to grow and develop into what might perhaps not unkindly be regarded as a second division of the HMC. Thus was born, again of prep school initiatives, The Society of Headmasters of Independent Schools (SHMIS), founded in 1959.

The preoccupying problem with The Hall was however the squeeze in Crossfield Road arising from the steady increase in numbers. The facilities a modern prep school needed were simply not there. The acquisition of more land or the better utilisation of existing spaces was the key to the improvements in mind. GAW had for long been convinced that an art room was the school's most pressing need. The old squash court, so much a pride and joy in its heyday, had deteriorated sorely during the war and was unusable without major repairs. Thanks to the generosity of a parent, H H Wingate, and the ingenuity of the architect, Alister MacDonald, there arose from the ruins of the squash court a fine, spacious and well-lit art studio, where Mrs Gregory could continue her excellent work in very much more pleasant conditions. GAW expressed a hope at the time that both squash and fives courts might be provided at a later date, when money was available. This has never subsequently been seriously contemplated.

GAW could perhaps boast that his thirty years of tenure had seen many major changes, and the buildings he was before long to bequeath to his successor were more than adequate for their purpose. The assembly hall and the library it contained was handsome. The new extension at its southern end provided for the sixth forms and beside it was the even newer art room. The Memorial Garden and playground had given the school more necessary space. The Junior School was in an even better state, with its capacious, airy rooms, beautiful central hall and properly equipped playground. By far the greatest change GAW was to effect, one that would secure the school's future, remains to be described in the next chapter. Meanwhile, he was readily achieving that other responsibility of the successful headmaster, that of filling his school.

PART II: THE WATHEN YEARS

Chapter 4
The Hall Unveiled: a post-war portrait 1946-1947

This selection from the pages of 'Uncommon Entrance' by Edward Blishen is published with the author's blessing and by kind permission of the publishers, Thames and Hudson Limited.

Edward Blishen was a master at The Hall between 1946 and 1949. After leaving grammar school, he spent a short time in journalism, but during his period of conscription his stance as a conscientious objector led him to work on the land. Unsure exactly what he wanted to do thereafter, he somehow found himself teaching. The school that snared him was The Hall. In 1971, Blishen wrote the second of a series of autobiographical books, *Uncommon Entrance*, thinly disguising the identities of the school, his colleagues and the boys. The Hall became 'The Vale', and its Headmaster, G A Wathen, 'Mr Juniper'.

> The Vale, I'd gathered, was a pretty important school. The Headmaster had referred to this quality himself, in a letter. 'Mr Bassett has spoken of you very warmly. I can make no promises, of course. We have many distinguished parents and they expect much of The Vale. But come along and let us have a chat.'
>
> I thought no more of it. The Vale was a prep school. That was a world I didn't belong to, and indeed was opposed to on the most insistent grounds of principle. Nine years before I had failed Higher School Certificate after a stormy career in the grammar school sixth form: if I was a ship, then academically I have been most fantastically holed.

What follows he describes as a 'comedy', and indeed, a joyous, far from unbelievable romp it is. Marvellously embroidered by comic insights and the deliciously apt descriptive skills of the gifted writer, it clearly enjoys some of the benefits of enhancement through the passage of time. He describes his attempts to come to terms with two unfamiliar experiences. Parallel with his struggles in and out of the classroom runs his even less propitious attempts to woo and win a young lady's favours. This second theme of the book is an integral part of *Uncommon Entrance* but clearly not relevant to the context of these extracts. The impression given throughout is that both pose totally unexpected and often insoluble problems. As far as teaching was concerned, he had neither training nor experience. The somewhat exotic world of a private preparatory school merely added to his bewilderment. The story that emerges however is remarkable for the number of insights and experiences that are totally recognisable. If much has changed since the later '40s, perhaps as much has, in essence, remained the same. Blishen wisely attempts to discount any suggestions that this is a precise portrait of The Hall. . . .

> I have (to use an interesting current term) re-cycled my memories. In pursuit of truth to experience rather than truth to fact, I have shaped the resulting pulp into people, places and episodes that are inventions entirely.

Well, not entirely invention. What follows provides a fascinating and vivid insight into the life of The Hall in the immediate post-war era, including impressions of the personalities of the remarkable collection of teachers at the school. He reminds us of that first harsh austerity winter of 1947. And of course, he demonstrates that, essentially, the boys of The Hall scarcely change from one generation to the next.

> From my own outer suburb I went to that inner one, where the poets lived and the clever and beautiful foreigners. The Vale was at the heart of it: two buildings side by side, the Junior School and the Senior School, among the tall houses that, on that summer evening, seemed husky with voices from Central Europe. Oh, I was out of my world again: no doubt about that. I need have no fear. Mr Juniper would see at once that I didn't belong.
>
> He was white-haired, brisk yet absent-minded. He had forgotten I was coming, but somehow was business-like about this. 'I forget rather easily,' he said, and it sounded like an assertion of soundness. 'The Vale is a great responsibility. It's an important school, and much is expected of it.'
>
> 'Yes,' I said, feeling comfortable. It was going to be a quick review of the many obvious reasons why I should on no account be appointed to the teaching staff of The Vale. 'You've had no previous experience at all? You went to . . . ah yes. I don't know the school. A good school, is it? . . .'

The Headmaster looked me up and down, as he had already done several times. I was wearing a baggy, cheap suit. I thought: 'They'd never have a teacher here wearing a suit like this.' My feeling of the unreality of the interview became sharper: and was crowned when Mr Juniper shook my hand and said, 'You have a telephone number – if I want to get in touch?' I had to say No. We had no telephone at home: had never had one. I was sensitive about that.

A week later the letter came. It gave the Headmaster great pleasure to appoint me to the staff of The Vale. He was certain from our discussion that I had made a proper choice of profession. He wasn't quite sure yet how he might use me. Some work would be in the Junior School, and I'd be expected to help with cubbing. Since I was wholly unqualified I would, of course, be regarded as a probationer, and it was understood that I should consider ways of obtaining qualifications. On the same grounds I was being offered a starting salary of £200 a year. I should attend the staff meeting that would take place on the day before the opening of the autumn term, three months away.

'I look forward to having you as a colleague,' was Mr Juniper's final astounding sentence.

In 1946, The Hall had a number of 'giants' in its common-room. 'Famous' Copinger had retired, but the names Blishen gave to his new-found colleagues – Diamond, Raisin, Hollow, Beesley – thinly disguised some formidable teachers, including Bathurst, Fyson, Rotherham, Prideaux and Sleigh. It is fair to say that his creations were composites, but the impact of these men – and some of the ladies of the Junior School too – was understandably very marked.

'The new young fellow, eh?' said Mr Diamond, history, one of the senior masters, taking my hand and pumping it with every appearance of scarcely containable delight. ''Normous pleasure! 'Normous pleasure!' He handed me on to another senior, Mr Hollow, mathematics. Mr Hollow spoke a form of English so beautiful that only an odd consonant or so emerged above its flowing surface. 'Extra sh'der to the wheel! Dam' g'd thing!' he seemed to be saying. These things done, I sat smiling anxiously at the edge of numerous bland conversations.

Extraordinary, the staffroom at The Vale, to someone fresh – but that was not the word – from five years of the humblest sorts of agriculture.

The conversation here was like the sandwiches we were eating: thin, dainty, swiftly digestible. I heard the voice of Mrs Leach, English: it seemed to be leaning back, her voice, away from the world, generally bent on avoidance. 'Personally,' she was saying, 'I believe that direct-method Latin will bring the whole system down about our ears. How *do* you examine what will have become . . . mere chatter?'

'Gentlemen, gentlemen!' cried Mr Juniper, bustling in with Miss Seakins. 'Let's get started at once, shall we?'

Impatience, I was to discover, was one of Mr Juniper's main characteristics. He swept through life in a constant state of being ahead of his own timetable. The world, on the whole, lagged a half an hour behind him. The school had adjusted to this oddity. Masters enjoying a legitimate and negotiated free period were resigned to being swept from it by the rapid passage of Mr Juniper. 'Oh, I say, do go and make yourself busy with some little chaps who are standing about in the garden room,' he'd cry.

At the staff meeting, Mr Juniper's first impetuous act was to flip through the pages of a book in which the educational ambitions of all the boys were set out. This boy aimed at Winchester, this at Eton, this at Westminster: a score of other places were mentioned, some of them quite unfamiliar to me. It sounded like a page from one of Shakespeare's histories. Today, it was a matter of emendations, reminders: decisions to be taken as to the aggrandisement or reduction of an ambition.

'Jones F E to Charterhouse.'

'Oh never, sir.'

'Absurd, Diamond?'

'Ludicrous, sir. He's Scarforth material at best.'

Some delicate laughter round the table. It seemed that to be material acceptable by Scarforth, wherever that might be, was to fall very low indeed.

Its imposing parental body has always been one of The Hall's more fascinating characteristics. Blishen noticed this on his very first morning.

My working life at The Vale began with assembly next morning in the Senior School.

Round the hall ran a gallery; and here parents stood, observing the scene below. I was amazed, noting an actor whose Macduff I'd much admired: two or three polemicists from whose incendiary writings I myself had drawn little rations of fire: a famous lady novelist: a marvellously infamous comedian. It seemed improbable, altogether – these celebrated masks, coupled with the consideration that small copies and fusions of the same were down in the hall among us and were soon to receive some of their notions of history, English – and the story of London – from me.

Anyone familiar with the school as it was prior to the major rebuilding of 1972 will recognise the feature of the gallery, from which visiting parents observed the assembly below. A newcomer into any school may well feel daunted by being subjected to the scrutiny of so many, young and old.

> As we dispersed, my terror was enormous. It seemed to me that I was being sternly scrutinized by those parents, drifting glamorously out of the gallery and into the entrance hall. They paid large sums of money to have their important children prepared, not simply for that distant lethal test we'd been singing about, but for the other one so much more imminent, and probably as crucial. I imagined them turning to one another, dismayed. 'An impostor, if ever we saw one . . .'
>
> It was quite without confidence that I walked into my first classroom. Lower Four: 'Give them dictation,' Mrs Leach had said. They were just up from the juniors. 'As new as you'll be,' I'd been assured by a friendly Junior School teacher. 'So they'll be no trouble. If you do find things awkward, read them a story.'

Every teacher, walking into his very first class, will know exactly the ordeal facing this innocent that morning. In anticipation, it may seem challenging, worrying perhaps; but, given some prior planning and some sensible thought, surely not impossible. The Hall was the same then as now: the 'fours' are still just 'up from the Juniors', and they are still highly articulate, garrulous, demanding and potentially unforgiving, typical offspring of north London homes.

> I imagined – to cram a huge error into a nutshell – that teaching was lecturing. The night before I had prepared a brief statement of principles as an introduction to my passage of dictation. I'd had in mind . . . oh, vaguely I'd had in mind a group of diminutive professors, who'd be at ease with the faintly sour cadences of my commentary. I was, surely, like a surgeon working out the details of an operation in total ignorance of the patient.
>
> In practice, everything was wrong. The faces, to begin with. They were not professorial, lecture-prone. They expressed amazement as I spoke. There was – I felt, panic-stricken – a mysterious but very definite feeling of unsuitability about those general propositions of mine as to the spelling and pointing of the English language.
>
> My lecture rapidly lost the sour crispness I'd designed for it. The room began to whisper. I hurried into the dictation itself. That was a relief – they looked aggrieved, but were busy. It was done: we stared at one another. I made a complex statement containing the idea that, owing to their incredibly sustained good behaviour, I proposed to read them a story of Rudyard Kipling's. This I had

> selected from a book on the staffroom shelves. It turned out to be far above their heads. They began again to look amazed. The story was also too long – five or six times too long – for the occasion. The bell went, and they began, loudly, to discuss among themselves the unexpected impenetrability of work in the Senior School. I dismissed them; but the effect was of their dismissing me.

At times, Blishen must have wondered just what he was doing at The Hall. Because he was no product of the system, he was to an extent able to view it objectively, quizzically, even critically. The fun he pokes is respectful and kindly. He was aware that this was, after all, 'a pretty important school', and so who was he to question its methods or its aims. Yet, at that first assembly, he could well have felt a wry sense of puzzlement at his situation.

> We sang the school song, which explored the idea that life was a long preparation for some final and fatal Common Entrance exam. Those who had done well would be received in the eternal public school above. The ultimate headmaster, unstinting in his praises, would offer them something in the nature of an infinite respite from scholarship. Prowess or simple doggedness in games would be taken into account.
>
> *What we've achieved on the field of sport*
> *Shall be noted down in the Great Report . . .*
>
> The fate of those who failed this exam was not glanced at. They would have trodden, one was left to assume, the primrose path to the everlasting State school.

Another characteristic of Hall boys over the ages, evident from its earliest days and unchanged still, is that they are inveterate chatter-boxes, and by and large, they are confident and out-going in the company of adults. Lunch time at The Hall is a noisy experience.

> It was lunch time. Bells went, boys raced impudently out of and into my presence. We were in the hall, having dinner, my head ached; I was in charge of a table, terrible boys were asking me questions of a personal kind . . . I was helping to distribute dishes. My hands were sticky with gravy. The Head, at the top table, was laughing uproariously at some joke told him by a boy. How could anyone smile, let alone laugh? How could one be at ease ever with a male person of prep school age?
>
> At The Vale, lunch was not a polite occasion. It had a vulturine quality. Food, an observer might have felt, was being torn here, fiercely ripped by ravenous beaks in a setting of plain uproar. There were eight boys to a table, and a master in charge of each. So it was

> Mr Beesley's table: Mr Hollow's table: Mr Blishen's table; and each was understood to have its place in a hierarchy of noisiness. Mr Diamond's was the most grave and seemly, and there was thereafter a sharp decline into a loose jocularity which had soon become characteristic of Harrod Parker's, and the plain quality of vocal violence by which my own table was distinguished.

As the very first London school to institute its own Scout troop, The Hall, with its insistence on the values of scouting, quickly swept Blishen into its way of thinking. He had been warned that he might be required to do 'some cubbing'. So there he was, on his very first afternoon roped in and unable to escape, largely one suspects, because he was far too nice and nervous to say no.

> It was after lunch: on waves of the most immense noise I'd ever heard I'd been washed over to the Junior School. I was in a hall, and cubs were shouting incredible phrases of salutation. I was assisting with a cub pack. . . . a tall, thin, intensely energetic woman called Miss Frome was announcing games. Mr Blishen would take a game of 'O'Grady Says', in the corner over there, with Blues. Blues were finding the mere existence of Mr Blishen stridently funny. All knowledge of 'O'Grady Says' had passed from my mind. I was rescued by Miss Frome, smiling thinly ('"O'Grady says" when you *do* want them to do it, my dear chap!'). The barrier of my skull, which had kept apart the noise in my head and the noise outside it, was suddenly removed, and the two spheres of din became one.
>
> I was making my way home, and my head was full of a red, sore uproar.

They always say that the greatest miseries occur in the second term. In Blishen's case, he had to wait only to the second day at The Hall, his baptism of fire in the Junior School.

> It was one of the most awful days of my life.
>
> Middle Three was my own form: the top but one class in the Junior School, a day later than the seniors in starting its term. We shared – it was all you could say – we shared the same room, before the opening assembly. Fifteen boys, most of them nine years old, inspected the stranger who stood, stamped fatally with diffidence and bewilderment, in the corner by the desk. I didn't understand how you began to deal with the problem represented by their relaxation and air of being casually and perfectly at home. It was as if all the supporting characters in a drama were masters of their lines, while the principal character hadn't even begun to study his part. I panicked, and made facile promises of punishment. 'Now, there's going to be very serious trouble if you don't . . .' They didn't, and I

> had no idea what forms of serious trouble might be at my command. I was not really capable of inflicting even frivolous trouble. I was lost.

To be fair, of course, here was a man who was untrained and unfamiliar with the style and mores of the school, or the ways of small boys.

> We were in different worlds. In their world, they laughed incredulously, fought one another, played with their toy motorcars – read comics. I, in my world, juggled with my huge unsuitable load of facts and theories, and intermitted this with appeals, threats, statements of my amazement. The noise grew, positively as if it were water rising within the walls and we were all drowning. Scraps of my lesson floated this way and that on the surface of this outrageous sound. In despair I began drawing on the board: a map of Roman London. It was my first attempt to draw a map with chalk on such a surface, and the unforeseen sideways nature of such work startled me. Alone with the blackboard, undistracted, I should have had problems. In the midst of all that noise, my head buzzing with dreadful thoughts – so I wasn't even going to last a day, a morning! – they would surely at any moment come and take me and thrust me out through the main door!

Hall boys do not change over the decades either.

> Again, enormous noise, enormous tendency of boys not to be sitting in their desks but to be –

⋆ ⋆ ⋆

This was 1946, and the start of a school year unforgettable for its weather.

> Mr Hollow roamed the staffroom, deploring the weather that made football impossible. There had to be an emergency timetable. His wrath was great. He looked constantly out at the wet world beyond the staffroom windows, hating the Labour government. I had already discovered that, among the staff of The Vale, Mr Attlee and his ministers were deemed to have Nature herself in their inept, seditious hands.
>
> 'D'm'd n'sance! W'st S'tember I c'n 'member! Oh, M'st' B'sley – k'p Upp' Four h'ppy, eh?'

One of the glories of the prep school age is that the grim realities of the outside world – perhaps weather excepted – do not impinge too harshly. The privations and tensions of the immediate post-war period scarcely feature in our picture of The Hall; yet . . .

> It was still wet: the football grounds were waterlogged, and Mr

Hollow continued to pace the staffroom after lunch, cursing the decline and fall of the British climate. Mr Raisin and I took a long crocodile to the peak of one of the suburb's green hills. There, German prisoners-of-war were levelling the site of a demolished air-raid shelter.

'Mr Raisin' was another of the stalwarts of The Hall, the senior classics master. In 1946, classics were very important.

The Hall was still a part-boarding school, a fact which has undoubtedly shaped its traditions and coloured its atmosphere.

Then came my first boarders' supper.

Masters stayed, according to a weekly rota, to supervise this occasion. Miss Pumphrey, the matron, smiled happily when I arrived in the corridor leading to the hall. 'They'll try to chip you,' she said. 'They always do a new master.'

I was fascinated by that word 'chip'. It was not descriptive of the torments with which The Vale had made me familiar. I smiled back, in a gloomy fashion, and went into the hall. The tables, with thirty boarders scattered among them, were screeching. From the walls, painted parsons and soldiers evaded my eye.

All the worst boys, I saw at once, were boarders. There was, for example, a whole tableful of my tormentors from Middle Four.

I murmured grace, and supper began. The noise remained steadily appalling. I stayed by the serving table, inhaling the excellent smells of the food and hoping that nothing much would happen.

I became aware of Mr Juniper's figure in the gallery above. He was peering down at us. How unruly, I wondered, did the scene appear? How could I guess what orderliness and whispering meekness might be achieved by other masters on supper duty? I tried to smile up at him. 'Masters shouldn't make faces at the Headmaster,' called a voice. 'Ahem,' said Mr Juniper. It sounded worse than a fullscale impeachment. He disappeared.

'And now, complete silence,' I cried, furiously . . .

When they'd gone, I stood amid the hastily piled crockery – I should have seen that it was neatly collected, but that was beyond me – and wondered again how I could possibly go on. I was being paid £200 a year for the privilege of being extensively humiliated by little boys from quite another social shelf than my own. What *was* the sense of that?

They'd gone up the stairs, shrilling, towards the staffroom, eager for the evening's instalment of the radio serial *Dick Barton*.

I leaned against a bookcase, weakly, and made a mental note of a necessary revision of the dictionary. '*Chip*, v.t., To torture, to

> subject to ingenious malice, to destroy a person's morale.'

There is every quality of the nightmare here. Yet, clearly, Blishen was surviving this baptism of fire better than he knew. Small boys can be hideously unforgiving and they will always put the newcomer to the test. But they have an uncanny sense that a teacher deserves respect and affection. It was not long before he had acquired a nickname and with it, acceptance. At this point in the saga, however, thank heaven for the BBC Light Programme at 6.45 and the unforgettable adventures of Dick Barton, Snowy and Jock.

> A long sequence of overnight rains came to a halt, and I experienced my first game of football.
>
> It was with juniors, and I was paired as supervisor with Mrs Cakebread, a gentle, amused woman whose instinct was to make people feel as important as possible. So she said, when I joined her that afternoon: 'They *are* lucky, you know – having a master to take them. It will make all the difference, I'm certain.'
>
> 'Mrs Cakebread,' I said. 'I wish you wouldn't think along such lines. I'm not really going to be . . . I'm not likely to be much good, you know.'
>
> Mrs Cakebread smiled at me gently. I had now just about enough confidence to believe that it was indeed a friendly smile, and not one springing from Mrs Cakebread's knowledge that, as a master in charge of football, I was an outrageous impostor. I even toyed with the idea of telling Mrs Cakebread that I didn't understand football: that my attempts to read it up, in more than one manual, had left me knowing rather less than when I began.

Every teacher who has served at The Hall over the decades will know the feats of imagination required to make many of the school's sporting activities match up to what more lavishly equipped establishments take for granted. A long walk to a scruffy meadow, muddy, unmown, markless and forlorn, this is the very stuff of junior games or senior leagues, with which hapless mistresses and frustrated masters have had to make do. And, of course, it was not just Blishen's total unfamiliarity with the finer points of the games or the niceties of coaching tactics and skills!

> But the game, I could see, might be the least of it. There was first, at the Junior School, the gathering of the players. For all the expertise of the Junior School ladies, this was like trying to organize a flock of birds for some un-birdlike purpose. Chittering, fluttering, they'd come together and then scatter again, and it was a tedious time before at last we were on our way to the sports ground. No public line of boys from The Vale, I was to discover, was ever easy to be

with, but this was perhaps the most difficult. They developed unforeseeable passions for unexpected features of the journey. Suddenly they'd have become a shrill cluster outside a women's outfitters – discussing, with great candour, the garments in the window. They might well be suddenly on their knees, peering into a drain. Amazing impulses would take them down some hopelessly unsuitable road, from which they had to be herded back to the correct route. Some of the time they were jostling for possession of my hands. Mrs Cakebread, tender though she was, had developed the sensible Junior School lady's immunity to this clutching for a teacher's hands. But mine were asking to be fought for. Mrs Cakebread sighed over this, rather, but seemed to take it as further evidence of the advantage conferred upon me by being masculine.

When we arrived at the ground it turned out that the laces of their boots, knotted together so the boots could be made to hang round their necks, had been so tethered since the last game a year before. 'Sir, my laces! Sir, quick – undo my laces!' I hurried up and down the twittering line, my fingernails shredded.

And that was a week of it, then. A week of shrill din, of the most intense nervous strain I'd ever experienced. It was, I thought – sitting bruised in the trolleybus on my way home – a lost, frightened week, on the whole. Oh, I'd surely never find happiness in school teaching. I felt so irritable, *irritable* – unable, at home, to endure questions about the The Vale.

Close to sleep, I imagined the hostile reports heaped on Mr Juniper's desk. In what shape would my dismissal come?

It didn't. Blishen's capacity to enjoy the life of the teacher developed. After all, he stayed at The Hall for three years, and remained involved in the profession for nine.

Staff common-rooms may in the folklore of fiction be indescribably parochial, philistine and petty, with narrow-minded and boring men or frustrated and spiteful women hiding behind clouds of pipe smoke or sheets of newspaper. At The Hall, this has never quite been the case. These men and women seemed to be so unexpectedly kind and welcoming, so unpredictably generous, so curiously quixotic.

Mr Beesley, a man of obvious rectitude, would express vast support for all spivs and layabouts. 'In a day such as ours, so full of *dullards*,' he opined, 'we *desperately* need our idlers and . . . *flashy* fellows. Eh?' 'Some contrast, simply,' said Capper, 'to Ernest Bevin and that most colourless of Prime Ministers, Mr Attlee.' 'May I congratulate you on the accuracy of that adjective?' called out Mr Raisin, strugglingly, from his asphyxiatingly deep armchair. 'Dull – beyond all conception – dull.' 'What we need,' said Capper, taking

> strength from Mr Raisin's praise, 'is a widespread revival of the orgy, the practical joke and the large-scale, lighthearted crime.' 'Oh *rather*!' smiled Mr Beesley.

Schools celebrate their distinctive traditions by adopting a private language. From the days of Montauban, there had been the Reading Over in front of parents, and the grading system of assessing effort via Overs and Unders. Blishen changed the first to the Running-over, and the latter to Ups and Downs. Of course, the mystique of such terminology can puzzle the newcomer.

> I worried helplessly about 'ups and downs', about the whole system of marking. No one had thought to tell me about this; and I shrank from asking.
>
> In fact, my strong secret sense of criminal incompetence made me behave with the utmost nervous oddity whenever I ran into Mr Juniper or the junior headmistress, Miss Seakins.

Miss Seakins was Blishen's name for another of the great figures of The Hall, Miss Gladstone.

> I'd discovered, in the end, what Running-over was. This followed from my discovery of the meaning of 'ups' and 'downs'. If a boy did good work, you put a little bar over the figure in the markbook. That was an up. If he did badly, you put a little bar under the figure, and that was a down.
>
> 'Then at Running-over,' I was told by Mr Capper, to whom at last I had taken my anxious curiosity, 'the Head reads out the number of ups and downs, or both, that a boy has been awarded in each subject. It's very tiresome. I mean, it's tiresome to listen to at Running-over; it's also tiresome to have to enter up in the markbooks.'
>
> I was too appalled to continue the attempt to conceal the full range of my ignorance, 'The Running-over . . .?'
>
> 'God, did no one tell you that? Typical! The Vale never imagines it has to explain itself in respect of any detail of its routine. The Vale's way is the world's way, forsooth! Oh well! Running-over is this fortnightly farrago when parents come and stand in the gallery round the hall and the Head runs over the marks, and calls out the ups and downs.'
>
> 'Marks every fortnight?' I cried.
>
> 'Marks, places, form orders. Oh, certainly. It would be every week if there weren't some limit to what can be done by flesh and blood. They have to be driven along, the little donkeys, you see, with kicks and carrots, if some of them are to have any hope of getting into decent schools.'

> The exhilaration I'd begun to feel, alongside a very great alarm, was pinched out when Mr Capper used the phrase 'decent schools'. I'd thought for a moment that he was a critic of this world of private education, a friend in the enemy's uniform; but his use of that phrase had been entirely without irony. 'Decent' was one of The Vale's keywords. Sometimes, when I heard it used, I thought, through faintly appalled inward laughter, of the many features of my own existence that would never qualify for it.

Marking and assessing is of the essence of the teacher's craft.

> I seemed to find it easy *not* to mark things: or having given marks, to discover that they seemed to bear no relationship to what I saw as true justice between boy and boy. And Running-over was like – oh, worse than any Day of Judgement could be. It was a complex festival of complacency and distress.
>
> I was simply glad, but rather incredulous, that the records of the staff were exempt from assessment and public announcement at Running-over. Huge quantities of downs would hardly have expressed my own disgrace.

He was lucky. Forty years on, teacher appraisal is accepted; he just might have found himself with some dreaded 'downs'!

Although it may perhaps have begun to feel like an eternity, our modest hero had, before long, reached half-term and with it his first salary cheque. The scale of his reimbursement for his labours seems, in these inflationary days, almost beyond comprehension.

> Some days before we broke up for half-term, Miss Cross, the school secretary, handed me my pay for those stunning six weeks. There was a cheque for £33 3s 8d.
>
> I was cursed with the most damnably unworldly economic outlook. I felt, as I tucked that cheque into my pocket, exactly as I had felt when being paid as a weekly newspaper reporter before the war, and as a landworker during it . . . a sense of very great embarrassment on behalf of my employer. Must he not be rueing the folly of paying out such large sums of money in return for my unimpressive labour?
>
> I felt this even more sharply in respect of my first payment from The Vale. They were getting from me, surely, some kind of anti-labour. I was a positive fraud. How could I blandly take their money?

But The Hall was greater than its component parts, and this greenhorn was perceptibly less green. Perhaps he didn't see it himself. After half-term. . . .

Mr Juniper wanted me at once in his room. I dissuaded Middle Six from providing me with a mock-solicitous escort ('Hard luck, sir!') and went down to the study where the Headmaster was accustomed to sit briefly between his impatient forays through the school. He said: 'Ah, would you like extra classes?'

'You mean –?'

'There are nine boys in Lower Six who are not far away from Common Entrance, and Mr Beesley says they can't spell or punctuate – in short, they are illiterate. You would take them twice a week – for half an hour . . .'

Mr Juniper then began to think, financially, aloud. The regular rate for extra lessons was 7s 6d an hour. If I took them, say, on Tuesdays and Thursdays, then nine times . . .

But somehow, being however implausibly asked to give extra lessons made me feel I belonged – I was edging my way into the picture.

A vivid picture of his formidable colleagues, opinionated yet sensitive, committed yet strangely vulnerable, emerges from the following description of a typical common-room discussion on teaching methods. How often, incidentally, has the wheel of educational theory revolved before and since 1946.

I had nightmares of being punished, in some huge unspecific fashion, by Mr Diamond and Mr Hollow together, for the slackness and general wretched character of my teaching.

But here I was, early in that second half-term, talking to Harrod Parker in the staffroom about the merits of certain kinds of parrot-like learning at an early age. Mr Diamond turned out to have been listening. He actually leapt to his feet and took up his place at my side, as if I'd raised a standard that he, for one, must flock to. 'My goodness, yes! My goodness, young man, how true that is! As practical men, we know it must be done.'

That phrase about being practical was a favourite with Mr Diamond. He used it as though throughout life he'd been the victim of a conspiracy to convict him of airily theoretical approaches to things. I was myself at this time deeply opposed to the idea of being practical, in any way whatever. There was a cluster of words that were devious ways of saying 'conservative'; and 'practical' was one of them. But I felt marvellously flattered by Mr Diamond's readiness to admit me to his club, even under such a heading.

'Oh, it must indeed be done,' I said. 'Better a little light-hearted misery at seven or eight than much real misery at a less flexible age.'

'I don't think it's even misery,' said Harrod Parker. 'They enjoy it. Acquiring useful knowledge by hammering it into your head with constant rhythmical repetition – oh, for a small fellow, very enjoyable!'

'Take,' I said, quite carried away, 'my maths division of Middle Four – you know, the lot I have here in the staffroom three times a week. . . . Part of their trouble is that in the juniors they were taught by a temporary wartime teacher – so Miss Seakins tells me – who believed that you learned your multiplication tables best by a process she called "absorption".'

'Good heavens,' cried Mr Diamond, ready to be apoplectic without hearing another word.

'The tables,' I said, 'were written out and hung round the room, and the idea was that the boys would absorb them just as they absorbed air, unconsciously.'

'Great Scott,' cried Mr Diamond. 'My hat!' He laughed in a rather broken fashion. 'You know, the war was a disaster in more ways than one. . . .!'

At this point Mr Hollow intervened. Interested, he said, to hear talk of that division of Middle Four. In his view, a great mistake.

'Oh, indeed,' I cried eagerly. 'They're the worst boys in the form and they positively enjoy being singled out and put together. They feel they're in quite glorious disgrace. They act upon one another.'

'Act 'pon 'noth'', Mr Hollow echoed, warmly.

I was positively in the club, now. One of my opinions on teaching (did I really hold it?) had been acclaimed. I had been commiserated with as a victim of Mr Juniper's impulsive rearrangements of the timetable.

Another glimpse is now afforded of the enthusiasm of the Wathen style, and the character of The Hall, which for decades had viewed education as being far wider than a mere classroom exercise. Further, there was a tradition, going back to the earliest days, that the organisation of affairs should never be spoon-fed to the boys.

The third incongruous step towards the increasing of my confidence followed almost at once, and resulted from yet another of Mr Juniper's seizures of decision. He bustled up to me during a break in the Senior School. 'This is for you,' he cried, taking me by a sleeve. Absent-mindedly he imparted a small correction to the angle of my spine. Himself, for all his age, a man of great spryness, bright with health, he equated youth with total hardihood. He tutted if he saw me wearing an overcoat. 'Stand up straight – *always*! give your chest a chance!' Now he hastily remoulded my torso, saying as he did this: 'The boys want to form an aeromodel club. You're of the generation that understands these things. You know all about aeromodels. There's a meeting on now. Come along.' I looked round at my colleagues, desperately, and saw no help in their grins. I had made my last model of any kind – oh, it must have been fifteen years before: one of those cardboard things, stick tab A to tab B; and my sad constructs had never lasted more than half an hour. I hurried miserably in Mr Juniper's wake and feared the worst as we entered the bellroom and I saw twenty or so senior faces turned in our direction. 'Here,' cried Mr Juniper, 'is your President. Ah, Ross-Stinson minor, this is your brainchild, isn't it? How's your father? Oh, and do something about that little brother of yours, won't you? Miss Seakins tells me he's been asleep solidly for six months. . . . Come on, someone! A chair for your President! You couldn't have a better man for the task. A thoroughly modern young man – knows all about it. . . . Carry on then, Mr Blishen.'

And they were eager. They were polite. I seemed to know what to do: referring sympathetically to the project, hastily appointing a secretary and treasurer, proposing certain initial tasks, dividing those present into the experienced and the beginners.

My reward I reaped at once. . . . Boys, with incredibly grave faces, pursued me along corridors, politely halted me on staircases. 'Sir, I've been thinking –' 'Sir, I wonder if you'd agree –?'

The gravity and earnestness of their manner brought me . . . oh, dammit, close to tears. I felt I'd had the most dramatic intimation of the remote possibility that, if I stayed long enough at The Vale and worked away at a total transformation of my character – and took, perhaps, a brilliant external degree – then I might become a teacher after all.

Was it with model aeroplanes – an area of skills and interests outside his comprehension – that Blishen became a true schoolmaster, and not with his exposition of the niceties of English syntax or the glories of our poetic heritage?

This unfamiliar world was kind to Blishen, and no one ever seems deliberately to have said or done anything to make him feel an outsider. He must have smiled wryly at some of the views expressed. The staff, many of them old hands, tended to regard the shifting post-war world with disfavour, and to air a somewhat other-worldly disapproval of the changes in society.

Mr Raisin put it bluntly once, over a staff room tea. 'One has never,' he said, 'seen a motor accident, has one? So curious, that! Just as one never seems to meet anyone who voted Labour.'

I opened my mouth, quite miserably. It would serve no useful purpose to inform Mr Raisin that I had myself voted in that extraordinary fashion. The news would merely perplex him. He liked me.

> Mrs Plenty was Senior School art, part-time. She took, very coolly, the brunt of Mr Juniper's views on art, as currently taught. These views, deeply disgruntled ones, he expressed from time to time at morning prayers. 'Paper', he would in fact inform the assembled Senior School when his irascibility ran away with him, 'costs goodness knows what a ream or packet or whatever one buys it in – and you'd be startled by the bills! The bills are frankly startling! But there it is, or there it seems to be! – there's this very odd idea that boys can be taught to paint only by being allowed *enormous* sheets of paper, and by being encouraged to – *ha*!' At such a point as this Mr Juniper's wrath would master him, and he would beat the table in front of him and make huge shapes in the air with his hands in an attempt to convey to the inattentive school the pointlessness of the kind of painting in which they were encouraged.

Oh dear! Art has ever been a favoured target of the conservative academic, fearful of the imagined licence and indiscipline of the bohemian.

The next nightmares to face Blishen were the examinations. His immediate problem was the internal school exam, but he was growing aware of that dread public exam, the Common Entrance.

> Suddenly there was talk of examinations. 'Let's see,' said Mr Diamond. 'Upper Five History – safe in your hands, eh?'
>
> It seemed monstrous to think of examining the results of my roaring encounters with Upper Five. In other fields, I attempted to add together the things I'd taught. There seemed nothing substantial enough in any direction to justify more than, say, five minutes of relaxed oral questioning. The formality of an examination paper was quite unsuitable, in all cases.
>
> 'Send your papers to Miss Cross to be duplicated,' I was told.
>
> Oh Lord! That meant I would be exposing to the entire world of The Vale the probably asinine questions that, when it came to it, I should bring myself to concoct! How dreadful! I had long been in the habit of rubbing my blackboard clean at the end of each lesson, to keep my work on it a secret from the world. But examinations threatened to make everything public.

Setting papers is a minor chore, providing a brief respite before harsher trials ahead.

> I marked my exam papers furtively, struggling with feelings of pure terror. Were these perhaps the worst exam papers ever completed in a school of the calibre of The Vale? I saw the expensive hopes of parent after parent being shattered by the incredibly inaccurate view

> of the medieval monastery expressed by Upper Five (could anyone hope to enter, say, Charterhouse, on the strength of such assertions as that 'they dinned in the refuctory'?); the pure anti-arithmetic of my backward set: the amazing stance in respect of simple parsing of my Middle Three: and Upper Three's cheerful willingness to regard the parts of speech as a sort of . . . general jam. The last was to me the most macabre: even clever children seemed, under my care, to have concluded that a noun might as well be an adjective if caprice didn't cause you to call it a verb.
>
> I wanted to burn all those papers, preferably at midnight, best of all in some remote spot where even the ashes would not betray me. But it was the convention that they should be returned so that boys might note their errors and repair them. . . . But the actual consequence of returning the papers was not one that, even in my madly sensitive anticipation of disaster, I had foreseen. Scores of boys were ready to dispute my marking. They questioned the marks given for each section of a paper: they demanded a recount of the total number of marks. At The Vale, I was to learn, boys took their revenge for the general terror of being examined by being extremely nasty about the results. I fought action after action, like some lawyer crazily over-employed. Till the very end of term I was beating off subtle attempts to have a mark added here or there, some readjustment made to a form order. Many boys kept files of their marks, as they accumulated, and of the points of complaint they were pursuing. It wasn't revenge only, I thought. It was also an example of the intense competitiveness of private education. You could expect to rise or fall, to realize your parents' ambition for you or to fail to do so, by the loss or gain of a mark.

This observation by a teacher who himself had never personally faced a structured system of examination at 13, or a tradition which readily accepts its inevitability, was understandable and fair comment. Indeed, forty years later, the situation has not materially altered.

> The savage academic demands of Common Entrance appalled me. All those exercises, in this subject and that, the ferocities of grammar, English, French and Latin: the massive mysteries of geometry, the schoolman's algebra. . . . At heart I had the morale, not of a teacher, but of a dunce. Heaps of exercise books filled me with much the same oppression and dismay as I'd have felt if I'd watched servants of the Inquisition hurrying about with the paraphernalia of torture and execution.

★ ★ ★

As the end of term approached, another test of stamina and skill emerged – report writing.

> The need to write reports had come as a final assault on my battered conscience. It seemed to me that I should be writing: 'I have taught this boy badly and offer, for the little they are worth, my apologies': or simply, 'I could have done better.' Instead I was required to add cowardly libel to my crimes. It might be true that Nye, in my arithmetic set, had made very little effort: but ought I not, in all decency, to add that he'd found himself in the hands of a teacher peculiarly unable to command effort?
>
> Worse – I'd discovered that the common quality of most report making at The Vale was one of wit, edge, a pleasant slyness. Of one boy, Mr Hollow had scrawled in a handwriting that seemed curiously to reflect the slurred character of his speech: 'Often absent: and when present, still absent.' 'James,' someone had written, 'seems indignant because Latin is not English. Once he withdraws this objection, all should be well.' I didn't know what contribution I could make at this level. And the things I wanted to say about boys were too complex to be rendered down to the phrases – conventional or not – of a school report.

Blishen was totally puzzled by the extraordinary discrepancy between The Hall boy's apparent stupidity in the classroom and his blissful talent outside it, a state of puzzlement that has perplexed staff before and since. It certainly has always applied in particular to that steady stream of gifted musicians that have attended the school.

> What, for example, could I say of little Tudor? He'd made an important contribution to the end-of-term concert, playing his cello most beautifully. The instrument had almost blotted him out. There'd been this large brown cello, with Tudor's nervous hands requiring music from it. Afterwards, he'd skipped up to me and said: 'So you see, sir – I *can* play!'
>
> It amazed me that this small gifted boy had believed that I'd had doubts about his talent. But then I'd exhibited very plain doubt of his power over formal English grammar. He'd danced up to me once in class – he seemed to think that approaching a master in a sort of demented jig would help to make the event imperceptible – and asked me if he was doing the right exercise. My eye had fallen on numerous very false assertions about various categories of noun. 'These are . . . not quite correct,' I'd murmured. Oh! how could such tenderly indefinite reproaches ever bring about an improvement in his work?

Part of the problem was that prep schools have been disgracefully slow to accept the educational role of music and art, and back in 1946 The Hall was somewhat abnormal to have any music within its walls at all. All too many of the staff remained depressingly unenlightened and in their perception of the glory of music, the boys may well have been ahead of their elders!

> 'Music,' said Mr Beesley, having Tudor in mind, 'is a kind of clever stupidity, I suppose.' He was rash enough to say this in the hearing of Mrs Dorset, the part-time music mistress, who gave him a brief, packed lecture on the mental majesty of, in the main, Bach and Mozart. Fond though I was of Mr Beesley, I enjoyed that. One at least of the staffroom's negligent aphorisms had been struck to the ground, and there beaten to dust by passionate conviction.
>
> But I enjoyed, I really did enjoy, that concert, as I was to feel ridiculous delight in so much end-of-termishness. Such occasions seemed to be festivals of forgiveness and forgetfulness as to the agonies and horrors of term. Mr Diamond became almost ungovernably affable.

And so, to the end of term, a habitually rather jolly affair, especially in December, with Christmas festivity beckoning excitingly.

> Mr Juniper had displayed his own, but more candid and impatient, delight in the concert, the final Running-over, house parties, and similar events: all of which seemed to turn The Vale for some days into a kind of panting indoor circus. I'd grown very fond of Mr Juniper – or perhaps I should say that I'd come to enjoy the legendary figure he'd been turned into: partly, I imagine, by accident, partly by such an accretion of mannerisms (and anecdotes relating to them) as might attach itself to any lively schoolmaster after forty years: but partly by his own manipulation. Mr Juniper enjoyed, one could see, being half-fictitious. He cultivated, among other things, a way of suddenly diving into a scene, and bringing it to a halt by some totally unlikely inquiry. So he'd enter a class and pose a grammatical puzzle.
>
> Mr Juniper was no grey figure, no invisible presence. He brought to any situation the preoccupations and problems that happened to be in his head at the time. So, on occasions, that startling entry of his into a classroom might herald some apparently quite inappropriate request for information. 'Who on earth won the county cricket championship in 1919?' It was often about cricket that he made these appeals or set his posers.

The Hall was about to endure the worst weather in living memory. Those who attended country boarding schools that winter of 1947 will vividly recall endless days with playing fields so deeply covered in snow that the domestic life-style of the eskimo became a practical, regularly rehearsed exercise. At The Hall, it was less glamorous. For Blishen, it gave a degree of welcome respite, for football was a sore trial.

> There was not to be much football that term, as it happened. At the end of January the most appalling winter of the century was to descend and turn the world to shuddering iron. In respect of football only, I was grateful to that savage weather when it came.

Meanwhile, he had to cope with senior football games.

> My senior game was at times happy to proceed in its own way: at other times, furious with my unhelpfulness. 'Sir,' I was asked at last, 'why don't you tell us where we're wrong?' I began nervously to do this: or rather, to utter loud cries of recommendation or dissuasion which had, to my ear, roughly the right sound. This new activity of mine seemed to increase the general enjoyment of the game. I even began to believe in the relevance of these shouts and urgings. The only times when I was overcome by bashfulness occurred when some passing workman stopped and peered over the fence into the ground. There were bad days when someone would do this for a quarter of an hour at a time. How odd it was, I thought, this English lust for football, that caused a grown man to stop and watch intently a game played by little boys of eight, nine or ten. At such moments, I became very self-conscious indeed, and would blur and mutter those exhortations out of which, at other times, I reckoned safely to compose my refereeship.
>
> It remained one of my greatest fears: being unmasked, as a pretender to the position of referee and coach, by some such passer-by, to whom the misinstruction in football of small British boys would be a hanging matter.

The deteriorating conditions that February seemed to come as little surprise to the stalwarts of The Hall common-room.

> It was towards the end of January that our traumatic winter really began. There was a day when the snow fell with a sort of idleness, a twist and flurry that was almost weary: it was caught in great sideways and upward sighings of air, deadly chill, that seemed capable of returning it to the sky it came from. But still it fell: and the temperature with it, to zero and then below. By the following day the snow had gained a fearful confidence, and came down in blinding masses, now with the character of pure ice. The ground became a horribly thick sluggish carpet that squeaked and groaned as we laboured across it. Falsely a weather forecast promised that the temperature might 'rise towards freezing point'. Buses were lucky and unlikely accidents. Coal disappeared; gas followed it. School lunches, for the dwindling number of boys, were lukewarm. Mr Juniper appeared in an overcoat: a personal defeat he

took hard. His revenge was to rearrange the timetable in quite an impressively unpractical fashion.

Mr Diamond was unsurprised by all this. He had expected nothing less from the election of a Labour government. 'They've cut the gas off now, y'see,' he pointed out. 'We shall grind to a halt. Everything will go. They simply don't know how to govern, y'see.' And he stared out of the staffroom window at the left wing snow lying where Mr Attlee and his team had allowed it to accumulate, in ungentlemanly heaps.

A town school can enjoy few of the compensations a major snowfall affords a country school.

Only someone with Mr Diamond's passion for pinning down the obvious would have commented on a commonplace blizzard. The world had become a prison of snow: we'd walked for weeks on thick floors of ice. They were floors of a glassy unevenness. Wireless programmes shrank: the Third Programme vanished. Every day brought some disappearance. Now the street lights were gone; now the weekly magazines. We collected amazing statistics of gloom: that, for example, in the month of February the sky was free of cloud for six minutes.

The school was filling up again, now it had become clear that the winter was not one you could see off with a few days in bed. The untapped energy of the boys grew greater daily. It appalled a new colleague of ours, Peter Nicholas.

Peter, on his way to Cambridge, was spending two terms in our company*. There was some tradition of teaching in the family, and the theory was that he would dip a toe into the professional experience, to see if it was for him or not. It was, I suspected from the start, a quite perfunctory toe. Peter had no air of the teacher whatever. His reaction to life at The Vale was one of polite startlement. I'd say, perhaps, 'I'm afraid my class might have deafened yours this morning. My maths teaching seems to excite them rather surprisingly.' Peter would smile, darkly, and then duck his head as if to prevent the smile escaping into general circulation. 'You flatter me,' he'd say. 'The noise in my own room's too great for me to hear anything beyond it.'

It was at this crisis stage in the school year that, almost to his consternation, Blishen became accepted as a proper schoolmaster.

It was about this time that, suddenly, appallingly, all the boys were calling me Gilbert.

* See below, page 213

The Hall has always had a problem over what to do if the weather placed its fields out of commission. When GAW first arrived at the school, back in 1924, he had introduced a programme of classroom activity, based somewhat loosely on the Dalton System. Non-field days were called 'Dalton afternoons'. In February and March 1947, the problem needed constant solution.

> Among the substitutes for games were walks to the great Common that spread across the brow of the borough. We'd go in crocodiles: and, given all that snow, it was like conducting parties of one's enemies to an unguarded ammunition dump. Back at school, senior members of the staff would be giving extra lessons: an essential operation of the private school industry. The hall would be full of boys polishing up their Latin, French, geometry.

Pressures brought their expected toll of both temper and health. The Hall has never eschewed political debate. Blishen would, forty years hence, have found a wider range of attitude among his colleagues but in 1947, the political persuasion of the common-room was predictable.

> Snow! At the beginning of March there was the promise of a thaw. It was ended by the wildest blizzard yet. Stinging storms of sleet were blown in waves and vicious spirals across the roads and back into the air. I waited an hour for a trolleybus to take me home.
>
> The conservatism of The Vale's staff had deepened during those weeks. It was as though the cruel weather were making a party political broadcast. They nodded at it, deeply in agreement with such icy exposure of socialist fallacy.
>
> I felt politically marooned: as when over staffroom tea Mr Juniper inquired about the Minister of Education. 'Not an educated person, I imagine? Self-educated, I assume.' His tone was not sharp or hostile – it was rather the tone of a man who discusses the baffling ways of total aliens.
>
> In fact, public dejection had become very deep. Grumbling had us all in its grip. I thought how sad it was that the doggedness of wartime had been allowed to slip away now that there'd been a change of enemies. Now we were faced by the consequences of a monstrously exhausting struggle, allied to a damnable winter for which no earthly agent could be blamed.

For reasons we can only guess, Blishen omits any description of the annual gym display. It certainly was not an institution with which he would easily have identified. In *Uncommon Entrance*, he explains that he was in bed with 'flu. Since he was describing 1947, this may well have been so. A piece of editorial licence is perhaps permissible at this juncture. It is very sad that no first-hand account by Blishen survives. Perhaps one does. An unsigned article in the 1950 magazine gives us just the gently irreverent picture one might have expected from him, one entirely in tune with the style of *Uncommon Entrance*, and it is included here:

> When you first go to a musical comedy, you may be misled into thinking that there are some hundreds of chorus girls; and it is not until you start wondering how many that you realise that there are only about a dozen who keep reappearing, and that all the rest is done by camouflage. The sophisticated may have thought that the same system was in use in the gym display and have been surprised rather than impressed. Your reporter is able to state officially that there were really five million Hall boys and – like the packet of foreign stamps – they were all different. There were also about four million watching mothers and fathers.
>
> The first March Past was excellently done, with precision which could have set any good General reminiscing about his last invasion. It was followed by wave upon wave of squads each one making life more difficult for itself and more amazing for us. The display was conducted by rather healthy instructors, but they were understanding and helpful and one could not help feeling that it was all rather fun. The Juniors did a 'Boat Race' and there were Chinese Fights and races to touch the top wall-bar (always the part of a gym most worth touching). Again, in the good old days, when discipline was discipline, there was always somebody who had not the ability or the figure to stand on his head. But take a random selection of Hall boys, tell them to turn upside-down on the wall-bars and they will to a man.

And so, to the Summer term, the final exam term, and with it, thoughts of the schools for which it was hoped these unlikely boys might aspire. It was another area of total mystery for Blishen.

> At staff meetings, the joke arose when, in the long review of boys' hopes of reaching the goals among the public schools that they'd been set down for on their arrival at The Vale, or even earlier – when, in that sequence of groans and hopeful cries, Mr Juniper came to Smith B J. His parents' aim was to get him into what I gathered was a very minor public school indeed. Mr Juniper had urged: 'We must not indulge ourselves! To sterner things! Will little Bolsher win a Winchester scholarship?'
>
> *That* was the area of the school's work about which I felt only a mildly terrified mystification. Here was I, engaged in dubious fashion with the Thirds and Fourths – roped in for peripheral, reparable activity with one of the Fifths. All that took me nowhere

near the main operations room of The Vale – seen as the setting for the very precise, very expert, very successful plotting of a campaign to get boys into the public schools. Some of my colleagues – with Mr Diamond, Mr Hollow and Mr Raisin at their head – were strict and seasoned strategists in this field.

The Hall has always endured as much as it has enjoyed its reputation for scholarship. The problem has been that not all the boys are scholarly. Indeed, its recruitment was random and entirely haphazard; some boys were (and incidentally, this remains entirely true still, in the 1980s) increasingly incapable of coping with the style, the atmosphere, the pace and the pressure. Others suffered a multiplicity of emotional defects or difficulties.

'Well, gentlemen – *he's* out of the window,' Mr Juniper would inform his staff. By which he meant that some child, unlikely to achieve the paradoxically named Common Entrance – it seemed only logical that it should be known instead as Uncommon Entrance – had been persuaded to leave the school.

It has to be said that usually a boy required some defect other than slowness of mind to qualify for ejection by way of Mr Juniper's window. Apart from Smith B J, there were not a few slow children among us, to balance that brightness that made Peter Nicholas dread a period of geometry with Upper Six. 'They would make Bertrand Russell pant a bit, I believe,' he said of those high-flyers.

Eccentrics are the joy of any good school. The Hall has had them in profusion. The trouble is that they do tend to clash with the authorities.

'You detention master, sir?'

I nodded, placed the heavy detention book on the desk, and looked round at my penitential charges. They didn't look very unhappy. For some reason, detention at The Vale was often a gay affair: like a meeting of some unorthodox club. From outside the window came the sounds of snarling dispute: the boarders were playing cricket in the yard.

Grayson was one of several obsessives at The Vale, whose earnestness as scholars, alas, was inspired by fields of inquiry unknown to Common Entrance examiners. That hopelessly slow boy, Radley, for example, was extremely quick of mind, and impressively well-informed, in the matter of aeromodelling. I'd once, on an afternoon too wet for sport, set Upper Four debating the relative advantages of living in town and country. Radley's contribution was brief and passionate. The town, he said, was infinitely better if one wanted to buy model aircraft: but the country

> had the edge when it came to flying them. He confessed that, as a result of this paradox, his whole life plan was painfully uncertain.
>
> Now Grayson dropped an exercise book in front of me. I saw what appeared to be a blueprint for a spider's web. 'These are the lines coming into Euston,' he said.
>
> '"Algebra Book, Exercise 17(a), Nos 1-5"', I read from the detention book. 'That's what you're supposed to be doing. "Flipping blotting paper at the ceiling" is Mr Parker's allegation.'
>
> 'Oh no, look,' said Grayson. 'This is absolutely your only chance of having the lines into Euston explained to you by an expert. Now, this is the down main –'

How utterly reassuring that, in the matter of characterful, original boys, as in so much else, The Hall has changed so little in forty years. At the same time, Blishen's colleagues seemed to combine philosophical resignation with total incredulity over anything outside the experience of their other-worldly background.

> Mr Beesley had said: 'They're poor devils, you know – at times I positively feel *compassion* for them. They simply aren't bright; nature has *not* been kind. The Common Entrance syllabus is beyond them. I am not at all sure' – and here he paused to give further consideration to the thought in his mind – 'yes, I'm not at all sure that in their circumstances I should not myself be . . . a little *intransigent.*'
>
> The Vale had a phrase. They should, it was said, be 'in an elementary school'. The passage of the 1944 Education Act had brought about no change in this language. Mr Juniper said to me once: '*Don't* send that boy Nye to me for anything whatever. He is . . . elementary school material.' I fancied he might have forgotten, or never understood, that I had myself been, in no figurative fashion, elementary school material. . . .

It speaks volumes for the kindly and civilised atmosphere of The Hall that 'Juniper' should express sentiments with such crashing insensitivity and yet inspire no resentment whatever!

★ ★ ★

The Summer term meant cricket, which offered little respite for an 'ungamesy' teacher.

> The summer bloomed enormously, and at times I seemed to have found my way into some gently haughty English middle-class fantasy of correct fairweather living, with perfectly kitted small boys performing the rites of cricket, and classes blinking over their books in the school yard. Mr Diamond went into shirt sleeves: and roared his apologies at any woman who appeared. You'd have

thought from the bluff fuss he made that he'd stripped to the skin. 'It's the heat, dear lady, you understand,' he'd explain to Mrs Leach; and no one would have been surprised to find that he'd put the sun down for a slippering.

Is Blishen turning his colleagues into quaint and comic caricatures?

Most afternoons were given to cricket: and I was not much better at taking that than I'd been at taking football. My mind would drift away from the bickering slowness with which a game developed. It was easy to absent myself for a whole over, to find I had no views at all about some sudden passionate allegation of lbw or run out. There were always, in any game, boys who claimed to know the rules by heart. They would appeal to a point that sounded at once slyly plausible and inane. If *A* did this at the same time that *B* did that, then *C*'s wicket was forfeit: 'It happened last week, Gilbert, in the game at Lord's!' What I really needed was to have the inner council of MCC in constant session on the edge of the pitch. My charges would climb on to the bus, on their way back to school, horribly inflamed.

When I could, I cut a game short so that we had time to walk back to The Vale. I shrank from what a couple of dozen small boys could do to a peaceful mid-afternoon bus. They turned it into a shrieking turmoil; other passengers would look stunned. Once as we surged forward on the pavement, the conductor took up a fighting position. 'You can get on,' he cried, sounding like some doomed general preparing for a famous defeat, 'but you'll keep your traps shut. This is a bus, not a blooming roundabout.' I smiled weakly at him: he muttered, 'Try to keep the little buggers quiet!' It was odd, and not unsatisfactory, to think for a moment of those expensively educated children as little buggers.

But the truth was, Blishen was growing enchanted by The Hall.

My noisy ease as a teacher increased daily. I might have been quite the master of my classes had I been able to control my instinct to tease. Perhaps it was because of some basic frivolity that I allowed myself to be overwhelmed by their desire for amusement. I would see the classroom situation heading towards a joke and would positively omit to change course. I would even do a little steering in that direction myself, anxious that they should achieve the enjoyment they'd promised themselves. I was also given to bursts of positively nonsensical rhetoric. 'Of all boys', I would cry, 'you are the most wretched in the world'; and they were thrilled, and sometimes actually cheered.

Problems still existed, some predictable and universal, some essentially characteristic of The Hall, and some – well, typical of the creatively accident-prone.

I found it difficult to restrain an absurd feeling of quite savage rage when a class failed to understand my explanation of a new piece of mathematics. It happened that term with Upper Four and simultaneous equations. I'd prepared myself with great care: setting myself problems, and solving them, till I felt I'd positively invented the process. The trouble was, as always, that their questions sprang out of areas of doubt as to the commonsense of mathematics that I'd never conceived of. So the whole notion of equality, without which one must naturally be rather cynical about any equation, was not acceptable to many. They retreated to a point of human development where this idea of one thing being equal to another had actually to be discovered and demonstrated. They nibbled away at the simultaneous equation till all I had left was a mass of pre-mathematical debris. Someone accustomed to dealing with primitive tribes might have moved forward from this point. I simply lost my temper.

And suddenly, all their exercise books had become scandals of untidiness – of blots and ill-formed letters and figures. From the Junior School they'd brought a mass of conventions as to setting-down, underlining: being rough over here, being neat over there. Mr Juniper had once said, with his eye on Mrs Leach, that ladies were too concerned with neatness. But I couldn't believe that the implication – that some kind of decent masculine raffishness might be aimed at – could possibly cover the grubby confusions that filled my own exercise books.

The academic year was reaching its hectic finale.

Back at The Vale, our days were in the grip of high summer and the events that belonged to that quite desperate season. Parts of the school were hushed, as scholastic emergencies arose; boys famous for their promise were known to be receiving their ultimate polish in the billiard room, a corner of Mr Juniper's study, the large cupboard known as the library. There was a rash of lecturers from outside, including a celebrated parent or two or a high-flying Old Boy. One of the latter gave an illustrated talk on a region of Africa: the illustrations consisting of his disappearing at intervals into a room off the hall and re-emerging in tropical garb – head-dresses, gowns, outrageously brilliant shirts, and a variety of exotic footwear. At times he brandished a spear or flourished a wicked-looking arrow. He loaded his ankles with bells intended to attract a lion. Mr Diamond found it necessary to forbid a certain quality of applause that greeted the early stages of this performance.

> In one of the lecturer's absences, he leapt on to a table, crashed his huge hands together, and, in a roaring whisper, intended to spare feelings as yet another costume was struggled with, declared: 'This is not a pierrot show, y'know. . . . We are not on the pier at Southend, Jenkins, Jameson, whatever your name is.' The rest of the lecture was received with a nervous bubbling of enthusiasm and disbelief. The lecturer certainly had a mild English boniness of feature and deportment that made his disguises seem a series of gaudy impertinences at his own oddly willing expense.

Hall boys have never suffered foolish lecturers very gladly!

> The Junior School sports were the earliest of the end-of-term galas. By then we could have done with a little of the cloud that had totally covered that now-incredible February.
>
> Massive manipulations were a feature of the junior sports. I had not before understood the lack of scruple that underlay the conduct of a good Junior School by its teachers. Certain boys must be jockeyed into winning positions for the sake of their morale – or indeed for their blue eyes or some other charming quality. Others, for the good of their characters, or for some special defect, must be excluded from triumph of any kind. The ladies of the Junior School were like illusionists as they convinced their audience of victories or defeats – sometimes in the face of the plainest visual evidence. No one – not even the most quarrelsome parent – was given an opportunity for complaint. All was most beautifully contrived. Said Miss Seakins, as the last officially favoured boy marched off, blushing, with his prize: 'It has been a thoroughly satisfactory afternoon.'

Blishen's saga includes singularly few encounters with one feature of The Hall which scares many a hardened teacher – the anxious, unrealistic parent.

> I was amused but my amusement was a little impaired by a growing sense of sickness. The afternoon had been very hot indeed. It was at the last moment, all prizes awarded, most boys safely surrendered to their parents or to nannies, that I ran into Headstone's mother.
>
> Headstone was a quarrelsome, sorely egotistic child in Upper Three. He was deeply detested by virtually everyone. Very simply, he set out to make as many people as possible as unhappy as possible. An unlikeable, dark-natured child. . . . Ugh! everyone said. Ugh! – Headstone!*

*Was Blishen's choice of this name for a boy for whom the expression 'ugh' was appropriate deliberately the same as the venue for the school's rugger, which resumed during his final year? He never actually described his attitude to the even more robust code of football than the one he had to endure. We can guess!

> And now, suddenly, here was his mother, announcing herself. Her own face dark, angry, sulky. What did I make of Bernard? No, no, I was not to be polite. She could see I was trying to be polite about him. Miss Seakins had been so dreadfully polite. Mrs Headstone wished me to understand that she couldn't bear the child herself. Don't be polite. He is so dreadfully unpopular. We can feel it! We know it! You see, Mr Headstone and I have such a very large circle of friends. Tell me, please tell me. Your true opinion. Why do people dislike Bernard so much? It causes Mr Headstone and me such distress. We ourselves . . .'
>
> My head was reeling. My sickness had become very acute and urgent. Her angry, egotistic eyes: the very hard line of her mouth, a hardness punched home by bright lipstick.
>
> 'Tell me, do. Tell me. Frankly. Mr Headstone and I would give anything to know why two such popular people . . .'
>
> I was going to be actually sick.
>
> 'You need not be polite. Miss Seakins . . .'
>
> Her angry, obsessive eye.
>
> 'Please,' I mumbled. 'I can't . . . must go . . .'
>
> Her face swam, a puzzle of revolving hard mouth and angry eyes, and I ran and ran until I reached the darkest corner behind the pavilion, and there was very sick. . . .

It is perhaps scarcely palatable to make the observation, yet the punch line above does perhaps symbolise the instinctive response of teachers over the ages to somewhat unreasonable pressures which parents can bring to bear.

Shortly after, another landmark was reached, and . . .

> I was called into Mr Juniper's presence. 'Ah – we said this was to be an experiment, didn't we? I think it's been a successful one. What do you say? Well, let's see – your salary as a probationer, I suppose that's the word, was £200 a year. From next term I think we ought to raise that to £300. Don't you?'
>
> I offered no objection.
>
> In the staff photo, posed in the sunny yard, my face looked much like those in other photos that hung along the corridors and that, among other things, enabled one to trace Mr Diamond backwards, to a bushy-haired youngster with unmistakable hands housed on his knees. The smile I wore seemed to be stamped into my face: a mark, I thought, of all the desperate good humour of that year. . . .*

And so to the last ritual of the term, and this included then, as it does still, demonstrations of enormous affection and generosity from

* See plate 21

hordes of boys whose behaviour often has required harshness and whose attitude has often implied hostility. They are an amazing and a wonderful lot of boys, at The Hall – and The Vale.

> The final Running-over of the year was a full-dress affair, revolving round an immense recital of marks awarded, expectations fulfilled or exceeded, hopes villainously dashed. A speech was made by a public school headmaster – a young, brisk, sharp man: I wondered, looking from him to Mr Juniper, if I'd have been tolerated on the staff of The Vale by a younger head. Mr Juniper had a capacity for eccentric action that might be no quality of a new generation of private school men, more managing – altogether less agreeably odd. This afternoon, for example, he was as nervous as an actor about to play Hamlet – and had made time for his routine correction of my spine and general posture. 'Chest out!' he'd urged, moulding me into a shape so unnatural that I was afraid a boy would catch sight of me before I could decently abandon it.
>
> Mr Diamond had received many gifts from grateful boys and parents: several boxes of cigarettes, a lighter, a dictionary ('Always jolly useful, you know!'), a bottle of wine. He had been excited into a state of quite alarming general friendliness. Some boys clearly found it difficult to believe that his hand might be descending between their shoulder blades for amiable purposes.

And what was Blishen going to do now? He talked of departing to take professional training, as he eventually did in 1949. But, in the way schools can, The Hall's charms had ensnared him. He had become part of the place, a willing prisoner.

> The Vale held me tight, anyway. I'd grown, as it were, nervously fond of it: or of certain colleagues, certain boys. I liked, childishly, the sensation of being at home in the school. I was quite ridiculously proud of having been accepted in so foreign a world.
>
> Still when I stepped on the stairs that led to the attic classrooms I'd hear the whispering running ahead of me: 'Gilbert! Gilbert's coming!' But that was now as oddly pleasant as it was professionally appalling. And in a recent prep a boy had called 'Gilbert!' and then looked guilty: whereupon Lightfoot ii had grinned at him, and then at me, and said: 'It's all right!' I concluded that he was reassuring us both.

PART II: THE WATHEN YEARS

Chapter 5
The End of the Wathen Era
1952-1955

The last years of GAW's long reign were marked by a number of signs and symbols that mighty change was due and, indeed, inevitable. The death of a tired and ailing monarch and the succession of a new, young and inspiring Queen was just one such. Quite apart from GAW's own realisation, long hinted at and increasingly anticipated, that he could not continue for ever, there was a steady trickle of retirements or departures of trusted staff, and, sadly, of deaths too. These must have been distressing, robbing this seemingly tireless man of key members of the team which had so strongly established The Hall through the post-war reconstruction years. Copinger had died in 1949. A year later, another death robbed GAW of a vital assistant, in the area where he was least interested or adept: administration. Miss J F Large, the school secretary and bursar, was first appointed in 1931 to assist with the ever-growing correspondence and office-work. She later became the resident secretary as well as the bursar and personal assistant to the Headmaster. She was in command of stationery and her eagle eye was quick to discover pages of exercise books unused and wasted. She hated the noise which boys make and how she hated interruptions, but she knew that all these things were part of the job and had to be endured.

Then in 1952 came another death of a key member of the staff, in office. Mr Rothwell was caretaker, cook and caterer in the Junior School. Within a year, Fyson and Wraith in the Senior and Miss Baker in the Junior School had retired, all three valued, long-serving teachers.

In 1952, the war had been over for seven years, but hints of austerity remained: things still were subject to shortages or even rationing. If changes were in the air, so were there the familiar minor excitements.

The Senior School boys had their simple pleasures. One of these was to roll motor-tyres like hoops about the yard. Some became very skilful in steering them through narrow gaps and avoiding the vast crowds of pedestrians and footballers who congregated in the playgrounds during the mid-morning breaks.

The recollections of prospective pupils and headmasters alike suggest that GAW regarded skill in propelling these tyres as the ultimate test of their worthiness!

Meanwhile at the Junior School a climbing pole and two ropes had been installed in the yard supported by those long-suffering friends of The Hall, the two pink may-trees. On their first appearance a curious silence spread over the Junior School break, and the neighbours must have wondered. True sons of their age, the boys had automatically formed themselves into silent queues waiting patiently with an abstracted air for a turn on the rope. This phenomenon lasted two days.

Later came the pleasant surprise of the appearance of a scramble-net in the Junior School playground. Rumour had it that Mrs Wathen was the first to climb its dizzy heights. Be that as it may, it was not long before Mr Wathen, fearing a domestic tragedy, put the net out of bounds for anyone weighing more than six stone.

Some remarkable scores were recorded in the cricket matches in 1952. Warwick House, our near neighbours in Lymington Road, scored a total of five to which The Hall replied with a total of six for two wickets. Gunnersbury, usually powerful opponents, were dismissed for only nineteen and once again The Hall were able to score the necessary runs for the loss of two wickets. The Father's XI also suffered a defeat. Only the Staff XI offered any positive resistance that year.

In the same year the Hampstead Borough Council decreed that, since their swimming-pools were public, any number of the latter could be admitted however many Hall boys were there. The organisation of swimming tests became more and more difficult. On one occasion, when an area had at last been cleared for a 'Pink Star' test, one of the public decided to join in. GAW, who was calling out the time every five seconds as was his custom, took no notice and the rightful candidates completed the course successfully. Boys were not even given cubicles in which to change but were sent to the spectators' gallery to change behind a moth-eaten piece of blackout material which they called 'The Iron Curtain'. This was the start of a long-drawn-out battle with the authorities, which continued even when the new baths were built at the corner of Avenue Road and Adelaide Road. By the 1970s the source of trouble was The Hall's status as an independent school. It led to the adoption of the principle that the school's responsibility lay primarily to teach water sense and basic skills. Swimming has remained a part of the curriculum for Junior School boys, but by the 1980s was purely a recreational option for Seniors.

GAW regarded gym – it was more what later generations would regard as a combination of drill and PE – as a vital part of the boys' preparation for life. One of the last of the gym displays of his regime, in 1952, was recorded by the recently appointed English master, John Watney, who was in his own right an author of some standing, with several novels including *The Unexpected Angel* and *The Enemy Within* to his name.

> It was the first week of spring. A north-easterly blizzard swept across Hampstead, bringing down the almond blossom and burying the daffodils beneath wet snow. The Finchley Road was a pneumonia trap.
>
> But the gymnasium was warm enough, as the mothers gathered on the balconies and the pipe-smoking fathers, with a 'Where's my boy?' glint in their eyes looked down upon the hall. It was a colourful scene. The dais upon which presently the Headmaster and the Mayor of Hampstead were to take their seats, was decorated with a strip of red, white and blue bunting, and supported seven orange chairs; while under the words 'Deep End' the pianist gingerly sat down at the upright piano, and the staff, still more or less on speaking terms, shepherded boys and parents alike to quiet restful corners.
>
> There was a movement at the doors, and the Mayor, not in his scarlet robes, but wearing his golden chain and medal, was shown to his seat; and almost at once there was a cry of 'Mark time – left, right, left – forward MARCH!' And the School, led by the smallest upright boy in the world, came marching in, the Junior School in white singlets, shorts and gym shoes, the Seniors bare to the waist. There was half a battalion of them, marching and counter-marching to the thump of the piano, and I could not help feeling that one day they would make fine soldiers.
>
> Parents leant eagerly forward, younger brothers hopped excitedly up and down, and fathers frowned as sons looked up and smiled at them. The Headmaster, a fine conductor, beat time with his hands and Mr Barron led the clapping as the School marched away.
>
> We settled more comfortably in our seats, and I saw a young boy of five or six, sitting beside me, watching, with a concentration worthy of a BBC commentator, for the arrival of the Squad C of the Junior School. They came racing on like circus ponies, cantering round the hall, and then formed themselves into three living stars, where under the direction of Mrs Davidson, they performed their simple feats. 'Down', said Mrs Davidson, and down they lay upon their backs, and the small boy beside me turned to his mother and said, anxiously, 'Are they going to bed now?' But before she could answer, they were up again, dragging a vaulting-horse into the middle of the hall. The small boy watched in fascination. 'What is

> it?' he asked at last. 'A horse', said his mother. The small boy considered this a while, and then said, 'But Mummy, where is its head?'
>
> Martial music and a slow handclap ushered in Squad B of the Junior School. They came forward four abreast, stamping their feet and moving with a fierce concentration to take up their positions in front of the dais. It was not until they were seated, however, that the small boy at my side spoke again. 'Where', he asked, 'is the food?'
>
> More music and more slow clapping greeted Squad A of the Junior School, as they entered slowly in files. Now, for the first time, the movements were performed without words of command, Mr Joint, their instructor, merely tapping with his whistle to note the change of exercise. Here, for the first time, were the wall-bars used, and those movements were watched with astonishment by the small boy who, unable to contain his indignation, suddenly said, 'Isn't that man going to hang himself too?'
>
> The first of the Senior Squads now marched out into the arena, and the timing and execution of more complicated exercises made an agreeable and ever-varying pattern upon the yellow floor. But it was Squad B of the Senior School that, to my mind, gave the most polished show. They marched in six abreast and then spread out into six files. Their complicated and unaided movements were precise and sure, while their vaulting and figure-work were excellent. Most effective to watch was the flying leap over the horse, a fine show of self-confidence and timing on the part of each performer. So excited became the small boy that it was all mother could do to prevent his taking a swallow-leap from the gallery to the floor below.
>
> Squad A of the Senior School brought the gym show to an end, with a complicated but co-ordinated display with three horses in use simultaneously, and as they marched out the instructors were already erecting the boxing-ring.
>
> After the boxing the Mayor gave away the prizes and made a speech, and there was nothing left for us to do but sing 'God save the Queen' and race each other through the arctic wind back to school and the excellent tea that Mrs Wathen had prepared for us.

In 1953, Mr Abbott, the Chief Instructor at the Hampstead Swimming-baths, who had done so much for the school over the previous thirty years, died quite suddenly. He had been responsible for the traditional gym displays for many years. They were never again to be quite what they had been in GAW's heyday. Educational attitudes and approaches were soon to begin to alter radically and the generations of retired ex-Army sergeant-majors perpetuating the military style of the training were dwindling. New instructors were out of sympathy with the old tradition, and displays were abruptly ended, probably to the relief of all concerned, after 1975.

Another post-war phenomenon was increasingly evident. The magazine of the day reveals just how simple had been the matter of passing the exams for transfer to public schools during the war and just after. Thus, at the end of the summer GAW was again firing warning shots across the bows of those who might have difficulties with Common Entrance. Whereas thirty-five or forty per cent marks overall average had been considered a reasonable pass at most schools, the better ones were now insisting on at least fifty per cent.* 'I cannot help thinking they are wise and we must accept the fact that places at the public schools of England are in greater demand and it is right and proper that they should be filled by the best boys available.'

GAW reminded the boys that if they benefited from the traditions of the school, they also benefited by the contributions which they made to school life. And, turning to the parents, he said: 'We do not claim to give our pupils one tenth of the things they derive from home but we do hope that in the atmosphere of The Hall the boys leaving today have learnt a love of laughter, of laughing with and not at people; a liking and respect for their fellow-men; that they have overcome inhibitions; that they have acquired that eminently British virtue of tolerance and learnt too to be good mixers and not bores; have unlearnt the habit of showing off, and developed a sense of humour and a sense of proportion, and have absorbed the teaching of the third chapter of Ecclesiastes, that there is a time for everything.'

Change and with it a lack of certainty seemed to pervade the school. The Headmaster had already reigned supreme for 28 years, but there were inescapable signs that GAW was now determined to look to the future of The Hall. In the summer of 1952 he announced the steps he was taking preparatory to the establishment of an Educational Trust to administer the school. He reminded his audience that there had been four headmasters since the Reverend F J Wrottesley had founded the school in 1889. Each had bought the school from his predecessor and sold it to his successor. GAW had felt for a long time that this system was not right. He had hankered after a permanent body to exercise authority, with the headmaster serving under such a body on a salary. He had found great sympathy with this idea from the Parents' Association and a special committee had been appointed to investigate the matter.

As a result of the committee's deliberations, The Hall School, Ltd

*In this, as in a whole range of things, standards have risen in the intervening years. By the '70s, the demands made of candidates for the most exacting schools were increased to 65%, at a time when the syllabus was increased and the number of subjects examined was extended to include science.

was converted from a profit-making school into a Charitable Trust and the first meeting of the new Governors took place on 30th July 1952.

The Governors were: Mr J Wrottesley, Chairman, Mr C W Myring, Mr David Robertson, Mr L Mackenzie Miall, (all members of the Committee of the Parents' Association), with Mr (later, Sir Denis) C D Hamilton, Miss K Gladstone and GAW himself. In addition to these original Governors, the Board was further strengthened by the appointment of Mr Walter Hamilton, Headmaster of Westminster, Dr R L James, the High Master of St Paul's, Mr F W Paish, Professor of Economics at London University and Mr W R Hornby-Steer, who had served for many years on the London County Council.

Now it would be the function of the Board of Governors to appoint future headmasters. It would also be within their competence to raise or lower the fees. Costs would be reduced for there would no longer be a tax on profits, no longer £1,000 to pay in rents and no longer dividends to shareholders.

The school's aims were defined in the third paragraph of the Articles of Association: 'To provide for the training and instruction of pupils at the said school in every branch of learning, in citizenship, in outdoor pursuits and in arts and crafts of all kinds, and on the basis of Christian principles to provide such pupils with spiritual, moral, mental and physical training.'

By happy chance, 1952 saw the completion of GAW's 50th year as a schoolmaster. To celebrate this remarkable achievement (almost impossible to conceive by succeeding generations), the staff presented him at the beginning of the summer term with a silver whistle and chain. This prompted some verse from one of The Hall's 'anonymous' poets.

Turned against the childish treble
May this pipe, this whistle sound,
Silencing the shrillest rebel,
Though you're now with silver crowned
That lustres ten have set the sheen on –
Crowned, yet fast in duty's chain –
May the Staff you chose to lean on
Never let you lean in vain.
Hall-marked, yet The Hall more marking,
Kindly, shrewd, revered, renowned,
May you, may we too, be harking
Years hence to your whistle's sound.

The new constitution of The Hall now firmly established, GAW was able to make a long-expected if nonetheless unwelcome announcement the very next year.

At the end of the summer term 1953, GAW said that he had now completed twenty-nine years as Headmaster of The Hall and he felt that the time had come when he should make way for a younger man. He had accordingly informed the Chairman of the Governors that he was prepared to be relieved at the end of the summer term 1954. If, when the time came, they had not found a man, he would not leave them in the lurch. To parents he said: 'I need not say how sorry I shall be to leave The Hall, where I have been most happy and where I have always met with kindness, consideration and sympathy. And to you, parents of this delightful present generation, I feel the same gratitude as I have felt to all earlier generations.' Mr Wrottesley put in a plea: 'Don't leave us unless you must and stay with us as long as you can.'

GAW stayed on for two more years while his successor was being secured. This must have been hard for him. He may well have anticipated retirement with little relish, for there is evidence that The Hall was his major preoccupation, and he had all too little to interest him outside it. Moreover, as already mentioned, his trusted colleagues were disappearing.

One of GAW's closest and oldest friends had already decided to hang up his gown. Hugh Fyson, who had been appointed senior classics master in 1932, had decided that he must retire. His learning, his scholarship, his ready wit and his many translations into Latin verse of psalms, hymns, poems and nursery rhymes had been appreciated by all the classical scholars and had given his teaching a rare distinction that his many able pupils recognised.

Mr Fyson's academic mantle fell on the shoulders of Mr Denzil Packard, formerly a Foundation Scholar of St Paul's and of Trinity College, Dublin. He had taught at King's College, Taunton, King Edward's School, Birmingham, Northampton Grammar School and Collyer's School. Horsham. He had recently been Lecturer in Greek and Latin at the Birmingham and Midland Institute.

The next year, the Senior School bade farewell to Mr Wraith. He had taught mathematics and geography. He was quiet and efficient, a man on whom a headmaster could rely for doing his job thoroughly and conscientiously. He was the last man to complain of overwork – rather like the wise old owl, 'the more he heard the less he spoke', never did a more benevolent 'spectre' haunt The Hall, never was a nickname less aptly chosen than 'Ratty', unless, perhaps, it was an echo from *The Wind in the Willows*.

Mrs Baker was compelled to give up her work in the Junior School owing to ill-health. She had been at the school longer than anybody else, except GAW and Miss Gladstone. Her cheerfulness had often given courage to the nervous and few were able to resist learning their tables under her guidance. GAW used to call her 'O C tears' because, if a boy were tearful, he used to be sent to Mrs Baker and the tears rapidly ceased and smiles returned. She earned the affectionate nickname of 'The Bear', but like so many nicknames, its origins were wrapped in mystery. She was never known to lose her temper and could easily understand the troubles of small boys and deal with them gently and firmly.

It would be entirely wrong to imagine that there was gloom within the school or any evidence of anything but vivid vitality about all that happened within it. The 1952 football XI was undefeated (despite the graphic but not totally unkind comment on one player – 'If only he moved quicker he would be first-class, but, alas, he runs very much as a policeman rides a bicycle.'). School clubs flourished, for stamps, chess, photography and, rather nicely – for all prep school boys are jackdaws at heart – for 'collecting'. Tennis was reintroduced, described by GAW (for once completely and demonstrably wrongly) as a 'comparatively easy game' for boys who preferred it to 'vegetating in the deep field wondering at their failure to become real cricketers'. Scouting remained as powerful at The Hall as ever, described by GAW once as 'one of the biggest contributions that this country has made to education'. And, perhaps most reassuring of all to GAW, competition to enter the school was as great as ever. Many candidates were having to be turned away. One lady had, so he reported gleefully in 1945, entered her 3 week-old baby.

And of course, in June 1953, there occured an event which captured the imagination of the nation. The Coronation of Her Majesty Queen Elizabeth II was marked by a whole holiday so that all could either watch the ceremony on television, listen to it on radio or even stand on the procession route. Some of the school Scouts were on duty on this route selling the official souvenir programmes. During the royal tour of north London, a crowd of pink-blazered boys cheered and waved flags as Her Majesty drove past the Junior School on her way to the Hampstead Town Hall. There she was greeted by members of the Upper VI, Scout Patrol Leaders and other privileged members of the school who cheered in a more dignified way without waving flags.

In recording this event for the magazine, the school correspondent added: 'It was a happy afternoon as nobody in the school fainted. Her Majesty was gracious enough to be late, so that we missed prep.'

To the end of his time in office, GAW continued to spell out his views on education. In some areas, he was inevitably a product of his generation, firmly conservative and traditional in his beliefs, somewhat inflexibly parading his prejudices.

If he was a firm advocate of the ancient target of a *mens sana in corpore sano*, his means of achieving the former was often as progressive and liberal as his approach to the latter was conventional and inflexible.

Thus it was that at the final Reading Over of the summer of 1954 he announced to the boys and parents that the Governors had appointed his successor, Mr R A Cooper, an ex-housemaster at Sedbergh. But he could not forbear to explain, even at this late stage in his long career, his aims.

> The practical headmaster of a preparatory school will probably emphasise the word *preparatory* but preparatory for what?
>
> Ideally one could take the high moral line and see in every lesson an effort for the foundation and development of such character as prepares a boy for the most difficult jobs in the world we live in; gives him initiative; readiness to take responsibility and put his ideals to practical effect.

At the same time he reminded everyone of the style by which The Hall achieved all that it had, the secret for its conspicuous successes and inimitable character.

Hall boys could not be accused of overwork; with school over every day by four-thirty, no compulsory prep, no school on Saturdays, no compulsory chapel on Sundays, the compensations were fresher minds, fuller life and zest for living, and the expectation that they would soon catch up with boys who had been having more and longer lessons.

Now the identity of the man to assume the mantle of Headmaster of The Hall was known. Those who were returning for further terms wondered who this Mr Cooper might be. It is always the way at schools. But boys remain much the same whatever happens, as the retiring Headmaster reminded them as he spoke to the school on the last day of that summer term.

> How often is the Headmaster's voice at Prayers raised to scold oftener than it is raised to praise. But the annual report makes no allusion to the many failings and fallings that have had to be mentioned. Perhaps a page or two out of the detention book would convince anybody that The Hall is not peopled by angels, for angels would not disturb prep by talking, they would not lose their books or their clothes, or if they did, they would make sure that they were marked. Angels would have hymn books and Bibles at Prayers and never a whisper would be heard. Nor would they ever be late or have their work returned for untidiness.

These were 'the angels' his successor was to inherit the following term.

PART III: THE SIXTH DECADE AND BEYOND

Chapter 1
Years of Transition
1955-1964

The sixth decade of The Hall's history was quite as eventful as any that had gone before. The 1950s saw The Hall Trust established under a Board of Governors. A headmaster left after 30 years and another arrived, destined to remain for over 20. Raymond Cooper came from Sussex and was educated at Brighton College. Before going up to St Edmund Hall, Oxford, he taught languages at Bickley Hall, a prep school in Kent, an experience which was destined to shape his future more than perhaps he could have imagined. At Oxford, he read geography when not playing rugby football for the University or cricket for the Authentics. He was a rugby player for both Blackheath and Kent, and a Free Forester and Sussex Martlet cricketer.

His first teaching appointment was at Sedbergh as a geographer, under the Headmastership of J H Bruce-Lockhart, famed for his advocacy of the direct method of teaching French, a subject Cooper also taught. The Army claimed him in the war and his military service was spent in Burma, where he was wounded in 1944. His experiences at this time were eventually recounted in the book published shortly after his retirement from The Hall, *'B' Company*. He was awarded the MC and earned the TD.

Returning to Sedbergh, he was made a housemaster in 1947 but seven years later he resigned, characteristically on a matter of principle, over which, unlike some of his colleagues, he refused to compromise. Thus it was that he came to be free to apply for The Hall, one of over 60 candidates for the post, demonstrating the fame which GAW had brought to the school. In anticipation of taking over GAW's teaching programme, Cooper went over to France to assist at the Ecole des Roches at Verneuil, before moving in to take over.

In March 1955 the school marked GAW's retirement with a large Presentation Party, held in Hampstead Town Hall. Sadly, and most unusually, GAW had fallen quite ill and was so poorly that even he had to abide by his doctor's orders and remain in bed. His son, Mark, accompanied Mrs Wathen to read his father's farewell speech. The occasion was rendered a shade the flatter by the absence of the guest of honour, but nevertheless, the speakers – a parent, the Chairman of Governors and the Senior Master – were eloquent, expressing heartfelt sentiments without ever succumbing to sentimentality. GAW's response was brief, unemotional and nicely laced with wit. The boys' views on their Headmaster's impending departure were included in the series of tributes published in the magazine that summer, to the man referred to by the *Evening Standard* as 'due to become a legend any minute'. The sixth-form boy who provided the word picture of GAW that follows was Hugh Pilkington, destined to become a remarkable scholar and rather exceptional human being before his untimely death in 1986.

> Suddenly the whole school scrambles to its feet, as an elderly man enters the hall at a curious cantering run, his body leaning slightly forward and his gown billowing out wide and brushing the ranks as he jogs towards his seat at the High Table. Behind him hurry with a sense of urgency several boys, one carrying a despatch case, another with a great mark book, the rest of them articles of lost clothing and Pandora, the foundling box. In a moment there is silence.
>
> It is not a hush of fear that accompanies Mr Wathen's entry, but a quiet of respect and affection for the man who for thirty years has been both the teacher and friend to thousands of boys throughout their years at the school which he has made famous. The affection and respect in which he is held by them includes a slight feeling of wonder too, for Mr Wathen has lived through very difficult periods of history, taking them all in his easy stride, but keeping echoes of them in his character and appearance. Many a town-worker driving through Swiss Cottage has briefly noticed the tall, distinguished-looking man, dressed in the long tweed jacket and breeches of a country squire in Edwardian days, walking briskly round the corner of Buckland Crescent, but he has driven on into the crowded streets without realising that the same figure might later that day appear in morning coat with striped trousers on his way to one of the few remaining society cricket matches, or might be seen sitting among the Governors of St. Paul's School, or dining with his fellow Mercers amid all the ancient ceremony of the City of London.
>
> Mr Wathen was not just a headmaster. He was the Spirit of The Hall, a force that has gone out into all the world through his deep influence on the lives and characters of doctors and engineers, teachers and public servants, who once were boys in his charge. We who have been with him in the last great years of his headmastership know that we could have had no better teacher or leader.
>
> It is more than a quarter of a century since Mr Wathen was in

> India, but Indians still remember him with affection. So too will it be with us. We shall never forget his friendship and his discipline tempered with kind humour, and each of us will imagine his figure hurrying, not through Swiss Cottage any more, but along some country lane as he enjoys retirement with the same vigour that has endeared him to us all.

Sadly, it was not to be quite as Pilkington supposed. When Mark Wathen accepted on his father's behalf the presents and good wishes of grateful and admiring parents, no one could foresee that only three years of retirement would be given him. It was as if this tireless, ever-active personality had too little to occupy him. Or perhaps, as the editor of the magazine hinted, he was bent upon some urgent task, such that, with the careless and absent-minded preoccupations of the elderly, he was 'hustling hard on some quest, the last of so many briefly noted in the very small pocket-book he always carried'. He thrust out his umbrella and strode across the Finchley Road. He was struck a fatal blow by a passing vehicle, and even so robust a spirit as GAW's could not resist. He was 80. Happily, the principal gift he received at his retirement, a cheque to enable him and Mrs Wathen to travel to Africa was well and truly spent. A long description of his trip was published in 1956. Mrs Wathen outlived her husband by some thirty years, retiring to the family homelands in Norfolk, and enjoying a remarkably vigorous and active widowhood. She is pictured in a subsequent magazine, on horseback, drinking a stirrup-cup of champagne, for all the world as if riding to hounds. The occasion was her 100th birthday.

The very last chapter in this particular part of the story concerns the GAW Memorial Appeal. It was perhaps faintly hoped that sufficient funds might accrue that a substantial extension to the school might be built: perhaps a new reading room or an improvement to the playgrounds. In the event, a trust fund was established to provide an annual Head Boy's prize. The idea was that enough money would be available to subsidise boys' travel to GAW's beloved France. This never fully materialised. Apart from the provision of new Junior School playground equipment, the other signficant use to which the money was put was a subsidy for the production of the short history of the school published as a special companion issue with the 1964 magazine, as part of the 75th anniversary celebrations. This 100 page production has provided much of the source material for this present volume.

As the regime under Cooper gathered momentum, links with the Wathen years gradually withered. Rotherham remained, of course. He had joined The Hall as Gladstone's partnership with Wathen ended in 1929. In November 1955, he celebrated his 70th birthday, and a jovial tea-party was held, presided over by Mrs Cooper. Not for him the more recent stipulation – that teachers retire at 60. He had already served The Hall for 27 inimitable years, and was due to soldier on, admittedly in declining health, until 1966, to complete a record 37 years on the staff. For all but eleven of the these, he commuted the 35 miles each way from Great Missenden. Clearly this daily rail journey was quite a noted feature of the school's life of those days. It was calculated that on his retirement, he had travelled over 330,000 miles to and from school.

An even more important link with the Wathen years was Miss Gladstone. She retired in 1960. It is easy to focus on the great men of The Hall story, whose length of service testified to their loyal commitment and was perhaps a measure of their character, as well as the worth of a school they served for so many years: Copinger, Earle, Wathen – as well as Rotherham – all topped 30 years. The ladies of the Junior School have heroines in their ranks too: Mrs Joan Barron joined the staff in 1938. Fifty years later, deep into official retirement, she was still to find a warm welcome in the Junior School, listening to laggard readers. Miss Vi Bearman was appointed a year earlier still, in 1937, so that on her retirement in 1968, she too had exceeded the 30-year mark. Miss Gladstone however outdid all but Rotherham for longevity. On her depature in 1960, she had been in Hampstead for nearly 34 years. A revealing farewell tribute to her appeared in the magazine.

> It's impossible to write impersonally about Miss Gladstone, or to use the clichés of farewell: and I'm not going to try. The test is whether one would have dared to enter her room and say, 'The place will not be the same without you,' or some phrase of the sort: there would have been a moment of the gentlest irony, mostly expressed in the eye, and then you'd have found yourself taking 1C for arithmetic. No: too dangerous, even at a distance.
>
> But, nonsense apart, it *is* difficult to think of The Hall Junior School without her sitting at the heart of it, putting the breath back into breathless situations, quietly regulating and steering so that over us all, fidgety boys and fluttery teachers, could be fitted that gentlest of harness – *her* daily programme, as laid out in that neatest of handwritings. She had the gift, without which schools founder, of sharply limiting the unpredictable that occured in her domain. She kept boys in touch with their caps, and if their wits were straying she knew kind ways of directing them where to find them. At least one old member of staff dares to declare in print that she was the Great Un-headmistress. Of course, she had 33 years (1927-1960 ungallant arithmetic, but then *she* won't mind) to acquire some

knowledge of what was likely to be happening in her warren of classrooms; but that wasn't *it*. *It* was her talent for calm; she could drive the vibration even out of shy male staff creeping across, on this morning or that, from the gruffness of Crossfield Road. We shall remember her voice, quiet and reassuring and her ready laughter, and the occasional sudden vagueness that gave you such pleasure – 'Catching K G nodding' was my own disrespectful formula for that; but one had to watch out, for she never nodded but as a prelude to a sharp coming-awake. ('I believe someone should take 1C for arithmetic.') For some reason I associated her with jelly, but that's because under her regime the Junior School always seemed to have a feast going on somewhere, or in the offing. But what everyone will want to say of her, and I will say for all, is that she held the Junior School with a most gentle firmness, and that laughter was never far away. And when an Un-headmistress is firm and kind *and* ready to be amused, then boys and staff are happy: that's the moral of it, and that was the way of it at the Junior School, for 33 years.

At the farewell party at the end of the Summer Term there were jellies, of course, and an incredible cake in the form of a Hall cap – good enough to wear, if you didn't mind icing on the brow: and there were lots of us from various points along those 33 years: and there was KG, who made a speech . . . Nonsense: it wasn't a speech: she *never* made speeches. It was just like those many morning assemblies, when the hurdy-gurdy tune on the piano stopped, and she spoke to us, in her soft and calming voice, and the day became possible. Well, she was given a watch, and we know it will tick for her, softly and calmingly, for a long time; and we hope that, using her gifts now in some unimaginable way – laying a gentle time-table on the flowers, perhaps, or the furniture – or on *jellies* – she will be happy as we all most sincerely would have her be.

Miss Gladstone retired to Sussex and kept an eager eye on developments at The Hall. Her death in September 1988 came sadly just before the centenary and the most revered figure from the Wathen era was never to read this history.

How difficult it must have been for Cooper, a relatively young and, for all the handicap of a war-wounded 'gammy' leg, a vigorously active man to succeed someone who clearly had become, in the eyes of all the boys, a grandfatherly figure. The problem of taking over as captain of such a conspicuously successful 'ship' was one he referred to in his first public speech in office, that July. It was the same problem that was to recur 21 years later, when he in turn bowed out to his successor.

Reviewing the evidence of both continuity and 'the new broom', as revealed in the pages of the magazine, significant themes almost immediately become clear. The Cooper years were to be marked by a notable surge in the scholarship record, with 1962 seeing twelve boys gain between them thirteen awards. At the same time, Cooper was from the outset adamant that extra coaching and cramming was unacceptable. He also raised the role of music in the curriculum: quite abruptly, from the very first term, lessons in violin, cello and clarinet were made available. An element of 'tightening up' of discipline was discernible too: boys were clearly required to attend school – and on time. The kindly, slightly indulgent old man, whose signature had been openly forged by generations of small boys who foolishly imagined that they were deceiving him, was replaced by a Headmaster who could be uncompromisingly firm in his stance. Another immediate sign of a new direction in the policy of the school was Cooper's commitment to the link between it and the local churches. So, from 1955, began the happy practice of beginning the school year with a Service in St Peter's Church, Belsize Square (the parish church of the Junior School) and of holding Carol Services in St Mary's, Primrose Hill (likewise the parish church of the Senior School).

By the mid-1950s, post-war uncertainties and austerities were being left far behind, and an immediate consequence was a surge in popularity for independent schooling. This caused what Cooper was to call the 'battle of the bulge': too many boys chasing too few places. This had clearly exhilarated GAW as he recalled harder times twenty years before. It led however to unsatisfied customers and to an inevitable swelling in numbers, noted in the Junior School by 1956, when 140 boys were being squeezed into accommodation never expected to receive more than 125. It led also to the public schools growing ever more selective in their admissions, with the Common Entrance becoming more and more competitive (rather than, as it has always been intended, qualifying). This was a problem that repeatedly exercised Cooper over the years. He constantly reminded parents of it, while equally recording the school's success at coping with it.

In the light of the curricular revolutions to sweep through all schools in subsequent decades, it is significant to note the changes Cooper tentatively introduced in these years. The inevitable development of the sciences in place of Greek was not seriously questioned. Parental pressure as much as his own personal conviction was inspiring this swing from the classics towards 'modern' subjects. Cooper felt unhappy at the ignorance of the natural and physical world, inevitable in the traditional curriculum. At the same time, he admitted that he 'would rather be in the position of the Headmaster at the Second Renaissance in the year 2057, reintroducing Greek as an alternative to science!' The situation reached thirty years after these words were spoken was that the classics survived with increasing difficulty, challenged on three formidable fronts: the pressure of ever more areas of study on the timetable, the mounting shortage of teachers familiar with the subject and an erosion of commitment, even in public schools, to its continuity.

What proved far more significant and, in its day remarkable, was Cooper's mounting conviction that the current Common Entrance exam was excessively long. In 1959, he was addressing guests, including the prize-giver and guest of honour, the Headmaster of Charterhouse. Only English, maths and a language need be the subjects of compulsory papers, he declared. The rest 'can be taught when teachers can plan a curriculum in freedom'. Did Cooper realise that, by strange coincidence, his predecessor almost exactly 30 years before had expressed similar revolutionary views on a similar occasion, again, to the Headmaster of Charterhouse? Could he have anticipated that 30 years later, such ideas were being positively advocated in wider circles? His successor would undoubtedly have used such an occasion to lend his support to such proposals – had Cooper not abandoned the formal prize-giving as an institution in 1969. Such events tend to accumulate many of the trappings of rather mindless tradition, their precise purpose and effectiveness being lost and forgotten in endless repetitions of ill-considered and oft-ignored platitudes. Cooper throughout his entire term in office was ready to make bold changes and accept the need to question established practices.

If the 75th anniversary celebration in 1964 can be seen in retrospect as something of a watershed between the 'old days' and the 'modern era', the years immediately preceding it saw a rapid expansion in that broad spread of activity which has always been such a feature of The Hall. The termly calendars were filled with lectures, expeditions, concerts, entertainments, competitions and sporting fixtures. A tremendous sense of bustling activity pervades the pages of every magazine. The school employed a professional bursar for the first time, and the parents were encouraged to support with increasing vigour an Amenities Fund, so that the facilities and equipment around the buildings improved. Clubs sprouted like mushrooms. Reading the pages of each issue of the magazine, one is left in no doubt as to the exceptional artistic and creative drive evident in every field. These years, in the 1960s, gave birth to The Hall's proud reputation as a school which took the arts seriously as a major function in its life. It is not surprising that out of this fruitful atmosphere sprang Cooper's dream to create a national prep schools' orchestra, a venture described in more detail in the following chapter.

The 75th year of the school's history came almost exactly half way through Cooper's reign. His second decade was to prove every bit as significant as the first. No slowing down by a tiring or complacent time-server here! In particular, it witnessed the one thing that The Hall needed with increasing urgency, a major facelift. The story of the years of the re-building and thereafter is told by another.

PART III: THE SIXTH DECADE AND BEYOND

Chapter 2
The Last Twenty-Five Years

A currently-serving master surveys the era from 1964 to the present

An authoritative picture of any school must in part stem from the recollections of its Old Boys. This naturally leads to a thought: how old is the oldest Old Boy of The Hall? How many survive who knew Marshall or Montauban? When that fine historian, Cecil Woodham Smith wrote her memorable volume *Under Six Reigns*, she reminded her readers that people are most unlikely to live through the reigns of more than four monarchs and most can recall with any clarity only two. A close parallel must arise with headmasters. The Hall is now in its seventh 'reign'. The majority of the old boy population of the school have *known* only one or two of the most recent; and it is of this period that this chapter speaks. Here will be set the scene showing the changes that occurred, things begun and things ended: the flow of ideas and with them, the characters who enlivened the career of many a developing Hall boy. In this period, since the 75th anniversary in 1964, there have been well over 1,200 of them.

'The past is a foreign country: they do things differently there.' So wrote L P Hartley in *The Go-Between*. How foreign really is the past of 25 years ago? For some, yesterday's newspaper is history, while for others the interval is too short for proper dispassionate judgement. Cooper was an established headmaster when this survey opens. Already much has been written of his arrival, his background in war and peace and of his achievements, aided by his wife, Ninette, during the first ten years of his reign. Of this period under review the time is almost equally divided between the end of Cooper's rule and the start of the Heazell era. For one who has spent a quarter of his life at The Hall it is hard to write impartially and, being currently on the staff, to offer a dispassionate view of the Heazell years. Yet it must be attempted.

A school may appear to have an inexorable life of its own but it presents a public *persona* as a result of the style of its head. Paradoxically, with two such seemingly different people as Cooper and Heazell, it may well be that in history it is their similarities which will be seen to have left the more permanent mark. Each in his time likened his role to that of a goalkeeper. And not just literally (both at various times turned out to defend the staff goal in matches with the 1st XI), nor in the pejorative sense of a Duke of Plaza Toro, futilely leading from behind; but more metaphorically, by monitoring the state of play going on before them, identifying the targets his team should pursue, and periodically offering stout defence when attacks became unduly fierce.

Each could be said to welcome and embrace change. Cooper was a noted innovator, trying to keep the school in the forefront of educational thinking and practice. He was also a loyal and independent-minded member of the IAPS, elected for two terms of three years to its Council. This distinction at various times came the way of both Montauban and Heazell. The latter was indeed the Vice-Chairman of Council on his arrival at The Hall in 1976. Cooper however was the only Hall Headmaster to become the Chairman of the Association, in 1970, the highest accolade the prep school world can grant a colleague. Cooper and Heazell were both awarded Walter Hines Page travel scholarships by the English Speaking Union to visit the USA, to study American educational methods, and both were sharply affected by their experience. Cooper was quick to react to the major curricular developments of the 1960s. The so-called 'new' maths was adopted and science became an integral part of the school's teaching. This was the decade when the first specialist room was allocated to its teaching, on the site of the former squash court.

At this point in the story, a major change in the Junior School must be recorded. Miss Gladstone retired in 1960, and her replacement, Miss Bearman, continued what might be regarded as the great tradition, until she in turn retired in 1968. By now she was almost the last of the team of teachers GAW had employed from before the Second World War. Hence, although Head for only eight years, she was a Hall teacher for over 30. She was replaced by a figure entirely in the mould of her predecessors. Miss Barbara Andrews was the first Head of Junior School to be recruited from outside The Hall: she had done war service in the WRNS, and had taught both abroad and in London before arriving at Hampstead. She was entirely in her element with Hall boys and an ideal foil for Cooper. She had a magic touch, at once authoritatively firm and philosophically sympathetic. She understood her boys and ruled with a gentle rod of iron. She saw Cooper out and Heazell in and then made it quite clear that the new man would gain by having his own appointment in charge of the

Juniors. In December 1976 she retired to an idyllic cottage in Suffolk, and another newcomer, Miss Julia Allen, entered the scene, to promote the dynamic changes in style and pace which the 1980s would demand.

Meanwhile, back at the Senior School, from 1970 an evident crisis was developing. Very little had been done to maintain the fabric. Photographs of the building taken in 1972 (a complete set, showing every nook and cranny, remains in the school's archives) reveal that major refurbishment was overdue. By now, too, the demand of a rapidly expanding teaching programme added to the pressures. What had been so admirable forty years earlier and was acceptable in post-war austerity years, was no longer adequate. Crisis was an emotive word and it was used to highlight the urgency of the Appeal, launched in 1972. Its purpose was to give the buildings a facelift, re-style them more efficiently and provide more essential facilities.

Many thought the sweeping away of the old hall a major act of vandalism. The south end gable window and the lean-to classrooms beneath it were demolished. The familiar gallery, and the hard-won panelling all disappeared, as did all but a token fragment of the Copnall mural. The hall was partially divided horizontally, with an ingenious arrangement of glass screens to bring light from the roof, which became flattened rather than pitched. The hall was then extended into a music area, and above it, a spacious new staff room was constructed. A new study – sadly too small and poorly ventilated – replaced the familiar room where GAW had held court for so long: that was converted into a small classroom.

The 1972 development, necessitating the raising of over £100,000 affected the science, art and music, provided a common-room/library for the boys, and greatly improved staff accommodation and changing-room space.

By way of explanation to both governors and parents, Cooper wrote a very detailed report to demonstrate just why these developments were needed, and to describe the new facilities that would be provided. Because this quite tightly argued 'note', as Cooper called it, is something of an historical document, it is reprinted in full.

PREPARATORY EDUCATION IN 1972

A note prepared for Governors and Parents
by the Headmaster, prior to re-building

Private education, which is more expensive than other varieties, has by no means been the best off materially.

The scholar, whose chrysalis years were spent at The Hall and who then went on to a public school may have felt himself king of infinite space, but in both places his bounds could well have been little more than a nutshell.

There are those today who see merit in such difficulties, but there are limits and today education needs more than space for the mind.

The State has to a large extent spent its money upon practical and convenient school buildings. In contrast private education has been spending more on staff and books. Gradually the ideals of the two systems and their practices have been coming closer together than either usually admits.

The first step was the idea that play and learning need not be separated in the early years. This led to a reconsideration of time-tables, examinable standards and fixed desks and to the use of more open planning, which freed teachers and children alike. How were such developments to be applied in buildings which were originally designed as large and desirable Victorian dwelling houses?

Initally, the answer lay in the training of teachers and not in altering buildings. As time passed then it became clear that our children still demanded a structured programme, a daily schedule of subjects, an element of order and discipline. However bracing the fresh air that blew through the corridors of open planning there are times when nothing can replace the intimacy of a class with its own form teacher.

In due course, the children learnt to link practical ways of expression with the more abstract problems of mathematics and literature. They discovered that in fact they knew their alphabet having first learned to read. They knew their mulitiplication and other tables having first computed the size of the area in which they worked and the shape of the furniture used in it or portrayed on the walls. Older boys had to learn to work under supervision but not always as a class under direct instruction.

These changes in techniques have probably been more far-reaching in the last ten years than any other during The Hall's 85 years. The changes stood the test of time, but space was preventing their full implementation.

In all this we have to remember what is the aim of the school, which can be interpreted very differently from the days when 'preparatory' simply meant 'prepared for' (i.e. the preparation of pupils to pass an entrance exam for) a public school.

In the 1970s the answer must be preparation for life, not just for Common Entrance examinations. Parents may well ask if passing entrance exams is included. The answer is that exams should be of a standard that well-educated boys of normal ability can take in their stride.

The non-competitive nature of the Common Entrance was designed just for this. When the content of education changes or widens then extra exams can be arranged. The Oral French exam, the arrival of science and an alternative maths syllabus have all followed teaching changes and not caused them.

Committees are always at work on one or more subjects, to prove and to illustrate this process of change.

These are some examples of the ways in which these developments have affected teaching.

Today science needs not one demonstration bench and twenty notebooks in which to copy the described result, but equipment for each pupil to record what is discovered, and also space for living things.

Languages need libraries, not just of books, but the sounds of foreign tongues, as well as the finest speakers of our own language. Space is vital, not just for a class to learn and listen on its own, but a place where groups within a class can turn when the need arises to find sound and vision readily at their disposal. One can learn more from painting or building a model of a Greek temple than by reading about it. Mathematicians, historians and geographers too must now have models. Scripture requires the visual just as much as art.

Music needs not just a piano in a cell but a centre for ensembles and space for them to join as an orchestra. A choir has to listen as well as practise in a room that is not already equipped or required for lunch or gym. Sport can profit when its techniques can be illustrated on a loop projector. New dimensions have become urgent as new horizons.

With one science laboratory and one art room, inflexible classrooms, a library shared with lunch and assemblies, and small, separated music rooms, the school clearly demanded not just expansion but a drastic re-arrangement if the work of the Senior School was not to be frustrated and if we were to continue to attract a first class staff.

Another part of the concept is that it will become possible to arrange 10 classrooms, which will remain the boys' 'home bases', into three groups, each with a resource area, audio-visual space, and library appropriate to its own age range.

With the staggering mental and physical development that takes place between the ages of 9 and 13½, this will make for unlimited possibilities for the eldest, and not let the youngest be overwhelmed.

At the same time, with all the improvements, we can be confident that we shall preserve the character and atmosphere of the

Senior School. Some changes will be evident, but it will still at once be recognisable as The Hall.

The price paid for this, apart from the obvious financial cost, was aesthetic; the internal grandeur of the building took something of a knock. Happily, the front façade was almost totally unaffected. The other loss was the tradition of boarding, which was abandoned to accommodate the upheavals occasioned by the actual building works, and never revived. This was almost certainly no bad thing. The Hall could never really offer the proper facilities parents demanded increasingly of a boarding school. Again happily, the traditions associated with a boarding prep school did not die with the departure of boarders. School life continued to exist after formal school hours and at weekends. Hall boys continued to tranfer to boarding public schools in much the same numbers as before.

Cooper was a progressive and not sentimental. Quite apart from this major building programme undertaken, it must be noted, some seventeen years after his arrival and hence scarcely a rash or impulsive gesture by an impatient newcomer, a number of other novel features were introduced. New teaching aids, modern resources and tutorial areas, ideas and techniques which have since come to seem commonplace were all being provided: audio-visual language teaching in French (this very much a special forté of Cooper's), and equipment for history and geography (how primitive the reel-to-reel tape recorder now appears). An article in the magazine of 1968 wondered: 'What did we do before we had a minibus?'. This, a second-hand Volkswagen, was purchased through the fund-raising efforts of the Parents' Association. The school at last had 'wheels'. Twenty years on, it had three buses, and those often were found scarcely adequate. How true the remark that yesterday's luxuries soon become tomorrow's necessities.

It was Cooper who confirmed the emphasis The Hall placed on the arts. Because of the artistic connection of so many parents over the years, there had always been a notion that the arts mattered. Cooper was personally committed to the idea, and his wife was a talented practising artist. So art, pottery, drama and music all were given far more genuine emphasis. More and more boys were persuaded to take up musical instruments. In Margaret Macdonald, Cooper had a vital ally as Director of Music. Music had a particular place in his affections. If Montauban before him had the distinction of imagining the foundation of a new public school, Cooper it was who gave life to an idea little less inspiring.

The creation of a prep school symphony orchestra was in large part the inspiration of Cooper. The story goes that he was ruminating on the achievement of Ruth Railton who in 1947 had started the National

Youth Orchestra. In twenty years it had gained world-wide fame. Perhaps, he thought, prep schools of the IAPS could at their more modest level create something similar. He approached Arthur Harrison who, quite apart from his enormous experience of the prep school world, happened to be a resident of Aldeburgh and a close friend of Benjamin Britten. Britten's enthusiastic support and the invitation to bring the orchestra to play at The Maltings, Snape, proved decisive.

Cooper began to assemble a team to make the dream a reality. One of the most committed and experienced musician headmasters in IAPS, Robin Wilson, Assistant Headmaster of Taverham Hall in Norfolk, was asked to take on the job of organising the routine of a residential music course. Cooper's last colleague in what he has referred to as his 'Gang of Four' was the Chairman of Council for the year of the inaugural concert, Donald Sewell, Headmaster of Old Buckenham Hall, Suffolk. The preliminary organisation all centred round The Hall, with the school secretary, the vivacious Helen Foggitt, appointed a member of the committee. The first orchestra assembled at Brandeston Hall, Suffolk, and thus, with the forging of a powerful East Anglian link, the Hampstead-Snape axis which has continued unbroken thereafter, was built.

The first IAPS concert was conducted by the Director of the Suffolk Rural Music Schools, Brian Lincoln, on 28th July 1972. The auditioning, assembling and training of the 75 or so boys from over 20 prep schools (and of course there were no girls involved at that stage) for that never-to-be-forgotten event was one of the major achievements of Cooper's career as a headmaster. Steuart Bedford and Bernard Keeffe were distinguished internationally recognised conductors whom Cooper involved with the IAPS Orchestra between 1973 and his departure from the scene, on his retirement, in 1976.

To complete the story, because it remains very much a part of The Hall's history, Heazell, by what was a remarkable coincidence, proved to have unmatched qualifications to take over the IAPS Orchestra from Cooper as well. He was intensely interested in music and marginally involved even before he arrived in Hampstead. So The Hall remained the focal point for the administration of music courses and witnessed the remarkable expansion of the whole organisation. One course grew to six. Pupils – boys and girls – rose from less than 100 each year to 500. On the death of Arthur Harrison, the organising committee was turned into a charitable trust. This has been Heazell's contribution to the Cooper legacy. And the Hall has been one of very few schools to have supplied at least one player for the IAPS Orchestra every single year of its existence. The association The Hall has had as a result with the world of music has grown, as can be judged by the list of international celebrities who have chosen the school for their sons, many of whom in their turn have proved to be highly talented.

Aside from music, the Cooper era saw an extension of The Hall's encouragement of other modes of creative expression. The poetry recitation competition, with a prize presented by Lord Janner, a declamation prize for speech making, a poetry writing prize awarded by Dame Peggy Ashcroft, and a prize for the best literary contribution to the magazine were all features of Cooper's years. The tradition for these competitions (in what is in fact not as hotly competitive a school as might be supposed from their existence, taking part as much as winning being their keynote) was extended by his successor, with Professor Lewis Wolpert's prize and medal replacing the Ashcroft prize, and an essay-writing competition, subscribed appropriately by the publisher, Tom Rosenthal, and a public reading competition for both juniors and seniors, most happily provided as a parting present by Cooper. It was in the Cooper years that an annual Summer Concert became a major festival of the year's musical and performing achievements. In these years, too, a Junior School play was instituted, designed to ensure that the entire school was involved. That upwards of 150 boys had to appear simultaneously at least once without squeezing the cramped audience clean out of the Junior School hall was not the least of the challenges to provoke the patient and always inspired ingenuity of the teachers.

What of the graphic arts? Here annual prizes and competitions have proliferated since the 1960s and the volume and quality of the work (both two and three dimensional) has left no one in any doubt that art matters at The Hall. Cooper began a policy, inspired by his artistic wife, of buying good art works for the decoration of the buildings. Heazell's wife, being the principal art teacher, emphasised the importance of the subject in a balanced curriculum, and the policies begun by Cooper have been greatly expanded.

Of the arts, drama has been the 'cinderella', not for lack of flair or imagination of staff or boys, but because of inadequate facilities, made worse by the constant pressure on time. While the boarding continued, house concerts and plays seemed easier to arrange, and Cooper's personal enthusiasm inspired periodic French plays. An annual Senior School play of full-scale proportions has remained a feature not fully realised, pending the completion of a hall more suited to such productions. In partial substitution for this omission, the school has tended to alternate biennial productions with major musical events: The Hall Choral Society has performed works of Handel, Mozart, Haydn and others, as well as two children's operas. Notable among the plays of these years was the school's first complete

Shakespeare, *The Merchant of Venice*, with a strikingly sensitive interpretation of the Jew's role; a highly creditable *Importance of Being Earnest*, and a chilling production of Giles Cooper's *Unman, Wittering and Zigo*, given in the Theatre of University College School while The Hall recovered from its fire, and significant for the imaginative casting, involving staff in adult roles and boys (frighteningly type-cast) as the pupils. The use of this splendid theatre was a concession to The Hall, a typically generous gesture by a near-neighbour which had suffered a similar misfortune.

It was Cooper who instituted a jealously guarded luxury in the timetable. He felt that breadth of programme could only be seen to be promoted if precious school time was allocated to it. Hence, Wednesday 'Options' for the sixth formers (matched by the more modest 'Groups' in the Junior School), were introduced and extended, to include at various times over the years, carpentry, wood-carving, mechanical engineering, jewellery and gemmology, heraldry, cookery, ballet, chess, computing, and art, drama, musical composition, model railways and bridge. In more recent years, 'minor' sports, squash, badminton and swimming, have been added. Options are highly popular and greatly valued.

Very shortly after his arrival, in 1957, Cooper created an institution scarcely matched in any other prep school. The Hall Sixth Form Society was designed to widen horizons of the more senior boys by facing them with interesting, often distinguished adults from outside the world of school, invited to stretch them. Three times a term thereafter, under their boy chairman, the members have enjoyed a rare privilege of sitting at the feet of a string of distinguished guest speakers. These have included over the years statesmen and politicians, academics and artists, professionals and men of affairs. A former Prime Minister, or a Chairman of a Nationalised Industry, a Trades Union General Secretary, High Court Judge, university professor, media celebrity, diplomat or industrialist, the list by the date of the centenary will reach 300. Many of these learned and busy people have been agreeably surprised by the evident sharpness of their cross-examination by their young hosts.*

All this emphasised the philosophy of The Hall propounded by Cooper, that it was the school's task not to teach what was to be examined but to seek to examine what was being taught. However, the timetable was being extended so much that it became necessary for two preps a week to be taken home from 1965. Up till then time at home was meant to be used for improving social awareness, pursuing hobbies and taking part in family life. The somewhat mindless ritual of homework being unwillingly carted home was never part of The Hall philosophy of education.

*See Appendix 6, page 243

Although a blue at Oxford for rugby and a member of the Blackheath Club, Cooper never boasted of his sporting prowess. He was a useful club cricketer too, until his war injury prevented him from playing properly again. At The Hall, he guided the colts in both rugby and cricket, patiently bearing with the ineptitude of referees and umpires. His support for rugby led to a new design for the school rugby shirt in 1968 and an inter-house seven-a-side competition. Athletics appeared (rather than just the traditional 'school sports') and volleyball and fencing. For Cooper, cricket was the summer sport, and few could opt elsewhere, but he allowed the old emphasis on swimming to relax, partly because, increasingly, politics reared an unwelcome head as the new Local Authority, Camden, assumed responsibility for the handsome sports complex at Swiss Cottage and made private schools rather less than welcome.

The school community consists of parents, governors, staff and boys. Cooper tended to seek to regard the last as his prime responsibility, and to protect the staff from the intrusiveness of the first. Nevertheless, termly 'Talk-Backs' on topics of educational interest were introduced for parents and staff, as were staff/parents evenings to discuss reports on the boys. Parents were even given the opportunity to visit the school while in session. The whole process of staff meetings was greatly developed compared with the rather casual, less formal ways of his predecessor. However, despite all this, Cooper's greatest interest was the care of the boys as individuals. He was not idiosyncratic like GAW and knew better than most how to fulfil each boy's need, whether in the trivial daily round or the ultimate choice of future schooling. He was concerned with the inner man (though, incidentally, he left the organisation of feeding it in the capable hands of Mrs Cooper), being himself a deeply spiritual person seeking to provide suitable means of expression for worship and prayer. Assemblies were reorganised so that Man's spiritual quest could be explored. Possibly not all the boys could always follow the way his mind was working; none could doubt that here was a man of the deepest integrity and true honesty, worthy of the utmost respect and attention. The needs of others were noted more positively than ever under his leadership. So, the termly support of particular charities was developed. Each House could organise the fund raising for the whole school on behalf of a number of causes, usually with a link with children: in particular, the NSPCC, the Save the Children Fund, and the Children's Country Holiday Fund. Cooper's own personal interest lay in a new charity, the Joint Educational Trust – JET, and because this was intimately linked with Cooper, a brief digression is warranted.

As the effective founder of this admirable institution, Cooper was closely involved in the early development of JET, and The Hall was from the outset a keen supporter of its purposes. During the 1970s, as the cost of education generally soared, so the option of choosing independent schooling, especially boarding, became more and more of a problem for many anxious parents, particularly in the swelling group that came to be identified as 'need cases'. JET was established as a charity to enable genuine problems – the children who were orphaned, handicapped or the product of broken homes, the gifted whose needs were being frustrated by bureaucracy or political ideology, indeed, any judged to be able to benefit by smaller classes, a more structured programme, a caring pastoral framework and stimulating academic teaching – to have all or part of the fees paid. Hall parents over the years have rallied to JET's aid and the school has offered a free place to the Trustees for a boy they would like to refer. Fittingly, it was to be as the Honorary Secretary to the Trustees of JET, that Cooper went when he retired from The Hall.

No less symptomatic of his deep sensitivity to the misfortunes of others was Cooper's leadership in the IAPS response to the hideous disaster in 1966 at Aberfan in South Wales. The loss of so many young lives inspired a wave of sympathy from fellow children in prep schools throughout the land. It was Cooper who organised the Trust, set up from donations from IAPS schools to support Aberfan Primary School which had been destroyed in the landslide. Each year, a joint expedition to bring the pupils of the village and of prep schools together was arranged. Hall boys were involved in these trips until after he left the school. By the early '80s, the scars were healed and his great initiative had served its purpose.

The pursuit of scholarship always concerned Cooper, even if not so much the compulsive pursuit of scholarships. Nonetheless, these in considerable number came to The Hall, notably in 1962. The old honours board was removed from the walls in his time, to be replaced by a less flauntingly ostentatious but no less beautiful honours book. Prefects at The Hall had always been limited in number, and he wished to extend their role, so more boys were involved, some as, in his phrase 'Gentle Giants', others as monitors. He arranged periodic School Meetings, to which each form sent an elected representative, the chair being taken by himself or his deputy. Though Cooper was not particularly autocratic, his presence was always felt and his authority seemed seldom capable of question. No one could escape the feeling that all were under his eye. The writer was once alone in the staff room when Cooper entered, demanding: 'Are you not aware that the Lower 5th are not supervised?', as though, because he knew it, all should be no less aware and have done something about it.

Even so, he had built up much loyalty and enormous respect when, after 21 years, the time came for him to retire. His chosen farewell was, typically, a special service on Ash Wednesday. All the hymns were in the key of E flat. The parents gave a large party, held in the hall at Highgate School, to bid farewell after so many years of truly historic progress for The Hall. Cooper's last words were, perhaps a trifle characteristically, equivocal. 'It would take a very bad headmaster to ruin The Hall!' Perhaps history will judge whether his successors have been so or not, but certainly he was right to the extent that no immediate ruin followed his departure.

So the summer of 1976 saw the arrival of the Heazell dynasty, for not only did The Hall have a new Headmaster, but a wife, a son and two daughters and a dog, together with his brother and growing family, who joined the staff the following September. The previous year's magazine had carried an article introducing Mr Heazell as Headmaster. It revealed his interests in music and the navy as well as sport, his connections by marriage with the Harrisons of IAPS, and suggested that, after four years on a public school staff and nearly twelve as a headmaster at another prep school, he was not exactly without experience.

At the start of this chapter I wrote that despite appearances both Cooper and Heazell had much in common. Admittedly, the latter was a Cambridge man, a scholar of Queens', but he had experience of Oxford too, as a post-graduate attached to Lincoln College. He too proved no less a progressive than his predecessor, looking to build for the future on the foundations of the past.

Heazell came to The Hall just 13 years short of the centenary of the school's foundation. Increasingly in his mind must have been the thought that this milestone should be fittingly marked. As early as 1980, the governors had received his first proposals for a major development of the site of the Senior School. Behind his thinking was the dual perception that the earlier re-building programme of 1972 had never really been fully completed and still failed to meet the school's needs, and also that the rapidly expanding pressure of the curriculum on a school aspiring to be a 'leader in the field' had to be met. Staff and parents were consulted, initially in rather general terms; a plan was devised; through the good offices of the Vice-Chairman of Governors, old boy, parent and good friend of The Hall, John Ritblat, of British Land plc, an outline planning consent to develop the school was secured from a, by now, slightly less unfriendly Camden Council.

The pressing needs were varied. Heazell foresaw a move towards subject-based classrooms, which would of course necessitate many more to be constructed. His bias favoured simultaneously the arts and the more practical sciences and technology. He was gratified when, as early as 1977, the school was given its first micro-computer, an American model 'Apple', thus laying some claim to be about the first prep school to provide facilities for computer education. Certainly, in the early years of the computer 'revolution', Hall boys found that they were quite as competent at manipulating computers as some of their public school teachers! This new area of learning activity was but one of many demanding space. Heazell wanted more space too for biology, history, geography and art. He was ashamed that the school still lacked a room dedicated to the sole use of the library. He wanted better facilities for music, drama, pottery, woodwork and technology. Ultimately, he hoped for a teaching room for each member of staff. He knew that the changing rooms were inadequate. Above all, he heard the parental pleas for a large weather-proof play area to compensate for The Hall's lack of games facilities.

It was with a degree of dramatic irony that the first phase of his dreams were shortly to be realised, phoenix-like, from the ash and grime of disaster. Late in the evening of Friday 1st October 1982, someone broke into 23 Crossfield Road, built a funeral pyre of art materials on the floor of the recently re-modelled basement area art room, sprinkled inflammable spirit and paint round the room, ignited this veritable time-bomb, closed the doors to let it gain strength undetected, and, stealing a few casual items as he passed through the silent building, he (or perhaps it was a she!) departed. For some 90 minutes the blaze was contained, before bursting through the relatively flimsy screen door into the main hall adjacent. With by now searing heat, billowing sooty smoke and flames flashing out and up, the contents of the hall were scorched and melted, the walls scarred, and in the nick of time, the fire alarm cables burnt through. The writer of these pages was the resident, asleep and entrusted with the safety of the building. His sharply provoked sense of self-preservation as much as any feeling of public spiritedness caused him to summon the local fire brigade, mercifully only a few hundred yards distant, and the inferno was subdued in minutes, just as it threatened to take irreversible hold. The whole building was fouled by the stain and smell. Two teaching rooms were put out of action and the hall reduced to the appearance of a veritable Valhalla. The Headmaster was recalled from a visit to Winchester College, all the parents were notified, messages of help and sympathy gratefully received from neighbours. Like the wartime Windmill Theatre, The Hall never closed. Examination boys were taught their full programme of lessons the following Monday, and within a week, school was as nearly back to normal as was reasonable to expect.

The first response to the trauma was to improve the fire alarms and equip the building with burglar alarms. The writer was indeed grateful for the reassurance these provided! It was clear that arson was the cause. It may be an occupational hazard for schools, for both

Bedford School and nearby UCS were victims of even more serious attacks shortly before, and Dulwich College Prep a few months after. The parallels between the style of the UCS fire and The Hall's were uncomfortably close. In neither case was the culprit discovered.

The happy outcome of all this was that a sudden, unexpected golden opportunity had presented itself to implement a phase of the development programme only recently sanctioned, as an addition to the repair and reinstatement which would begin in July 1983. Thus, out of the fire, The Hall gained a specialised computer centre, a history and a geography room, achieved by adding two new classrooms on the southern corner of the main building. This permitted another room to be transferred to the sole use of the library, which by the parents' generosity, was provided with a completely restocked supply of books. The biggest changes in this 1983 building programme involved the site of the old central hall which had been 'vandalised' ten years before. The lower half was remodelled in a more stylish and integrated manner, as the dining and assembly area, while directly above, a circulation/recreation space, dubbed appropriately the 'Old Library' had beside it a miniature arena, 'the pit'. One footnote to this unexpected, but ultimately rather fortunate episode involved the handsome, unique collection of public school shields which had ringed the walls from the 1930s. They were all ruined quite beyond any repair. A chance meeting with the Windsor Herald from the College of Arms prompted a request that the College replace the entire set. Their researches revealed the embarrassing fact that a number of major schools had habitually used arms to which, by heraldic law, they were not entitled. This included several to which The Hall regularly sent boys, like Highgate, St Paul's, Winchester and Marlborough, as well as the Headmaster's own old school, Sherborne. A possible impasse was eventually resolved and slowly but surely a new, even more beautiful and heraldically impeccable collection of shields was assembled.

The rebuilding was completed and the Vice-Provost of Eton, as representative of the landlord, unveiled a small commemorative plaque. The Hall was now back on an even keel and ready to contemplate the second phase of Heazell's longer-term plan. Before a start was made on it, however, the need to develop switched to the Junior School.

The Junior School, situated at 69 Belsize Park, in a building which was largely adequate for its purposes, had seen far less development than the Senior. In 1977, an important step was taken by the Governors when an opportunity to purchase the freehold from the Church Commissioners was avidly seized, and this inspired a small reconstruction programme in the basement area. A decision, on ground of economy, to concentrate all the catering centrally in the Senior School created the chance to convert the dining room into a very admirable library and a small caretaker flat, as well as some other lesser facilities. Under Julia Allen's vigorous leadership, a steady programme of repair and restoration was implemented, designed to restore, as far as its school functions permitted, the architectural character of a handsome building.

By the 1980s, a new issue was clearly arising. Demand for places was swelling. Meanwhile, parents who wished to send their child to a maintained primary school for a year until he was 6 and ready for the Junior School, found themselves under fire. Primary heads were unwilling to see their schools used as a temporary stopgap. The Hall had in the past accepted a few 5-year olds, but the standards of infant school provision had risen and the existing Junior School was in no way properly equipped. So in 1984, a kindergarten, soon to be given the title of 'the zeros', was opened in the basement area of 2 Buckland Crescent, under the Headmaster's home next door to the Junior School. A highly successful, attractive conversion was completed and some 28 boys enrolled in two classes, increasing the overall numbers at The Hall to a new high figure of 360.

It is time now to turn back to the Senior School, to comment on a number of rather more trivial developments, which mark perhaps a characteristic of The Hall, its constant impulse to move at least with, and sometimes ahead of the times, and its great reluctance to drift complacently in a wash of backward-facing tradition. The attitude to uniform has been a case in point. The issue is one which has over the years been met by pragmatic realism: a uniform, yes, but simple, practical and flexible. The views of the boys have always been heard, if not always heeded. So pink and black remained, in recognition that the heritage of the past was not to be ignored; but a relaxation of the degree that senior boys in particular were expected to wear them became evident.

The irregular School Meetings were developed by Heazell into a more formal School Council, chaired each term by the Head Boy, with the Deputy Headmaster in attendance. It considered a host of ideas, raised by the representatives of each class: some were even acted upon! Here is a modest exercise in democracy. Such democracy sits uneasily in a conventional framework of the formal school autocracy, governed by prefects. The logic of sharing the prefectorial responsibilities among more boys by creating plenty of them inevitably cheapened their status and value and left far too little of real worth in the tasks any boy was given. There were just too few 'indians' for the numbers of relatively plentiful 'chiefs'. So in 1984, the role of prefect was abolished, and the duties and responsibilities attached to that office were shared among all the boys, in short spells, under the organisation of each of the four Houses, in rotation. This had the effect of making every boy appreciate the true realities of leadership and duty: it also enhanced the status of the one boy elevated to the titular dignity of Head Boy of the school.

In its sporting activities, The Hall moved perceptibly during the first decade of the Heazell era to a more broad-based approach. The importance of greater regular training in skills was marked by a policy of appointing a young school-leaver as a sports assistant, to encourage the athletic development in both parts of The Hall. The first such appointment, Philip MacLeod, came for two terms, stayed for eight, and after qualifying at St Luke's, Exeter, became Eton's first Physical Education specialist. The range of sports available to the senior boys began to widen. Softball, shooting, badminton and hockey all grew in popularity. At the same time, the traditional and distinctive Hall Gym Display had clearly outrun its usefulness and in the rather moribund form to which it had degenerated, its demise after 1976 was regretted by none. Rugby football, always the 'cinderella' of the major sports, was relegated to a recreational/fun status from 1985. With no less enthusiasm, boys learnt to throw an oval ball around the unpromising slopes of Primrose Hill, as they always had. Indeed, the last relatively successful XV the Hall produced, in 1982, gave Stowe one of its best players of the decade and no less than four public schools their rugby captains for the 1987 season: at Eton, Radley, Marlborough and St Paul's. For The Hall, however, there would be no more inept referees or inadequate grounds. The writer once witnessed The Hall line up for its kick-off from the 25-yard (as it then was) line, for they had never seen the lines marked out on a proper pitch before!

The same year that rugby was demoted, hockey pitches became available at Hampstead Cricket Club, and hockey rapidly developed into the Spring term school team sport. Mention of Hampstead CC prompts reference to a major renewal of the lease negotiated with the club, which helped it to embark on its development programme and secured for The Hall its access to the ground well into the next century. Football continued to be The Hall's best game, and in 1983, an unusually competent all-round squad of players was unbeaten in what was a formidable programme of matches and tournaments, against opponents which included boarding schools.

One victim of the age was boxing. The Hall became quite a boxing school in 1965, through the passionate brilliance of one man, Mr Pat Newman, who made this controversial activity safe, fun and physically admirable. By combining with the less favoured boys from St Pancras's Tonbridge Club, an excellent element of social mix was added. Newman was an amateur with rare enthusiasm and quite unquestioned talent at training boys at every level of skill and courage. He held a senior appointment at the BBC and he gave unsparingly of his time, organising every detail of his Saturday sessions meticulously. But during the 1970s, attitudes began to change, as school after school gave up the sport, including Eton where he was for a period the principal instructor, so that, as the pages of the magazine report in words of increasingly evident dismay, support even for his dynamic instruction declined. His untimely death came soon after the demise of boxing at The Hall, in 1983, but he will be remembered affectionately as a truly gentle gentleman. The school choir was pleased and proud to be invited to sing at his memorial service in Westminster Cathedral.

Another feature of the sporting scene in the Heazell years was a marked widening of the range of inter-school fixtures. In particular, week-end tours in football, rugby and cricket to boarding schools in the country provided a greater variety and often a stronger competition for Hall teams, as well as offering a brief experience of boarding.

Can all this activity be justified by the conventional yard-stick of success? Over the years, Hall teams have had to learn to be courteous and civilised in defeat! The 1980s saw the school teams begin to develop a greater reputation for success however. At shooting and hockey, they did well, and at football they were always respected opponents. From time to time old boys have gained their blue at Oxford or Cambridge. In 1976, John Carr was captain of The Hall cricket XI and just eleven years later he became the first Hall boy to win his county cap for Middlesex. In 1987, a Hall boy won the Prep School golf championship, appropriately at Stowe. The Hall produced three successive keepers of fencing at Eton, the captain of cricket at Charterhouse, and strings of competent oarsmen. For a school with almost no sporting facilities of its own, this tradition was gratifying, the more so in the knowledge that the school is no 'sportocracy', and non-games players are respected and understood no less than the keen athletes. The element too of option has been good. Boys have not been forced to idle away endless daisy-chaining hours pretending to play cricket merely because the authorities regarded it as the only manly sport for a summer term. Field and track athletics and tennis have both swelled in importance and surged in their standards of performance, as only those keen to play 'the national game' have been required to do so.

This philosophy can be nicely illustrated by an occasion when Heazell was approached by two dismayed, highly articulate seniors, eager to explain their predicament. Being quite hopeless at football, they found themselves perpetually condemned to playing in defence, since there was no possible chance they could ever score goals. By very definition therefore they could only be responsible for conceding goals. This made them not only discomfited, cold and bored, but positively unpopular with their hapless team-mates. They were both promptly given a crash course in refereeing, and thereafter enjoyed themselves in a new, less humiliating role.

All is in a state of flux, reckoned Heraclitus, and so things at The Hall continued to change and evolve over the years. The academic programme of the 1980s was increasingly shaken by uncertainties inspired by external educational pressures. Those dread letters, CE, so long haunting prep school examination candidates, were mysteriously expanded – into GCSE, a new spectre of unclear portent. The Heazell reign saw the programme widen and the traditional subjects groan under the consequent pressures on an unyielding school week. Major academic laurels were won, including a top scholarship to Eton. In 1985, the History department, under Mr Andrew Corbett, a worthy successor to the redoubtable Bathurst, scored a notable triumph. Two boys finished top respectively of the Batsford Townsend-Warner History Competition and the Harrow History Essay Prize, and the Hall team emerged top of the list. It was the centenary year of perhaps the oldest of all the inter-school competitions.

Heazell always passionately believed that boys should learn by looking beyond the cloistered walls of school. The formal affiliation between The Hall and HMS *Invincible*, granted by the Admiralty in September 1979, was an example. Every year thereafter, boys and staff have visited or been to sea in her. On one trip, boys were sent to 'work ship' as part of the ship's company. On another, they lined the side, as the ship entered harbour for the unforgettable experience of a decommissioning. The link with *Invincible* was made the more poignant by the outbreak of hostilities in the South Atlantic. A senior Latin set despatched a congratulatory telegram once the fighting ended. It was a tribute to the educational tradition of the Senior Service that the reply of thanks was in no less elegant Latin. The Hall's links with the Royal Navy were less happily marked by the sad news that the very first fatal naval casualty in the Falklands was a former Hall boy, Lt Nicholas Taylor RN. His memorial, funded by a school classmate then resident in South America, was a picture of his ship, HMS *Hermes*, which was hung in the entrance hall of the school.

An even greater commitment to external links took Heazell several fruitless years to complete, this time with manufacturing industry. Just as Hampstead boys are unlikely to have many ready opportunities to go to sea with the Royal Navy, so he felt that all too many of them, sons of professional, media or artistic fathers, bankers, publishers, teachers and their like, could have too little understanding of the role of industry and manufacture in the economy. As a result of *Industry Year* in 1986, (which was run by a Hall Old Boy, Sir Geoffrey Chandler) and encouragement from the Industrial Society (which was run by another Old Boy, John Garnett), an official School and Industry Liaison was established with the 'hi-tech' electronics company, Hypertac Ltd., a subsidiary of Smiths Industries, in Cricklewood. From May 1986, a regular programme of visits and educational exchanges was begun. The Hall was given an award for its enterprise from the Royal Society of Arts which had sponsored *Industry Year*.

In no time at all, so it seemed, Heazell had been at The Hall for ten years. The centenary was just three short years off. This was the point when the second and by far the larger phase of the building programme which had been started after the fire was to be implemented. Designs were drawn up, not always without difficulty; costings were made; a decision to launch an appeal was taken . . . and the writer is no longer in the realms of history, he is describing the present and straying into the future.

Yet we may be falling now into the trap of thinking a school is its headmaster, like Arnold – Rugby, Thring – Uppingham, or a parish its vicar, so that assistant staff are often forgotten. Let us make amends. Many of the staff have served long and loyally so that when they retire their absence is more than apparent. By 1970 came the end of an era with the departure of Rotherham, Bathurst, Barron and Packard in the Senior School and Mrs Barron and Miss Bearman from the Junior. Between them, they had given The Hall more than one and a half centuries of service!

Their memorial is the deep impression made on the minds of generations of Hall Boys. The picture of Rotherham, painted by Mrs Cooper, catches his stern glare. The words painted on the blackboard 'Ne Dum Quis' form a punning motto – loosely translated 'Make hay while the sun shines' (Ne – imperative of neo, spin; Dum – while; Quis – second singular of queo, to be able: – Spin while you can.) With the subsequent retirement of three stalwarts in the catering department, Mrs Dow, Mrs King and Miss Chapman, another century of service had been achieved. When 'Jimmy' Earle left in 1982, after 33 years on the staff, came the end of the era of the giants. Is it probable that their like will be seen again?

This very question makes it the more difficult to mention names of more recent servants of the school without invidious omissions. Some of the more important members of staff have spent but brief spells at The Hall. Such was John Brett, a personal friend of Cooper's from Oxford days, who joined as 'second' master following retirement from his headmastership of Durham School. He succeeded

Rotherham, and was in turn followed by Tim Thornton, a vigorous representative of a new generation of schoolmasters, well attuned to the thinking of the 1970s. He left in 1976 to assume a taxing job at Dean Close Junior and subsequently take over and dramatically expand The Croft School, Stratford-upon-Avon. When Earle retired, he was succeeded by another Oxbridge blue and ex-headmaster, Bob Chambers. After a short stay, he in turn departed to resume headmastering at The Park School, Bath. In the Junior School, no teacher made a greater mark on the community during these years than the irrepressible 'Fidge' Sutherland, a teacher of amazing energy and personality.

The academic tradition of The Hall was sustained by men and women, some of whose names have occurred in the preceding pages, some who may be recorded here. Packard was followed by a scholar/poet, Robert Imlay, in charge of the classics. The English department saw Richard Dawson in charge for some thirteen years, followed by Charles Guttmann, both highly respected teachers. The introduction of science as a major examination subject in the curriculum, a development that occured in the early 1970s, fell to the capable hands of Charles Buxton, formerly head of department at Trent. In Michael Fitzmaurice, the school gained a remarkably versatile schoolmaster, able at once to run the games programme, head the mathematics department and mastermind the introduction of computing.

And so, by now, the story reaches the contemporary scene and it all ceases to be history.

The Hall has always managed to generate the genuine atmosphere of a community with greater depths than its scholastic function alone could create. The affection and loyalty this can breed may be well illustrated by the impact of the Frais family on the story of the last quarter of this century of The Hall's history. Their contribution to the cubbing and scouting is referred to elsewhere, but it is proper to stress that in quality no less than in quantity, their devotion to the boys of the school, and their families, has been truly remarkable. Perhaps as a climax to his service, always so freely given, Tony Frais undertook to administer the Centenary Appeal as its Honorary Director. Not only did he vigorously embark on the burdensome task with rare imagination and enthusiasm, he saw the value of renewing contact with so many Old Boys and former members of staff, that the idea of reviving The Hall Old Boys Association, put in abeyance in 1966, was promoted.

This account of the recent past, as it imperceptibly slides into the immediate present, ends with a personal reflection. Among many events which were organised to mark the Appeal and direct attention towards the date of the 100th anniversary of the school's foundation, was an evening spent with several Old Boys, some of whom had left over 50 years ago, and one who first entered the Junior School in its very first term, 70 years before. Their conversation and manners were charming, witty, courteous and urbane. May this be said by my successor of those who have left The Hall during the years which I have described, when the sequel to this volume comes to be written, to celebrate the sesquicentennial in 2039.

PART IV: MEMORIES AND REMINISCENCES

In preparation for this volume, a call was put out to all Old Boys for any contributions they would like to make to the history of the school. The response was such that far less than all the material received could possibly be used, and a fair amount of repetition was to be expected. This has necessitated some pruning and editing. Every effort has been made to ensure that the essential flavour of the original writing is preserved.

Chapter 1
1889-1939

Recording the history of the earliest days of the school is, by the very nature of things, precarious and uncertain. More than one of those Old Boys who have sent contributions have died, sadly, before their handiwork could see the light of day. E W Lindeck was one such. He was one of three brothers at The Hall during the Marshall/Montauban years. He recalled the days when boys travelled to and from school by horse-drawn cab or bus and the vast majority lived so near that they went home for lunch each day. Another posthumous contributor was Frank Ballin who was one of the eight scholarship winners in that *annus mirabilis* year of 1915. A fascinating and unexpected cameo came from Mrs Prior, the sister of another Old Boy, R A Bartholomew, who like Ballin, left The Hall during the First World War. She recalled regular visits for ballroom dancing classes with the smartly be-suited boys, all wearing their shiny black patent-leather pumps.

The eight-year-old A R Kennedy arrived at The Hall at this time, and vividly recalled the RFC fighters chasing the German bombers. Kennedy, in common with surprisingly many Hall boys, made the Royal Navy his career, retiring as a Captain. Anthony Rogers was one of those 'uprooted' from Hampstead and taken off to 'the fat of the land' at Balmore, where they all feasted on ham and home-made cream and were introduced to the mysteries of golf (on a special course Montauban constructed for the purpose). Many, many years later, Rogers revisited Caversham to see whether any trace of Balmore survived. Alas, subsequent building development has submerged it and its grounds under a sea of houses.

A contemporary of Rogers provides the first contribution to be included verbatim in this chapter. The Worshipful Chancellor the Reverend Garth Moore recalls his days during and just after the Great War. He became a barrister, and as a clergyman, one of the leading canon lawyers of his time, and a fellow of Corpus Christi College, Cambridge.

On the opening day of term in September 1915, my mother took me up the front steps of The Hall and handed me over to the Headmaster, E H Montauban, always known as 'Monty'. He immediately passed me on to a boy who conducted me to the upper changing room, near the boys' entrance, and thence into the big hall. In 1915 it was laid out with benches for the boys facing a table at the far end, at which sat the Headmaster in front of a semicircle formed by members of the staff and prefects, with, at his extreme left, a grand piano where daily Mrs Montauban played the opening hymn. There was a large Jewish contingent at The Hall, and they gathered together in one of the classrooms leading off the hall for their own prayers, after which they filed into the hall for roll-call with the rest of us. This was normally taken by a prefect; but on the first day of the new school year the Headmaster himself took it. When he reached 'Moore', I immediately answered, but so did another boy, the son of a General and himself destined to become a General, who died in 1985. He had been there for at least a year before my arrival, and so he became Moore I and I was Moore II.

I was already in possession of my school cap (or perhaps it was my brother's), which in those days was black with a pink Maltese cross and pink stripes. But inappropriately I was also wearing a green jersey and blue shorts, and it immediately became apparent that I should get a pink jersey with black collar together with black shorts and a black blazer with pink stripes. All these came from John Barnes, the store in the Finchley Road (closed since 1980).

'Monty' was undoubtedly a good headmaster, and perhaps even a great one. He was a firm but kind disciplinarian and an excellent teacher and man of business. His weakness was in having favourites among the parents, and this favour could subtly flow over to the boys, or at least appear to do so.

His staff was well chosen, despite the difficulties of the war. W H Copinger took us for maths and J H Carpenter for a number of other subjects, including elementary Latin and English. There was also Mr Duggan, a handsome Irishman with a fiery temper, and later a Mr Sandberg who left to be ordained and Mr Betts from South Africa. At one stage we had a young Swiss to teach French. He did not last long. One day he seized a boy called Wicke by the hair:

Wicke, however, remained in his place, but his hair was left in this master's hand. Wicke did not appear to be any the worse, but the story got around and at the end of the term the Swiss left. He was succeeded by an elderly and kindly Belgian with a beard, called Monsieur d'Ouffet. For the most part masters were replaced by mistresses, most of whom were first-class teachers. For the small boys there was both Mrs Montauban and Miss Lang. Then there was the universally popular Mrs Mason who took a variety of subjects. For more advanced classics there was Miss Bolton, who was a first-class classicist and teacher, though a bit prim. On one occasion Walther, who was sitting next to me in Miss Bolton's class, surreptitiously conducted a swap with a boy behind whereby Walther acquired a tiny brass cannon. He was happily poking at it with a pin, when suddenly it exploded with a surprisingly large bang, singeing Walther's eyebrows. Eventually Miss Bolton rose from her desk and gingerly picked up the cannon and placed it outside on the windowsill. She then resumed her seat and we waited fearfully for whatever judgement such a heinous offence would call forth. 'Walther,' she said magisterially, 'for that you shall lose three marks.'

For boxing Mr Keegan used to visit the school. His face must have been made of rubber, for he would encourage boys to hit him on the nose as hard as they could, and he never seemed to be any the worse for it. For soccer and cricket at one time we went to a field in Finchley, travelling there in a bus hired from the London and General Omnibus Company. Later we migrated by Metropolitan Railway from Swiss Cottage to a wayside halt at Preston Road, one stop before Harrow and in unspoilt country. If it was too wet for orthodox games, we were allowed to go to Hampstead Heath, where we played a glorified version of French and English.

When London became a target for air-raids (at first by Zeppelins at night and later by Gothas during the day), about half the school migrated to the country with 'Monty' while the other half, including myself, remained in London where Carpenter acted as deputy Headmaster and we all enjoyed ourselves immensely.

About October 1918, the great and often fatal 'flu epidemic hit London. I was one of the victims and was very ill indeed. My first day back at school was on the 11th November 1918, and at 11 o'clock the maroons went off to signal the Armistice. But, since hitherto maroons had been used as an air-raid warning, there was some dispute in the school as to what on this occasion they signified. Mr Carpenter thought they were an air-raid; we boys maintained that it was peace at last. Eventually the noise of cheering in the streets convinced him that we were right. He assembled us in the hall, where we had a brief service of thanksgiving and sang *God Save the King* and then were released for the rest of the day. Most of us rushed up to Finchley Road and joined the frenzied cheering crowds in one of the most remarkable spontaneous events I have ever witnessed.

With the end of hostilities the school was reunited in London. It was growing rapidly and two new houses had been added. But not long after that 'Monty' retired and the school was taken over jointly by Mr Gladstone and Mr Chitty, both of whom proved very popular and very efficient. On their first Speech Day (and my last), they said that, coming as they did from boarding schools, they had expected to find the boys at what was then predominantly a day school less independent. They were surprised to find that the opposite was the case. They obviously had not realised that we were accustomed from a very early age to go all over London by ourselves.

The teaching at the school was of a very high standard, especially in English and Latin. No science was taught, which was a pity, and scripture was almost confined to the Old Testament, no doubt because Christians and Jews could be taught this together. Apart from the excellent grounding we received, what in retrospect impresses me most is the remarkable degree of tolerance with which we were treated. I was chronically unpunctual and not a bit interested in orthodox pastimes such as cricket and soccer, though I did become a leader at drill; but I was treated by boys and staff alike with a great degree of understanding and given every encouragement in the things at which I was good, in particular at writing, and I was made the nominal editor of the school's magazine, which enabled me successfully to evade all sorts of (to me) less attractive obligations. I look back to my time at The Hall with very real gratitude.

Contemporaries of Moore were the Salvi brothers, the older, 'Beppo', a formidable cricketer and the younger, one of the key founder members of the Scouts. He reminds us of the uniform they wore – shorts, of course, and the Baden-Powell hat; and a five foot pole, marked at one end in inches, and useful if, in those far-off days, there had been the attacks on young people which darken our society these days. The Salvis were very active members of the Old Boys' Club in its early days.

Hardy Lee entered The Hall in 1919, and tells of his time as a day boy in the early 1920s.

Living in Highgate I had the (usually) happy experience of bicycling each day across the Heath and returning in the winter evenings, having lit, sometimes with difficulty, my front and back oil lamps. For the toil up Fitzjohns Avenue, I would hang on to the tail of an Express Dairy Sentinel steam wagon, which was often available.

When there was snow or severe rain my parents would advise me to go by public transport. This meant starting at least half an hour earlier and a complicated journey involving walking, tram, bus and tube. My father, believing that my memory might fail me during it, made me memorize a piece of doggerel which went: 'Addie laid an egg for the King and he eat on until he crossed the field to The Hall', all of which gave me Adelaide Road, King's College Road, Eton Avenue and Crossfield Road. It worked.

Another incident involving my father was not so benign. He had always been interested in geography and believing that my knowledge of this subject, as well as that of the other boys, might be improved with an appropriate stimulus, donated a cup (I believe it was) to be competed for as a geography prize. My embarrassment was twofold: first, because none of my fellow students, as far as I was aware, really thought that the study of geography would further their prospects of entering the public school of their choice, and secondly, because it put great psychological pressure on me (as I thought) to be first winner of this trophy. I forget how it all turned out, but I imagine the Geography Prize was soon forgotten after the Lee connection with the school had ceased.

My memories of the teachers are in some cases vague, in some cases strong. I recall Mr Chitty, memorable for his dashing GN sports car, and Mr Singleton for his knowledge of other cars. ('All Morris cars now have windscreen wipers' – hand-operated, of course!). There was Mr Blakiston telling boys at lunch 'You won't like it' when they tried to take his beer. Then the most memorable of all, Mr Copinger, supreme teacher of maths – and purveyor of puns. ('Catch up, like the tomato'.) For games we had, for me, the enormous pleasure of travelling by Metropolitan train to Wembley Park, with the great stadium looming over the playing field and the gleaming Great Central trains providing glamorous excitement on the way there and back.

And as age increases so do the memories. Even to the roll-call, preparing to shout 'here': '. . . Lack, de Laszlo, Lee . . .'

Lee himself went on to Rugby and Cambridge to read law. After military service during the war, he moved to the USA, joining the US Foreign Service, and then becoming a banker in California. Marrying late in life, he retired to Cambridge. The geography prize he refers to was not won that Christmas by Lee, but by M L Rosenheim, who was shortly to win a scholarship to Shrewsbury. A Shield for Geography is still awarded, though research fails to reveal whether this trophy is a direct successor of the Lee Prize.

Lee's immediate contemporary was L M Miall, whose recollections span some thirty years, as boy, parent and governor. Miall was one of the tribe inspired by Montauban to enter his new school, Stowe. Then he went to Trinity Hall, Cambridge and later became an industrial chemist and biotechnologist. He gives us a view of the period of transition from Montauban to Wathen.

> I spent a year at the Junior School, still run by E H Montauban. I cannot pretend to remember him well, but I think of him as a very old-style headmaster, always wearing a dark suit and a high stiff collar.
>
> When I moved to the Senior, the Headmasters were Gladstone and Chitty, two much younger men who would not be out of place as schoolmasters today. Chitty soon left and was replaced by Gladstone's uncle, G A Wathen, who descended on the school in a whirl of enthusiasm with many what then seemed revolutionary ideas. The chief innovation that I remember was called the Dalton plan, which in some way involved having periods when the boys could do what work they liked. Strangely I do not recall this being popular with the boys, who were intensely conservative in anything that concerned the school, which had so far been very conventional.
>
> My chief memory among the masters and I think inevitably of anyone who was at the school at that time was W H Copinger. Like Montauban he was of the old school in dress, though his appearance often looked rather down at heel. But he was a genius with preparatory school boys; he knew brilliantly how to appeal to their sense of humour and they loved him for it. Lessons with him were a delight.

Over the years, certain families with a prolific supply of sons make a special mark on The Hall. None in this category outmatch the Earles, four of whom joined the school during the 1920s. Sons of a senior army officer, the tribe's oldest member was W H Earle, who recalls his last term, in the summer of 1926:

> Some sixty years have elapsed since my last term, but I can still remember some not entirely happy occasions . . .
>
> Firstly, I had failed to get into Winchester College which was, of course, a great blow to me, my family and the staff. Fortunately my father knew a master at Rugby who had been his adjutant in the war, so I took the CE for Rugby and passed.
>
> Secondly, my performances on the cricket field – rather fortuitously, I feel, I had been appointed Captain of Cricket – were

very disappointing and, at the end of the term, I clearly could not be awarded either the batting or bowling cup. So a fielding cup had to be instituted and presented to a rather indifferent wicket-keeper!

Thirdly, it was customary for the games master, after prayers, to call out the names of those who had been given colours, whereupon these budding Bothams would advance to the Captain who placed the appropriate caps on the heads. On this occasion it was somewhat embarrassing when, owing to a misunderstanding, a boy approached me eager to be capped and, in front of the whole school, had to be told that I had not got his First Eleven cap. Doubtless no-one will recall this incident. I certainly have never forgotten it.

This tradition of 'capping' has been modified over the years, and replaced by a captain's handshake and the presentation of the appropriate colour tie. W H Earle, went from Rugby to Christ Church, Oxford, and thence to the British Council, serving abroad, chiefly in the Middle East and India. He was awarded the CBE for his work in New Delhi. His youngest brother, F J Earle, was a pupil from 1929 to 1934 and then returned to serve on the staff under three headmasters for 33 years before retiring in 1982, to assume a role of assistant editor and researcher for this volume. His personal contribution at this juncture is especially valuable.

Memories of nearly sixty years ago do not come flooding back but I do recall my first day at the Junior School. I remember joining the other new boy and marching round the hall to the tune of *The British Grenadiers* played on the piano by Mrs Baker. Mrs Baker played the piano not only at school but also at the Hampstead Baths in the Finchley Road for the annual gym display. This was a formidable task and quite unpredictable, for the Finchley Road instrument had many missing notes and a number of the others were out of tune; so whether it was meant to be Schubert's *Marche Militaire* or *The Teddy Bears' Picnic* made no difference.

I cannot believe that I was anything but apprehensive and a little afraid when I made the step from the Junior to the Senior. Here was a world of men. In fact I had little to fear. French was my best subject, and I believe it was Mr Dodd who taught me first. He was an advocate of the 'direct method', and I thrived on the system. I have since learned to sympathise with those who find it difficult. I remember too the other masters of the time, Mr Millard for English and drama, as well as scouting, Mr Rotherham for geography – and woe betide any slacker in his lessons – and Captain Forrest, who, poor man, suffered terribly from shell-shock. Then there was Mr Copinger, 'Famous', who taught maths and was never happier than when playing chess, or sharing his store of jokes and puns. Mrs d'Ouffet taught English literature and art and was responsible for training several very successful teams which used to be entered regularly for the Inter-Preparatory School Spelling Competition. Miss Bolton – 'Sally Bee' – used to teach Latin. We had been grounded in elementary grammar in the Junior School. We now moved on to the adjectives, pronouns and verbs. All had to be learned by heart. Latin grammar played a large part in the Common Entrance exam and we were expected to know our grammar thoroughly. I can remember the first sentence of one of our first translation books which, oddly enough, was not about Caesar. It ran: *Non procul est ora maritima*. I recall no more. It might have been a quotation from the brochure of a Roman boarding-house. There were three standard text books, by Kennedy, by North and Hillard and by Hillard and Botting. Hillard must have made a fortune out of his Latin books. North's brother was cashier at the Swiss Cottage branch of the National Provincial Bank.

Reading Over used to take place weekly and parents used to crowd onto the gallery to listen to the results. We received positions in every subject and these were sometimes accompanied by an 'over', a 'plus', an 'under' or a 'minus'. Some boys did exceptionally well and qualified for a 'gold star' while a few earned what was called a 'red cross'. This was considered a terrible disgrace and usually caused considerable embarrassment!

Parents, particularly mothers, had far more spare time in those days. Many had resident help, at least a cook and a maid, and probably a nanny or a governess to look after the younger members of a family. They were therefore able to attend more school functions. One of the favourite entertainments was the regular gym class held at the Hampstead Baths. Here, as at school, there was a gallery for the parents. Our chief instructor was a burly red-faced man, Sergeant-Major Biggs. Woe betide any boy who made a mistake or failed to perform to his standard. He would go up to the miscreant, stick his face close to the boy's and announce in a clear voice so that all could hear: 'You've got a big 'ead and nuffin' in it!' The embarrassed parent of the boy would take it out on the little wretch later that day.

Next to the Baths there was a toy shop called Porters and I used to gaze longingly at the displays of Hornby trains. Nearer Swiss Cottage there was a sweet shop which had a 'halfpenny tray', a display of humbugs, sherbet, lollipops and liquorice, none costing more than a ha'penny. I am surprised we were allowed to go there, as eating in the street was surely forbidden then as it is now, but perhaps that was part of the attraction!

I became a boarder for my last two terms. I lodged at 2 Buckland Crescent with Mr Wathen who would wake us each morning. We would do our daily exercises with him in the dormitory. We would perform the same exercises several times, counting as we did them in English, French, German and Latin.

Another boy destined to return to The Hall as a master was a contemporary of James Earle. John Dizer in fact attended the Junior School only, before going away to boarding school. He went up to Oxford and then joined the RAF. After the war he became a schoolmaster in public and prep schools. His descriptions of his time under Miss Gladstone has the sharpness of focus which countless pupils have long since come to associate with this remarkable teller of tales.

To all of us, even that long ago, Miss Gladstone seemed venerable, standing about, usually chatting to another mistress and beaming austerely on the world in general and us in particular. Mr Wathen, lean, dark and genial, we saw so much of, I thought that he was the Headmaster only of the Junior School. I never visited the Senior. To me it was a remote place for terribly big boys round an infinitely long corner or two. I once arrived far too early for school and was allowed into No. 2 (Buckland Crescent) to watch some boys finishing their breakfast there. I remember them putting away vast quantities of toast and marmalade and wishing someone would offer me some.

My elder brother Jim and I were in the Junior together for a time. We were driven to school daily in a great, square Buick by my father's chauffeur, a veteran of the Great War, named Salmon. He had been captured by the Turks at Kut, in Mesopotamia, and had had to walk for days through the desert with his hands tied together and roped to a camel. One day, just as he was delivering us to the school, my brother thought it a good joke to push his chauffeur's cap down over his eyes. The old man's reactions were none too quick, and our stately vehicle mounted the pavement. Nobody was struck, but once home, my brother was punished for what he did, and I was punished for thinking it was funny!

On another day, just as we were being collected at 3 pm or 3.30, the ill-fated R101 airship flew quite low overhead. It must have been its trial flight, on 1st October 1930, three days before its fatal crash in France. My know-all brother later insisted that it had had an ominous list to starboard.

Jim was always hard-working and did all the right things, including being a most enthusiastic Cub. But my mother had some illusions shattered when she had some of his friends to a birthday party. They ran amok in the house and did quite a lot of damage. Unlike Jim, I lived life in a perpetual dream, and had consistently bad reports. I hated both work and games, especially cricket, and seemed to spend all and every day being ticked off for not paying attention. Therefore, feeling discouraged, I paid less attention than ever – and did worse than ever. One day, however, at Sunday lunch, I reduced the family to stunned silence by announcing that I wanted, above all things, to have a good education. My father put his knife and fork down, rose from his chair and solemnly shook my hand. I could not understand what all the fuss was about. All that had happened was that, during the morning, I had read in a comic a story about a man who had been captured by a band of brigands, but had amazingly managed in only a few months to become their leader '. . . because of a good education. . . .' Clearly, this was an important thing to have. I don't think that, in those days, I even knew what the word meant. And I'm sure I couldn't spell it.

The only things I remember enjoying in the Junior School were singing and wrestling. The latter was not actually in the curriculum. But it must have been tolerated because on one occasion, when my form was having an indoor break in the hall, I remember trying to persuade them all to sit cross-legged in a semi-circle, and watch me have an exhibition wrestling match with a boy I knew I could beat. I could not understand, at the time, why they were all so unco-operative. And even in singing I was frustrated because I was made to stand beside a boy called D'Avigdor, who was not only taller than me but wagged his head from side to side when he sang. Thus he was noticed and got all the praise.

Was I happy in the Junior School? Not particularly. But I was a lot less happy at the boarding school to which I was sent at 9, and I don't think I much enjoyed any school until I was 15 or 16. Some boys just hate being chivvied, and react against it either by rebellion or, as I did, by quietly 'switching off'. I can certainly detect the odd 'Dizer' in most forms in the present Senior School. I only hope that I am as patient with them as my teachers must have been with me.

In every decade, some pretty distinguished names appear in the class-lists of The Hall, sons of famous parents or boys destined for notable careers in their own right. Such a name in the 1920s was Croom-Johnson. The son of an eminent judge, Sir David Croom-Johnson went to Stowe and Trinity Hall, Cambridge and served in the Royal Navy. A notable legal career brought him the appointment as a Lord Justice of Appeal.

My brother Oliver (killed in the RAF in 1940) went to The Hall a year before me. E H Montauban was at that time still running the

> Junior School. He and my father worked together to get Stowe School founded. 'Monty's' was the inspiration and my father was Chairman of the original committee. I can still remember 'Monty' telling the boys at the Junior School how he had helped to select Roxburgh for the headmastership of Stowe and that, when Roxburgh was told, he was deeply moved and betrayed it only by a movement of his throat. The first library at Stowe was subscribed for by parents at The Hall and I remember my mother busying herself with the lists of books to be bought, at the book department of the *Army and Navy*. This was all done in secret from EHM.
>
> Other boys at The Hall at that time and friends of mine included Frank Byers (later Lord Byers, the Liberal peer), Anthony West (son of H G Wells and Rebecca West) and Freddie Erroll (later Lord Erroll of Hale). Of my two headmasters, 'Monty' had the gift of treating boys as equals, so you were never afraid of him. He stimulated imagination. Wathen was a wise schoolmaster. He must have known we made fun of him – 'When I was in India, very many years ago . . .' – and was prepared to let us. A great deal of my love of English literature and language I owe to Wathen. He and Montauban are two of the four schoolmasters to whom I really owe such education as I possess.

Sir David's classmate, Anthony West, who died in 1987, was at The Hall for only a few terms, having encountered severe difficulties at his previous school, not least because of his illegitimacy, a problem that tainted his whole life. GAW's reputation even after only a year or so in Hampstead was such that Rebecca West decided to entrust her sensitive son to a school where, so she confidently believed, there was no bullying. GAW was, she wrote, 'a real fine liberal' and West himself regarded him as 'a saintly man'.

Another distinguished name of this period was Del Mar. Norman, to become a distinguished musician, was the youngest of the brothers. His elder brother, R O Del Mar writes:

> I can't pretend to remember a lot about the Junior School, presided over at the time by Mr Montauban. We were taught cricket by a certain Miss Malley, probably a mere girl, but she impressed us enormously by bowling over-arm and taking huge, unlady-like strides. And we were taught singing by a very nasty man who, for a slight misdemeanour, would make a boy lie spread-eagled on the floor and would proceed to spank him at intervals. I don't know why a parent did not report this, but nobody did. We were graded according to ability and voice. There were nightingales and blackbirds. I was a corncrake.

One was automatically transferred to the Senior School, and when I went there in 1923, it was run by two Headmasters, Mr Chitty ('Chitty-bang-bang') and Mr Gladstone. Gladstone was a huge man and I was always rather afraid of him. He had a very loud voice and had the uncomfortable habit of coming out of what we assumed was the door of his private rooms onto the balcony overlooking the main hall and watching unnoticed what was going on below. If a boy was transgressing a voice like thunder would bellow out and scare us all into fits.

Then appeared Mr Wathen, a first-rate Headmaster and under him the school undoubtedly flourished. While I cannot remember much about the staff, I do recall Mr Singleton who taught classics and if, as happened not infrequently, a boy nodded off, he would throw a full-sized dictionary at him with unerring aim. Some would feign sleep and field the dictionary which infuriated Singleton. I was hopeless at Latin and suffered the dictionary more than once. But the master who stood out was Mr Copinger, a superb teacher. His overriding passion was chess, and he encouraged and taught any willing boy how to play. He used to play boys in batches of eight during the lunch break. I don't know how good a player he was but he used to beat us all with ease. I can see him still walking up and down the eight chess boards, admonishing a stupid move, moving his own piece and praising a boy who had made him pause to think.

In those days there were about half a dozen boarders. We felt sorry for them but they always maintained they had a splendid time once we day boys had gone home. Our day began at nine o'clock but some of us would get there before nine so as to squeeze in a game of squash or half an hour of nets before prayers. Most of us lunched in the big assembly hall and pretty terrible it was too! I enjoyed my food but even I rebelled against great tough broad beans, wet cabbage, parsnips *ad nauseam*, cold fatty meat and skinny milk puddings. It shows the impression they made in that I remember these lunches so vividly.

Games were a major part of one's life, especially if one was lucky enough to be any good. The real joy in summer was to go by the 'Met' from Finchley Road to Selfridge's Sports Ground at Preston Road. The great ploy was to get on an express by accident on purpose when homeward bound and get whisked through to Baker Street! My memories are of many victories over other schools in matches but inevitably the defeats have been forgotten. Squash featured very highly in my life. Boxing was voluntary, with the fearful Sergeant-Major Biggs. He would take out his false teeth, put his hands behind his back, stick his chin out and shout "it me boy, 'it

PORTRAIT GALLERY 1 – The Staff of the Junior School

19: In 1949, under Miss Gladstone (Miss Bearman on her left)

20: In 1987, under Miss Allen
Back Row: Milly Polacek, Jan Mance, Julyan Heazell, Clare Hardy, Stuart Millar, Joanna Newton, Elona Cooper, Julia Hobhouse, Jill Le Moine *Front Row:* Cilla Sharpe, Nicky Fletcher, Priscilla Weld, Julia Allen, Sue Dallyn, Camilla Awdry

PORTRAIT GALLERY 2 – The Staff of the Senior School

21: Group taken in 1947
Back Row: Mr Maclagan, Mr Mayhew, Miss Large, Mr Sleigh, Mr Chitty, Mr Murray, Mr Blishen, Mr Bathurst
Front Row: Miss Harbord, Mr Barron, Mr Rotherham, Mr Wathen, Mr Fyson, Mr Prideaux, Miss MacGilvray

PORTRAIT GALLERY 3 – The post-GAW years

22: Top left: R A Cooper, Headmaster 1955-1976
23: Left: Paddy Heazell (Headmaster) and Julia Allen (Head of Junior School) at Junior School Sports, 1980
24: Above: Miss Gladstone presents prizes to Junior School, 1960
25: Below: F J Earle, pupil 1928-1934, assistant master 1949-1976, senior master 1976-1982

26: Senior historians, winners of the Batsford Townsend-Warner History Prize

27: A Kindergarten opens – the 'Zeros'

28: **The Hall School in 1986**

FRIENDS OF THE HALL

29 and inset: The school aboard HMS *Invincible,* off Portsmouth

30: Educational visit to Hypertac Ltd, Cricklewood

THE SITE OF EXPANSION

31: The original Strathray Garden plot, purchased in 1947, site of the War Memorial and tennis court, being prepared for excavation for the Centenary Building, 1987.

32: The 6th form yard, pre-1972

33: **The Centenary Building nearing completion, September 1988.**

me. Go on, that was a butterfly kiss, 'it me!' However hard we tried we never seemed to hurt him. But he taught well and it stood me in good stead in later life; but that's another story.

Del Mar was wrong – and right. The Hall lost more soccer and rugger matches than they won, and were far from invincible at cricket during his final year. He left for Marlborough in 1926.

For all its enthusiasm for sport, The Hall has produced few distinguished performers. Truth to tell, the heroes of Hall school teams were never quite talented enough to make 'the big time'. It is fitting that a 'name' from this period was to become such as a writer about sport, and cricket in particular, rather than as a first-class performer. Michael Melford was for many years an eminent commentator, succeeding the renowned E W Swanton as chief cricket correspondent on *The Daily Telegraph.* A chance encounter in the Long Room at Lord's with the Headmaster elicited the information that Melford had joined the school via the Minimi (referred to already on page 36). Its precise constitution was not altogether clear and Melford ventured an explanation:

> I can only guess at the *raison d'être* of the Minimi. I presume some sort of population bulge manifesting itself in the Junior School; it was certainly an overflow and was sited in Avenue Road in the early 1920s. Having spent my first term at The Hall in Belsize Park, I was drafted to the Minimi for the two winter terms of 1923-24 before returning to the Junior School. The Minimi was situated at the junction with Elsworthy Road and I dimly remember assaulting a football for the first time in the garden there but otherwise the episode remains a great mystery to me.
>
> Casting about for other events unlikely to be widely remembered, I hit on the return to his house in Buckland Crescent of Sir Alan Cobham after one of his epic flights to Australia or South Africa. He must have had a nasty shock when he found a large contingent from The Hall lining the pavement outside his front door. If this sounds creditable, the very opposite was the case when Hugh Lofting, the distinguished creator of Doctor Dolittle came to speak in the Senior School. He was a speaker given to long pauses which were a severe test of the boys' self-control. Eventually half-smothered sniggering broke out. The more circumspect did not help by hissing for silence and the next day Mr Wathen very properly delivered a severe reprimand.

Melford was reminded of his feat, as a Hall colt cricketer, in scoring half centuries twice in a season – against the Mothers' XI! In those days – the late 1920s – ladies seem to have played rather more regularly and proficiently than in more recent times. Melford explained his pride in what was one of his rarer cricketing achievements.

> Now to the most kind and stimulating references to my prolific batting against the mothers. I never felt entirely guilty at hogging it because Mrs Wilson was by no means a pushover as a bowler. She came, I think, of a Kentish cricketing family and had done a lot of bowling at her brothers. Her son, Dick, was, I recall, vice-captain to me in 1930. We both went to Charterhouse where, in 1935, he was captain of cricket and I was abroad, learning French in Paris, never having reached the first XI. I suppose I was already 'over the top'.

Melford's contribution concludes with a delightful tribute to Gladstone, who perhaps receives less than his due in these pages.

> GAW of course went on for many years but fewer will remember Robin Gladstone. We were already dabbling in clichés even at that early age and would often proclaim that 'old Gladdy's bark was worse than his bite'. We were shrewd judges. He was a most kindly man. He was the staunchest possible supporter of rugby football and the Harlequins. When he was packing up and leaving The Hall soon after the end of his last term, he rang up and said that he had something for me. I rode up to Crossfield Road on my bicycle and he said: 'As you're going to a soccer school,' (this with mild disgust), 'you had better have this.' I still have the charming, perfectly proportioned bronze-plated figure of a footballer which he gave me. I last met him at a cricket match at Hove more than 20 years later. He had become a great lover of Glyndebourne and invited my wife and myself there. We had baby-sitter problems and only one of us could go. There was no question which of us would appreciate the finer points of *Cosi Fan Tutte* more, so my wife set off from Victoria in full evening dress on a Sunday afternoon, an afternoon of such rain and tempest that lifeboats were out all along the South Coast. Glyndebourne can scarcely have been at its best, but Mozart and Gladstone between them seem to have made it a day to remember.

Colonel D W Robertson was another of Gladstone's pupils, and a keen games player. He recalls with pleasure the emphasis on sport which he created, with his enthusiasm for rugger. He explains the origins of the squash court:

> Some oak pannelling, I think from a room in Haddon Hall, was up for sale and my father who was prominent in the advertising world led an Appeal Committee to purchase it for the school's main hall.

> Fortunately many parents were disinclined to make what amounted to a personal present to the Headmaster and the appeal failed dismally. I say 'fortunately' because, from the money which was received, it was decided to build a squash court. Over sixty years ago this was a fairly rare game and those interested got enormous pleasure out of it. I remember how delighted I was to win the Squash Cup in 1923!
>
> Robin Gladstone, with his exuberant and forthright personality, had no doubt an excellent effect on not only individual boys but on the whole school. But there can be no doubt that the greatest influence at that time was exerted by Mr Copinger, one of those people who can really be described as a 'character'. He was, in his outlook, way out on the right. He had what almost amounted to obsessions about *The Morning Post*, Lancashire cricket, English grammar and chess. I don't think he ever got over the demise of *The Morning Post*. He was an inspiring teacher of maths and English. Now sixty years later, I would never dream of splitting an infinitive or saying anything but 'different from' and his guidelines on how to solve a problem, however complex, remain with me always.

Day schools in London inevitably attract boys destined to be just 'birds of passage'. Robert Maclean, like Robertson, was destined for a military career:

> I arrived at The Hall in 1926 at the age of six, from Sumatra, which at that time was in the Dutch East Indies, and hitherto I had been in the charge of a Dutch governess and was trilingual, with English my weakest language. This reminds me of the time I got lost on Hampstead Heath in my early days at the school. I remember quite distinctly sitting on a bench and weeping bitterly while a kindly old lady tried to comfort me. Unfortunately, in the circumstances, my English deserted me and I could only speak in Dutch or Malay. This naturally led to some difficulty and attracted a good deal of attention.
>
> I remember quite clearly meeting Mr Wathen for the first time. We visited the school with my mother and had tea in the drawing-room where he showed us his wife's splendid collection of butterflies. He was very interested in natural history and we used to visit the Zoological Gardens regularly on Sundays after attending church. The main object seemed to be to see if all the lynxes were still surviving. I believe Mr Wathen had some connection with their presentation to the Zoo. We were given a penny to buy monkey-nuts for the birds and monkeys. Needless to say neither got very many.

> How well and how gratefully do I recall my first introduction to cricket, one of my abiding passions ever since! The first ball I received I managed to strike away quite firmly and began to run. Several fielders immediately raced to retrieve the ball but there was a considerable difference of opinion as to who should throw it in. I ran six. I never forgot that I had hit a six off my first ball.

Maclean left The Hall prematurely. He contracted pleurisy, went to the Isle of Wight to convalesce and never returned. Such a vivid recollection after a relatively brief and youthful period at The Hall is striking. Alas, such departures on grounds of ill-health were far from uncommon in those days, when sickly children were advised to seek the curative air of the seaside, thereby contributing to the boom in preparatory schooling in such bracing resorts as Bexhill-on-Sea, Weston-Super-Mare, Ramsgate and Cromer. Improvements in medicine quite as much as changes in fashion have forced the closure of almost all of these schools in more recent years.

Another reason for premature departures from The Hall has always been the parental determination to send their 9 year-old offspring to board away from London. No school has been more favoured for this purpose over the years than The Dragon School, Oxford, an establishment which under the Lynam family seemed to share many of the values and attitudes to be found in Gladstone and Wathen. Two brothers who followed this route were the Garnetts. John, the younger, explains:

> I went to the Junior School when I was 8, in 1929. After only a year in the Senior, I followed my brother to The Dragon, in 1932. I expect today I would have been labelled as dyslexic, but in those days, it was known as being a bad reader. I was also quite unable to remember which was my left foot and which was my right. I was taught that if you stood in the hall of the school facing the curved windows, my left foot was on the side of the door. For many years afterwards, I would turn myself in the direction of that window and remember that left was on the side of that door. When I joined the Navy, during the war, I had the same problems with port and starboard. I always resorted to a similar exercise, too, aboard the battleship *Malaya* in which I served as a rating, lying alongside the mole at Gibraltar: it was port-side to! To this day, when I need to remember which is port, I picture myself in Gibraltar harbour.
>
> Of my earliest memories, I recall in the playground there was great gang warfare between two rival gangs, who occupied the two corners. I was in the gang in the north-west corner. While we ran and ragged about, a beautiful golden-haired lady sat on a bench

> against the wall, seeing that we came to no serious harm. She was Miss Gladstone.
>
> We were great walkers in those days. One remembers the crocodile that went to the swimming baths or Lymington Road. My parents had no car. We lived in Well Walk, and every day from the age of eight onwards, we walked to The Hall and back. At the end of the day, Rosslyn Hill seemed to go on for ever.
>
> The great excitement of the term was the invitation to lunch with Mr Wathen in his house. He was a very impressive man and treated you with great dignity even though you were only nine. I have a vivid memory of sitting round that big table, eating macaroni, because he seemed to have views on vegetarianism, with a little, fair haired boy sitting opposite. This was, of course, Julian Wathen, now chairman of the governors, who was I suppose two years younger than me, but when you are nine and the other chap is seven, the difference in age is enormous. My other vivid memory, always with me, especially when I am doing carpentry, is of making picture frames in what was, I imagine, a garage attached to the back of the building. One Saturday morning a boy let his chisel slip and it cut an artery in his wrist. It was said that the blood hit the ceiling. I never use a chisel without taking care it doesn't happen to me!

In each decade of the school's history, the community suffers that most unbearable of tragedies, the death of a pupil. Happily, the incidence of fatal illnesses has over the years declined. Death from accident, especially on the streets of London, is a constant threat, and the pages of the magazine are from time to time darkened by memorials to such calamities.

Elphin Lloyd Jones was at The Hall for only a year, a 'fugitive' from a Kent boarding school which he clearly disliked. His parents were typically cultured Hampstead folk, with a remarkable circle of acquaintances. The boy was articulate, precocious and sensitive to a degree, remarkable even by Hall standards. On a shopping expedition to purchase Christmas cards, he was knocked down by a car in December 1928, just a month short of his 13th birthday. In 1984, a class-mate came across a copy of a beautifully produced *In Memoriam* which comprised three essays, one by each of the parents, and the third, an astonishing autobiography, written for GAW only weeks before his tragic death. As a tribute to all those Hall boys who would have matched and outmatched their contemporaries had they lived, two short excerpts from this volume are reprinted overleaf.

ON MYSELF

by Elphin Lloyd Jones

(Note on 'Myself'. The school essay here reproduced was written for Mr Wathen in October 1928. Elphin learned about atoms from Sir William Bragg's 'Concerning the Nature of Things', and the suggestion for his list of 'likes' – omitted from these extracts – came from a similar list of T E Lawrence which he remembered reading in 'Lawrence and the Arabs' by Robert Graves.)

To begin with I had better inform my reader that I am a schoolboy. Now, as many will know, one of a schoolboy's worst plights is having to write an essay on a given subject by a given time. I am at this moment in such a position.

Let me enlarge on the circumstances. I am seated in front of a table drawing pictures on the blotting paper, trying to arouse one spark of imagination. But these very circumstances, comfortable though they may appear, are nevertheless annoying.

I have to write about myself. Perhaps the obvious course to some is to send an apologetic note to the merciless human who set such a task, asking him to excuse them this once on the ground that they thought themselves not worth writing about.

Now when I sat down to the problem, I naturally bethought myself from what point of view to deal with it. I meditated thus. I might review my past, but being no Pepys I have no diary to consult; I might discuss the present, but my reader knows it; I might speculate on my future, like an H G Wells, but I have no vision. On the other hand, I might compress all three into a short biographical note such as one finds in 'Who's Who' . . . .

But we learn from the eastern sage that 'Man is like unto a grain of sand on the ocean's floor'; and modern astronomers tell us a man is a speck in the universe, a mite in God's creation. And if we consider a man's brain as his self, think then of its size compared with the vastness of space. But on the other hand, within this grain or speck, there is the mind that has grasped with such accuracy the very heavens themselves. 'What is man that thou art mindful of him? But thou hast made him but little lower than God.'

But enough. These are waters too deep for such a pen.

★ ★ ★

It is less than thirteen years since our younger boy was lent to us. Yet into those years he packed more laughter, more lovingkindness, more philosophy than most people get into a lifetime. He was wise with the deep wisdom of the young. To a mother's mind, Elphin seems to have been smoothing the road which we are now travelling by giving us happy recollections on which to dwell. All his life was a joy to us. This last year was particularly full of fragrance.

From March onwards he lived at home almost without a break in order to undergo special treatment, which I had to carry out. We were much together. His patience and cheerfulness under treatment were unbounded. He went about the house whistling fine tunes. He was full of thought for other people. His constant question was, 'Is there anything I can do to help you Mummy?' At table, before starting his dinner, he would often say, 'Are you sure you have kept plenty for yourself?' Nearly all his pocket money went on presents for one and another of us. He seldom addressed me without adding an endearing word. He kissed my hair as he went out to school. It was like a benediction.

Another boy of this period was A H Elt, whose recollections are clear about the delights of his years:

GAW conducted a French course by the then no means universal 'direct' method, not a word of English being uttered in class, thus grounding me in a language I like to think I still speak with some fluency. He also devised and had printed a leaflet – *Wathen's Symbols for Correcting English Composition* – with signs for various defects of style, such as '1d' – for turgid, or penny-a-line journalistic writing. Another novel feature for the senior boys was a class known as Civics, to which Major Williams would bring a copy of the day's *Times* and comment on some item of news.

When we travelled to games, there was a charge for the fare, as there was also for dinner and tea. At the beginning of the day the form master would call for what were known as the 'DIT's which stood for Dinner, Iter (journey) and Tea.

Of the masters, outstanding was Copinger, intensely religious (no unseemly pursuits on Sundays), a staunch Conservative, and for some reason known to, and addressed by, us the boys as 'Famous', a soubriquet he did nothing to discourage. Among the boys of my time, Frank Byers later became Lord Byers. Another, Michael Ayrton, achieved fame and distinction in many spheres of artistic expression, particularly as a painter and sculptor. He was in fact Michael Ayrton Gould; his father was for many years literary editor of *The Observer*, whilst his mother was a leading figure in the affairs of the Labour Party and an MP just after the war. Peter

> Fraser, another friend of mine, was the son of the novelist Ronald Fraser.

Harrison Elt was a scholar at Highgate, before pursuing a business career in the City. Retired in 1976 to Blackheath, he recalls that his mother used to send the school a cheque each year for the *A E Prize* for original writing. The evidence of the magazine suggests that it was not sent for very long after his departure.

There was seldom any danger that Hall boys might remain so happily and laudably immersed in the life of school that they failed to be aware of the wider world outside. Quite apart from their upbringing in energetic Hampstead, the policy of the school seems always to have aimed to keep boys aware of current affairs. A newcomer in 1932 was P H Venn, who recalls various events, signficant and trivial alike.

> One incident I recall at this time, which shows how history in the making goes by unnoticed – it would have been in January1933 – was when Major Williams told us that there had been a change of government in Germany. He pronounced it 'Nahrzionelle Zozialiste', attempting to sound like a German. Little did we realise .... Later we were all taken by train to Portsmouth for the Spithead Review. There seemed to be interminable lines of warships and we were firmly of the opinion that Britian and the Empire could easily defeat the rest of the world with one hand tied. I remember – it must have been a year later – when we were all marched to the John Barnes shop in Finchley Road to see television when it first started. There was a tiny screen in a huge cabinet, with a picture which flickered all the time. This was yet another epoch-making memory from my youth!
>
> I had a number of friends – Darke, the son of Harold Darke, the organist, Gordon Hadfield, who became an orthopaedic surgeon in Bristol, Peter Howes, the son of Bobby Howes the actor. I also remember Clement Freud when he was at The Hall, and many others.

Paul Venn qualified as a doctor, and after military service, settled in Sussex and became a consultant anaesthetist, as well as father-in-law of the daughter of his class-mate, Victor Levison.

GAW was universally regarded as a truly liberal educationalist, and liberal attitudes were inspired in many of the boys. One such benificiary, later to emerge, after a slight shift in his viewpoint, as a conservative MP and Chairman of the Monday Club, was Harold Soref.

> I took an active part in school debates and at the time I was a keen and active Liberal. The only contemporary of mine to become a

Liberal politician was Frank Byers, although at the time, he was an outstanding athelete, only interested in sport. Major Williams had been a Liberal MP, and the liberal tradition was exemplified by the keen support for the League of Nations Union, of which I was always suspicious. Of course, Mr Robin Gladstone was also a descendant of the famous Prime Minister.

Another Old Boy of the 1930s who enjoyed those seemingly halcyon years was Sir Nigel Foulkes, who confirms this judgement of GAW as a liberal influence, in its broadest sense.

GAW was a fitness freak. I have vivid memories of his presiding over a dormitory of small boys for PT first thing in the morning, full of energy, clad in a diminutive bathing 'slip' – a vanished Edwardian version of the bikini – urging the reluctant children to greater efforts in the cold early morning: a lasting impression of boisterous energy and geniality. I seem to remember he frequently broke into French on these occasions.

Another dormitory memory – the 'Indian Boy'. As a special treat, he would occasionally respond to our shrill requests for his rendering of a dramatic dialogue between himself, (when principal of Khalsa College, Amritsar) and a pupil about to be caned for some offence. 'Oh, sir, please do the Indian Boy!' GAW played both parts – a series of magisterial admonitions to the boy, punctuated by falsetto screams as the cane descended, and eloquent pleas for a remission of sentence. The whole was of course in Hindustani. It was immensely popular, and the noise simply deafening.

In recollection, he was a man of huge energy and enthusiasm; a born teacher and, I would guess, a very good picker of other teachers. The academic standards of The Hall were impressive. In the classroom he had the gift of putting boys at their ease and getting them to learn without anxiety. As a housemaster he seemed very large but not frightening; there was, I think, something of the child in him. He commanded our respect but we thought of him almost as one of us – quite different from the other adults around him. I have always understood that the character of Fielding in E M Forster's *Passage to India* was partly inspired by him. I wouldn't be surprised.

Major Williams was the housemaster when I moved to the Senior School. A former gunner in the Regular Army and Liberal MP, he was tall, thin, quietly humorous, laconic, disciplined. The two men could not have been more different in style. I remember both with gratitude. Though not by profession a schoolmaster, Ronald

> Williams left his mark, giving us a precocious interest in the adult world of politics, crime, war and science, which all came in handy later. He ran a very happy house at Crossfield Road. He was blessed with a vivacious and affectionate wife, Cicely, whom we all loved.
>
> In hindsight, GAW was what nowadays would be called a liberal. The combination of exuberant skill as a schoolmaster and the traditional framework of an urban preparatory school produced, I think, a remarkable education for us – an orderly framework within which we enjoyed freedom of thought and action. You can't ask for anything better.

Sir Nigel went on to Gresham's School and to Balliol, and after service in the RAF, spent a long and distinguished career in industry and in public service, variously running Rank Xerox and the Civil Aviation Authority.

Michael Rubinstein qualified as a highly distinguished solicitor, whilst his brother, Hilary, became a noted literary agent. The former was asked to submit a description of his experiences at The Hall as part of a project by the Camden Historical Society. A pertinent extract follows. It includes a reference to one deeply painful episode, remembered only by those at the school at the time, an episode which for a time shook local confidence in The Hall.

> When I was at The Hall, we were fortunate in having GAW as Headmaster. He was a genuinely friendly father-figure, who conveyed his spirit of goodwill to the boys and the staff alike.
>
> The sanction of corporal punishment in English preparatory schools was universal in those days but at The Hall only the Headmaster exercised the right to inflict it and although I am sure that occasionally recalcitrant boys were whacked I did not encounter that punishment until I went to St Paul's School (then in Hammersmith) where it taught me invaluable lessons, notably that life can be grossly unfair and never to own up to anything.
>
> At The Hall, however, it did apparently get GAW into terrible trouble. There was a scandalous trial of which all I know is that a committee of parents was formed to support him and at the end he was acquitted. Two of the three boys involved in the case were brothers, unpopular for being generally obstreperous and aggressive, and no-one was sorry to see them go. GAW's return completely exonerated him from whatever he had been accused of and was greeted with relief as a vindication of British justice.
>
> One of the many pleasures which I first encountered at The Hall was scouting. My first camp was memorable because it rained and I had gone without a mackintosh. I had deeply impressed on me the relevance of the motto, *Be Prepared*! We used to gather for our

weekly meeting on Hampstead Heath on Saturday mornings. There we played games, generally 'fighting', either ankle tapping with our staves or with a woollen band tied round the upper arm to be snapped by the victor in a tussle. When I resumed scouting at St Paul's, I was sure that its training in initiative and self-reliance was more valuable than the Officer Training Corps which others joined.

As I know from my experience of a smaller prep school I had attended previously, The Hall under GAW was a happy school. I can remember no bullying by masters and hardly any between boys either – perhaps in consequence. For a period one of the boys in my class frequently broke down and cried for no apparent reason. Later it transpired that his father had been guilty of frauds and had involved his son in one of them at least. I do not believe the boy was shunned or treated otherwise than with sympathy when he was, as we later learned, desperately worried about his father's forthcoming trial. I think he left by the time the trial was making the newspaper headlines.

In retrospect I can recognise the disadvantages of a hot-house private prep school education for boys. We were fortunate at The Hall to enjoy a friendly, liberal atmosphere without any sacrifice of the academic pressures essential if we were to make the grade and pass the necessary entrance exams into our chosen public schools. Yet this was achieved with a curriculum which enabled the pupils to experiment in a variety of recreational activities *and* to complete virtually all their 'home work' within the school timetable. The Hall of fifty years ago gave me an experience of such an institution at its best. I cannot be sure that it was responsible for sowing the seeds of such wisdom as I now possess but it certainly provided a nourishing seed-bed.

The last memoir of the pre-war era comes from E G Cohen, who went on to Harrow, and after war service in the Far East, to Jesus College, Cambridge, before a career in business. His seven years at The Hall ended in 1940, and hence he became an evacuee to Claydon House.

When I arrived for my first day at The Hall in September 1932, I had to be carried in, in tears. I was nearly in tears again in April 1940 when my last day arrived and it was time to say my good-byes at Claydon House.

Over and above a profusion of personal memories is the sense of having been to a really well-run, disciplined but tolerant school, which tried to bring out the best in everyone from the most academic to the less gifted; which tried to win its matches but didn't put games players on a pedestal; and which liked its academic success but tried to turn out a rounded individual.

Mr Wathen formed round him a team of excellent masters, two of whom I got to know well. 'Famous' Copinger was the housemaster of Blue, my house, a keen Lancastrian, with a great sense of humour. Rotherham was an even keener Yorkshireman, an outstanding cricket and soccer coach, who loved us to win our matches, but not at any cost. He instilled the will to win, believing that what mattered was effort and guts. On those rare occasions when Yorkshire lost a County Championship match in the 1930s, we would tremble before and during his lessons the next day! The supporting cast of Dodd, who taught French so well that I knew more at 13 than I did at 16, Clair and Millard, who both became headmasters, Castle and Fyson – an incredibly strong team. And at the Junior, there was Miss Gladstone maintaining an easy authority. One's early learning couldn't have been in better hands.

So many memories come flooding back. The caretaker, Roberts, playing cricket and soccer with us in the yard; singing *Let us with a Gladstone mind* and other hymns at the Junior; speaking English in a French lesson and having to put *un sou dans la boite de charité*; the Reading Overs, awaited longingly or with dread. Above all, one remembers the boys – the Shaffer twins and John Schlesinger, Clement Freud and Greville Janner, Anthony Sampson, who all became eminent in their various fields; Tony van Gelder, destined to be killed on the Italian front and Gordon Langner, to die from a germ picked up in a liberated concentration camp, and many, many others.

Perhaps my strongest memories are of my last two terms at Claydon House, where Mr Wathen and the staff made such valiant attempts to keep the school going in most difficult circumstances, including an incredibly cold, snowy spell lasting many weeks. On a visit to Claydon House many years later I said to one of the Verney family, whose property it is, that I hoped The Hall boys hadn't done too much damage. 'Far from it', he replied, 'but the girls' school that followed you really wrecked the place!'

PART IV: MEMORIES AND REMINISCENCES

Chapter 2
1939 to the present

Few people at the time seemed to notice the significance of the year 1939 in the history of The Hall. Most would be forgiven for their rather greater concern with affairs on the European stage and beyond. These of course seriously impinged upon the life of the school, swamping any thoughts of a fiftieth birthday celebration. A closer scrutiny of the school prospectus of the time would offer another explanation for this omission: it clearly attributes the foundation to 1884! No obvious explanation for this error exists, other than perhaps the false supposition that a school which did exist in Buckland Villas (no longer standing) and which was also called the Belsize School was the precursor of The Hall. The Wrottesley family are quite clear on this point. F J Wrottesley's establishment was founded in 1889 in Buckland Crescent and had absolutely no connection with any previous institution of the same name. So, 1939 was indeed the Golden Jubilee.

If the minds of The Hall staff were fully occupied with ensuring the survival of their charges in the face of mass bombing and other horrors of modern warfare, the young seem to have been blissfully innocent of any real sense of impending disaster, if their memories, even in extended retrospect are anything to go by. It is with the recollections of the evacuation to the country that this chapter opens. Here was high drama indeed, an exciting break with routine, offering enticing possibilities of a total breakdown of schooling. J A Lemkin was nearing the end of his time at The Hall, and hence enjoyed to the full the thrill of both the projected evacuations.

> With great prescience GAW had made arrangements in the summer of 1938 to evacuate the school, and as the international crisis hotted up, families were contacted with a view to Hall boys reporting to school on a Saturday and then embarking in charabancs to be transported down for the start of the Autumn term. I said *au revoir* to my parents. I had planned to have tea with a friend and travel down with him. I remember vividly we were having tea in his father's comfortable study and in the corner was a wireless. We

switched it on in time to hear Chamberlain's voice from Heston on his return from Germany when he made his famous 'peace with honour' speech. Shortly after this The Hall was in touch by telephone and our trip was cancelled – though some boys did actually get to Codford.

A year later, it was for real. My mother and I motored from our home in Sussex to Claydon for the first day of term. It was not my first experience of boarding – I had been a boarder at The Hall in 1937 when my parents had gone on a long trip to South Africa – but as we turned up the long drive a chill came over me. The house was gaunt and the drive in the late afternoon was empty apart from a number of baa-ing sheep. However, the house was light and well occupied by boys.

Because the main staircase was roped off in case we damaged it, we had to walk down long passages to reach our rooms. Some of these were a bit scary at dusk and in the evening. The cellars were soon open, both for a chemistry lab and as a rifle range but boys found a number of coffins of Verney ancestors down there and used to dare each other to walk round them. This gave rise to two ghost stories.

The first concerned Mr Millard who had been deputed by GAW to open up the house before term and had I think slept alone in it. He had woken up in the middle of the night to hear a terrible grinding noise which he could not understand. With considerable courage he had walked the length of the house only to find that a cow was rubbing its hide against the wall! The other story was told us by a member of the family who gave us a lecture on the house and the Verneys. His distinguished ancestor, Sir Edmund Verney, had been Charles I's standard bearer at the Battle of Edgehill. He clutched the Royal Standard so firmly that the Parliamentarian soldiers had to hack off his hand at the wrist. This flag was restored to the family many years later, and was there in the saloon – one of the large public rooms – when The Hall arrived. We were told that on the anniversary of Edgehill the hand would appear clutching the pole supporting the standard. The saloon was used as a dormitory and one boy claimed he had woken in the night, seen the hand and on checking next morning had discovered that the date – October 23 – was the anniversary of the battle.

That winter was very cold and there was snow through much of the Lent term. I broke my foot and had to be taken to the Radcliffe Hospital at Oxford by the splendid matron, Lady Patterson-Ross, wife of the distinguished doctor, Sir James Patterson-Ross, and mother of two contemporaries of mine at The Hall, who subsequently also became celebrated doctors.

> Two final memories. Grace on the December day that the news of the sinking of the *Graf Spee* arrived was altered to: 'For what we are about to receive thank God and the Royal Navy'. And PT on the lawn during the snow in early 1940, at 7.15 am, the parade overshadowed by two or three great cedars, and GAW, dressed in a kimono, vigorously enjoying it, even if the boys did not.

Regular mention has been made in these pages of E V Millard. His daughter, who witnessed these war-time evacuations, later had the good sense to marry the young master who was to take over the school which evolved from the departure of The Hall from Hampstead, Long Close School. Her account of these days now follows:

> As my father was the Scoutmaster for The Hall Troop and had taken many boys on camp, some of the parents asked him whether he would take their boys into the country to get away from the bombs. This was how it came that he led the evacuation to Claydon.
>
> I was an only child and I suppose was lucky to have so many boys as companions. I remember performing *Peter Pan* in the drawing room, and finding sheep and cows grazing right outside the windows of our cottage in the grounds. We had no electricity, and I remember my mother having to learn to trim the oil lamps and give me a hip bath by the kitchen fire. I still recall the names of some of those Hall boys.
>
> We returned to London for a while, but when the bombing started in earnest, my father was asked, yet again, to take boys into the country. This time he was helped by a colleague from The Hall, Miss Barrett, whose aunt was principal of an agricultural college near Oxford. Thus it was that my father took just six boys and established a branch of The Hall at Waterperry. Shortly after he had to move out. He found a house called The Long Close in Farnham Royal, and obtained GAW's blessing to make the final break with Hampstead and set up his own school. We moved in on 24th June 1941. It was a very hot day, and we were all feeling quite exhausted, when a huge bowl of strawberries and a jug of cream arrived. It was from our very near neighbours, another prep school, Caldicott. We existed there until the end of the war when we moved to Slough.

A further reminiscence from Claydon days is provided by another Old Boy who also, like Lemkin, became a parent of sons at The Hall. Stephen Danos was a representative of the signficant group among Hall boys who were recent refugees from troubled Europe and often referred to as 'Mr Wathen's International Zoo'.

My first memories of the school all had to be about the great informality of the place, as compared with schools in Hungary. Even then, masters were called by their nicknames – unheard of on the Continent. Some seemed more fierce than others. We all had a feeling of reverence towards W H Copinger, who even then seemed very old, as against a more familiar attitude to E V Millard – 'Millie' I think we called him. I do remember a gorgeous matron, a young woman we called 'Snow White', who introduced me to dripping on toast with Marmite!

I moved to Claydon, a dreadful place. Oddly enough, I seem to have forgotten everything about the classes; my main memory is of my hunger. I think I must have been hungry every day of my life at Claydon and used to get very envious when boys with parents in England received food parcels. At night, everything was blacked out, and I slept in a huge dormitory. I remember one night when I had to go and spend a penny. I found my way into the hall, where I got totally disorientated. The floor was of some porous kind of sandstone, and in the end I couldn't contain myself any longer ...

I tried to find my way back, but in the end had to shout for help. GAW eventually came with a torch and took me back. Imagine my humiliation the next day when my footsteps were firmly visible in the puddles I'd made!

My best friend was John Gilbert, who for a while went to work for another friend, Paul Hamburger, better known as Paul Hamlyn, the publisher. There was 'Pokey' Cole, whose father was Professor G D H Cole, and there was the comedian Bud Flanagan's son, in whose slipper I put a stink bomb. I had never seen a stink bomb; they didn't have such things in Hungary. He stepped on it and got blood poisoning. At assembly the next day, GAW referred to 'a boy of foreign extraction' doing this terrible thing, and had his parents not lived abroad, he would certainly have been expelled. Bud junior died a few years back of leukaemia, and I've often wondered ....

My memories of being back in London centre around air raids. In class, I would pray for an alarm if some bad lesson was in progress; my prayers were often answered. During raids, we slept in the Junior School, in what is now the library, which had been reinforced with girders. When a bomb struck some houses just across the road, the light shone through the ventilation brick on to a girder, making it appear as if it were buckling.

I have other memories: learning the school song. I wonder how many of us knew what '.... it's a call to the sluggard' really meant. I didn't. It took me years to understand that the 'Altiora' in the chorus referred to the public schools.* I remember the blazer and cap and it

* See Appendix 1, *Carmina Aulariensia*, page 225

is to be regretted that the rule to wear them is relaxed now. I remember the bomb which hit the block of buildings right at the bottom of Fitzjohn's Avenue. There was a greengrocer there where we used to buy huge, juicy pears for a penny each ..... there, I'm back to food again.

By his second marriage, Danos has had two sons at The Hall. The war has generated a host of experiences which remain most vividly in the memories of those who stayed in Hampstead. Of these, Peter Woolf gives a particularly graphic account of this emotive period.

It was the Luftwaffe which caused me to join The Hall. In 1940, they dropped bombs on our road when aiming for Hendon Aerodrome, and my parents, with a logic that escapes me, decided to move right into the centre of London, to Regent's Park. Thus, I entered Lower One, then located in the Senior School, and at the end of my first term my progress was crowned with immediate success – a prize. This was notable because it was the only tangible recognition of my entire scholastic career.

It must be appreciated that these years were a period of severe restriction and deprivation, especially in respect of food, books and travelling. In addition, there were particularly bad spells of daytime alerts and bombing which sent us bounding down the stairs to the makeshift shelters.

When it became clear that the war would carry on for some considerable time, it was necessary to introduce a system of rationing of stationery. Pencils and rubbers were carefully checked by Miss Large who entered them in her ledger and we were expected to write on both sides of the paper before a new issue was allowed.

Rationing was affecting what we wore, what we ate and how we lived. Everything seemed to have coupons of one sort or another. The simple pleasures of to-day, which we take so readily for granted, such as fruit, ice-cream and chocolates, were not freely available and later on even bread was rationed so that boys, hungry after a day at school, could not find enough to satisfy their hunger in the shops on the way home and even, when they reached home, the disciplines of restraint were necessarily imposed, bringing home to us the handicaps of living on an island. School lunches, I recall, remained of a particularly high quality. Lining up for second helpings was a definite feature which GAW would announce, giving first place to those who had a birthday or the victorious football and cricket teams, to the cheers of those who recognised that excellence deserved a better deal than they had to accept.

I also recall hanging my gas-mask on my clothes-peg but never having to use it except in practices, against attacks which were considered possible in 1940 and 1941. I also remember the barrage balloon which was sited at the corner of the cricket field, often a loose heap of silvery fabric on the ground but more often filled with gas and flying high over the field. The RAF was in charge of it.

Recreation was dependent upon whether anybody possessed a tennis ball or not. Tennis balls were essential for playing football or cricket in the playground and they had to be returned to a master at the end of break. Some were accidentally kicked over the fence into the neighbour's garden, alas, never to be seen again!

In order to understand to the full what The Hall represented to its boys one has to acknowledge the strong personality and brilliant organisation of Gerrard Anstruther Wathen and his seasoned team of masters. As headmaster GAW totally dominated the school in every aspect. He towered above us, devoting enormous energy and time in making his relatively small school an important establishment to be recognised by the public schools to which his boys would be going, and by his eminent contacts who were invited to give lectures or make presentations. GAW was a brilliant communicator who loved talking, especially to boys. During lunch he would blow his whistle for silence and then keep us abreast of world affairs or other interesting topics. He often spoke of his times in India and I remember him walking into the school and sadly showing me the newspaper on the day Gandhi was assassinated. All the boys admired GAW – initials many, I am afraid, learnt to forge expertly on their fake excuse notes. In all the time I knew him he was plagued with ill-fitting false teeth which shot out when he became over-excited or very cross.

Sport continued but we were not able to wear whites for cricket and an odd assortment of clothes began to appear. The masters tried hard to keep us in pink blazers and in the correct gear or uniform for cricket, football and scouting but it became increasingly difficult and standards lapsed for some, while others managed to get hold of second-hand items and looked immaculate in comparison.

Our parents were involved either in the armed forces or in government work. We had to get about by ourselves, usually by bus. The services were more frequent than today and moved more quickly because there were fewer vehicles to cause congestion on the roads. The Underground also provided a good service getting people to and from work and everybody had that indomitable spirit boosted by Churchill's speeches, a forceful press and radio and the Movietone News at the cinemas showing films depicting bravery and daring. Sometimes, when the bombing became so constant and threatening, we would spend the night on the platform at Maida

Vale Station, although I had my doubts as to whether or not this was the wisest course in the event of a near hit which would have trapped us all. But we lived very close to Primrose Hill and Regent's Park which had large gun-emplacements and the noise of the guns shook our building and, of course, meant that the area was a marked target for bombing. Our parents had to fulfil their duties as fire-watchers and frequently they stayed out all night, leaving us to read or listen to Tommy Handley on the radio.

At school we were encouraged to go to Lord's where, if GAW saw us, he would give us a shilling each. We played our games of 'conkers' in the autumn but most other things seemed unobtainable and I regard that time as particularly dull. We would go train-spotting, or fishing from one of the bridges over the Regent's Park Canal and shrapnel-collecting after the previous night's raid. Every evening we put up our black-out shutters and frequently a bomb would affect the power supply, plunging us into darkness with only candles to brighten the gloom but with no heat against the cold or to dry us from the rain. Even water for baths was rationed and each bath had a measure beyond which it was considered unpatriotic to fill it.

So between the ages of five and ten I went to school, sometimes past buildings which had been demolished the night before and where the fire-brigade and rescue services were still in attendance. At school the lessons went on and we learned as best we could. Boys were recruited to be cleaners or librarians or to carry out some other service for the good of the school. If a father had the influence to obtain some special treat, GAW would see we got it. I recall the first time, thanks to Mackenzie's father who owned the Chicken Inn restaurants, we had ice-cream at lunch. The excitement was electric.

From the age of eight I spent my holidays in the country. I was evacuated to a 'holiday school' where we were able to enjoy games without the constant reminder of the war and where food was in better supply. I had a bicycle then and that was a real luxury, enabling me to enjoy the country and later London more freely.

What struck me most during the war years was the spirit of the people and their single-minded purpose to do their best for their country. We boys gave our pocket-money to National Savings, collected ship half-pennies for sailors and even prepared tea and bread and butter for servicemen billeted in flats near our home. Our faith in God seemed to play a large part in our lives. At The Hall our spirit never flagged because GAW never allowed us to think anything but positively and I shall always remember the joy when the war was over.

Peter Woolf was to qualify as a chartered accountant with Price Waterhouse, in Paris, before switching to senior management posts with Total Oil and then running his own business, appropriately in view of the elegance of his writing, restoring and repairing pens! Ted Harris also endured the war years and confirms the impression that, despite being so near the centre of a capital city under aerial bombardment, the school managed to shelter its pupils rather effectively from most of the grimmer realities of the blitz.

> I was at The Hall from 1940 until 1949 throughout most of the war. I think I must have joined the school just as they came back after their abortive evacuation trip and was proud to have been there throughout the danger period. I remember one day that we counted 34 boys in the whole school, the rest not having been able to make the journey due to bombardment. As a child I loved the war and found it very exciting and I cannot remember ever being frightened. My father used to take me out in the middle of the blitz to see the bombs exploding and the searchlights. I cannot think of any more exciting time in my life.
>
> The fun the next day on the way to school was to find the shrapnel. You had to be careful that you didn't pick up dogs droppings but after a while you were able to discern one from the other. If one was able to find a piece of shrapnel with writing on, it was worth more, and if you could find a bomb fragment with German writing on, that was worth even more still! All of these were proudly exhibited in the playground on arrival.
>
> Most of my reminiscences of The Hall are of being rather naughty. I confess I was a naughty boy although I would like to feel I wasn't wicked. The main punishments were detention or whacking and if one did not attend detention and absented oneself one was automatically whacked the following morning. I can well remember in the evening finding that one was going to be kept in and that the sound of leather on willow was far too hard to resist and opting for the whacking the next morning. These were painful but short and sharp and I think there was no grudge given or felt. I remember the injustice of being whacked for something I didn't do and trying to trade it off as a credit for a future whacking that I was due for something I certainly had done: sadly, this didn't work.
>
> Mr Wathen for whom we all had great affection was recognised by us even as young as we were as a character. He had a strange habit of beckoning one to him using the outstretched palm of his hand facing upwards and beckoning with all fingers joined together. If the hand was pointing upwards, it was good news, but if he beckoned you with his hand pointing downwards it was rather like

> the Roman Emperor at the Christian Games, it was bad news indeed and one was invariably whacked.
>
> One thing Mr Wathen didn't like was seeing boys sent out of the room and standing outside because they had misbehaved. I suppose he felt that since it was a fee-paying school the parents weren't really getting good value for money. He used to resolve the problem by correcting the boy whenever he saw him standing outside the room, despatching four sharp whacks and then sending him back into the class. I remember standing outside one of the classrooms in the Long Gallery and trying to press myself in the corner knowing full well that my punishment was about to be sharply curtailed. Cur*tailed* with the emphasis on the tail being the word of the moment.
>
> I had the privilege and the dubious pleasure of living two roads away from the school. This meant that I was able to get to school early and enjoy myself with my friends in the playground. I remember enjoying myself so much that one half term I turned up to school only to be bitterly disappointed that the school was closed.
>
> I remember walking down Finchley Road in the holidays wearing my blazer, eating an ice-cream and being spotted by the Headmaster. Sure enough the first day of term I was summoned to him and was beaten for disgracing the uniform by eating an ice-cream in public. Even to this day 40 years later if ever I am on holiday and we buy an ice-cream I still eat it cringing in shop doorways for fear Mr Wathen may walk by and see me and consider that I am a disgrace.

Harris became an engineer, his business often taking him to France. His francophile attitude he largely attributes to the grounding The Hall gave him.

Many Old Boys have recalled their memories of events during the blitz, which is hardly to be wondered at. A Churchillian tone of stout defiance is evident in every line. John Prideaux did not enter the school until 1951, but he writes:

> I can remember my father telling me that the standard reply, on picking up the telephone during the war, was 'Hall School still standing', after which the caller would be asked if there was anything else he or she wished to know. The standard instructions for air raids were that, at the first warning the boys were to move to the edge of the form-room and teaching continued and then, with the danger becoming imminent, boys were made to lie flat on their faces.

Mrs Barron amplifies this by observing that when the siren sounded, boys would drop to the floor and continue their work *underneath* their desks. It did not improve their handwriting, but it showed that the school was not to be interrupted by the antics of the Luftwaffe.

Dr W J Jory was another war-time pupil:

> There were few of us at the school but this had two distinct advantages. In a class of only three boys my statistical chances of being top increased, and when not in school the streets were almost deserted and became our neighbourhood football pitch. Only air raids – and class – interrupted our routine, and at night we five boarders slept on bunks in a basement room at the Senior School.
>
> We woke one night with the smell of burning, and a red glow in the corridor. There was the usual noise of an air raid, with distant explosions, and the occasional crack of the Naval 4.7″ gun on Primrose Hill. Apart from that, we had heard nothing but having woken we wondered if the school was on fire. We were not encouraged to go wandering around at night and it seemed ages before the Headmaster appeared in his dressing-gown. 'It's all right,' Mr Wathen told us, 'just a fire across the road.' We went back to sleep. In the morning we looked across Crossfield Road. The fine house on the corner was just a pile of bricks, smoke still drifting up out of the rubble, struck by a 1,000lb bomb. We weren't too impressed. Twenty yards closer and we would have had the day off school, and anyway we had to mark new goal posts on our street football pitch.

The Hall, doubtless in company with all other schools, refused to adopt a passive role. Much though they might have wanted to, they could not man the guns, but they could raise the money to buy them. Patrick McNair-Wilson, with his brother, also to enter politics and become an MP, was a war pupil.

> During the war, schools throughout the country were encouraged to assist the war effort in a multiplicity of ways.
>
> One such was a slogan competition organised by the Hampstead Borough Council in 1941. The aim of the competition was to find a slogan which could be used to help raise money to pay for a new vessel for the Royal Navy.
>
> The ship chosen was HMS *Quilliam.*
>
> The Hall was invited to take part, and as an eleven year-old at that time and being taught by that most British of teachers, Mr Rotherham, I decided to try my poetic luck.
>
> Not perhaps surprisingly there was considerable interest, and I was therefore delighted to find that I had won with the slogan 'Three quarters of a million will pay for the *Quilliam*'.
>
> Clearly ships in those days were relatively cheap, but my £1 prize in the shape of a savings certificate seemed to be a substantial reward.

With the war over, the numbers of boys rose again, and perhaps significantly, the recollections of Old Boys seem even more plentiful. Gavin Ross, member of the 'Class of '46', subsequently moved through the conventional route of scholarships to Westminster and Trinity College, Cambridge, via National Service in the RAF, to the world of computing and technical aid and advice in agriculture to the Third World. With all the authority of forty years of retrospection, grounded in that liberalism that The Hall has never decried, he comes to voice doubts and irreverences that may in fact be a measure of his affection for his old school. His political sympathies lie with the less favoured but he has positive and vivid recollections which would seem to suggest a lasting respect for all that it did for him. His views on the lessons he had in French provide a rather contrary interpretation to that just expressed.

I hear a jumble of voices:

– Levez-vous mes camarades et restez debout jusqu'a ce que le Directeur dit 'Asseyez-vous!'

– One more squeak out of you and I'll send you straight for the Detention Book!

– Come on, you old women!

– Lord behold us with thy blessing, once again assembled here ...

– There's a motto that rings in the ears of all ...

– Paish-Trevor-Jay-Griller-Landry-Dove-Bairnsfather-Rea-Price-Marshall-Nedas-Cotton-Himsworth-Hawkes-Whale-Myring-Ross!

★ ★ ★

Being asked by James Earle to put on my pink blazer and cap once more, and to write an essay on *The Class of '46*, or *The Unhappiest Days of My Life*, how can I refuse? The 'powers that be' that glower on us may not approve, but they cannot control our thoughts. Two points lost to Orange House, I'm afraid, one for untidiness, one for non-conformity.

I was sent for just a term to the Junior School and placed in the top class. Being a new boy in it was a curious experience. The work was relatively easy, some of it repeating what I had learnt before. But you were expected to know all about the place and nobody told you anything, not even where the toilets were. It was such a highly organised place – marks, roll calls and crocodile marches – and staff with imposing names: Gladstone, Noble, Barron, Earle – quite coincidental of course, but it made quite an impression.

Of that term I remember mainly the dinners in the 'Hot Pot', that underground room nearby, and the melée in the playground, with an enormous blank wall of the adjoining house against which we threw our balls. Mr Barron was the most jovial figure, we had some good fun-lessons with him: 'I draw a triangle LMN, no, that's too elementary – shall I call it PQR, or is that a bit peculiar?'

Next term I was promoted to Middle 4 of the Senior School and said goodbye to my friends. Here I was much younger than the rest and was very shy. For the next three terms I was promoted again, ending up in Upper 5B. While this did not matter for Latin, which seemed to be the school's main concern, for other subjects the effect was chaotic; either I was doing the same subjects again and again in history and geography, or I was expected to know things I had missed out on.

The spring of 1947 was very cold, and epidemics took their toll – sometimes there were only five boys in a class. An icy slide in the playground ended in a brick wall – its use was banned after someone got concussion. School meals were nourishing, in spite of rationing – the custard was rather thin, of course. A well-wisher from down-under sent some lamb carcases – I was surprised how quickly we disposed of the them. Lunch in the billiard room under the stern eye of Mr Rotherham was an ordeal at first – arbitrary punishments were meted out for minor indiscretions.

Mr Blishen was the most interesting teacher at that time. He encouraged imaginative writing and was in tune with the boy's interests. He is of course now a successful author and has penned his own memories of that period.* But I was moved up again, and had Mr Mayhew instead. Mr Mayhew did not seem to appreciate our sense of humour, and we soon began to tease him mercilessly. He did try to teach us structure in writing: an arresting opening, logical development and a good summing up. Apart from one or two lessons from him, writing as a craft was never taught – it was probably something else I missed out on. Perhaps he was not happy with us, for he left a year or two later, to the Latin epigram: 'Vale Mayhew, May You Fare Well!'

Arriving in Upper 5B in autumn 1947, I was at last stretched and out of my depth. The first to discover this was the irascible Mr Prideaux, to whom I owe an unexpected debt. We were given some graph paper and told to draw a graph of some function. I had not a clue what we were supposed to do, so just made a large J shape in the middle of the page, a bit like one of the book illustrations. The blue pencil came out: 'Don't you know how to draw graphs?' – 'No, sir' – 'Then you shouldn't be in this form!' Since my teacher apparently had no intention of explaining what was wrong, I felt very low, and spent a long time staring at the book illustration. Then it clicked,

* See page 100

and I found you could not only draw graphs given a formula, but also discover the formula given the graph.

Since my later research career has been particularly related to fitting curves to data, this incident has a certain piquancy. Equally important was the discovery that in maths, at least, you did not have to wait for the teacher to explain something: the textbooks could be read and understood in advance. The other boys thought this a most immoral practice, but as I acquired some books on recreational mathematics the subject became a bit of an obsession.

It was soon clear that we were the scholarship stream: the idiosyncratic form numbering could not disguise the fact that some were destined for the top, others for Common Entrance (how low that sounded) or worse (the eleven-plus). Intellectual snobbery was compounded with social snobbery. Whether the obsession with marks and competitiveness really helped those who couldn't keep the pace, I doubt: it probably just bred inferiority feelings. The curriculum was highly distorted towards scholarship-passing: Latin, Greek, maths, French and history. English and geography were light relief, science, art, music and current affairs non-existent. A chance encounter with a beautifully illustrated book of human anatomy revealed a whole fascinating world outside the curriculum: encyclopedias and hobby books were my real education at this time, and the fantastic world of newpapers. (I often bought an evening paper to read on the bus home).

School games were an extension of the same authorities: crocodile marches to Lymington Road and later, journeys to Wembley Park. In football I had two left feet, and later became linesman, and finally caterer (providing bits of lemon at half time). In cricket I scored six runs in all, comprising four overthrows (the throw that was to run me out missed and proceeded to the boundary), and two accidental runs; my best stroke cost Himsworth a front tooth. So I became scorer instead, and enjoyed forming patterns of six dots and converting them to M or W. My scoring skills developed from hours of practice with a six sided pencil rolled surreptitiously on the desk during Latin lessons: Denis Compton and Gavin Ross formed fantastic partnerships, scoring six after six against the incompetent bowling of Caesar, J and Virgil, P.

The gym periods at the Hampstead Baths in Finchley Road were a very different experience. We were under the care of those splendid men, Sergeant McMahon and Sergeant Pow and others whose names elude me. With memorable phrases they brought our intellectual pretensions down to earth. One thumped away on the old piano, and we marched past to the tune of old army favourites like *Underneath the lamplight, by the barrack gate* .... One day the pianist was ill, and we were asked to find a substitute. Breaking the deathly silence one horrid boy said 'Ross plays the piano' and I was hauled to the front and told to play. My repertoire was limited to Grade 4 pieces in triple time, and the only remotely suitable piece was *The Arrival of the Queen of Sheba*, which could be classified as a march for the first eight bars. When I reached the pianissimo interlude the march collapsed in confusion and I was dismissed on the spot: the beginning and end of my public career as a pianist. Our favourite was Sergeant Pow: when he left he gave us the memorable farewell: 'Boys of the 'All, I loves you all.'

There were occasional outbursts of mass hysteria. The victim would be chosen for no obvious reason, and I never knew who was the instigator, but at its height 'baiting' was cruel and terrifying as the victim fled from the mob, not knowing whether to seek protection from the staff or brazen it out. One incident made *Lord of the Flies* a very credible tale: here were the sons of professors and bankers rushing after a poor fat boy, who collapsed in exhaustion at the feet of a master. No doubt it was only play but I cannot forget the scene.

There was some anti-semitism, in spite of recent history, but it was more in the form of awareness that about half the boys were Jewish and half were not, and that on feast days school attendance was very thin. Scripture teaching was a little low-key, no doubt because of the sensitivity to the Jewish question. Perhaps an opportunity was missed to explain more about Jewish worship and observances, which otherwise seemed like incomprehensible superstitions. For instance, my sister was called into a house one Saturday and asked to light the gas: the lady was unwilling to 'make fire on the Sabbath' herself.

Political prejudice mainly came out at election time. In my innocence I said that my parents had voted Labour, only to find myself accused of the worst excesses of Joe Stalin. However I found allies, as Hampstead socialists were not yet ready to send their sons to state schools, and Jasper Ungoed-Thomas organised us with his John Bull printing set to make and distribute 'Vote Labour' slips into desks all over the school: no doubt he had committee-room experience at home. Our awareness of the arguments was limited: current affairs was in the hands of the Headmaster, whose homilies at assembly were rather obscure, but tended to be about the loss of the empire rather than the birth of the welfare state.

Sexual prejudice was total. With absolutely no contact with girls of the same age, and with sisters often relegated to the state system, the assumed superiority of the male was unquestioned. The only women in the place were Miss Harbord, who taught the lowest form, Miss Large, the Headmaster's secretary, and Matron, of whom I remember nothing but her departure, announced as follows by Mr Wathen: 'Matron has a job in a hospital, and a good job too!' We were sternly reprimanded for giggling at that one.

There was of course a rich culture of dirty stories, but we were sexual innocents, and did not appreciate their deeper humour until much later. Daring and prudishness were curiously mixed: one boy who could recite no end of risqué stories appeared very shocked by the pictures of Greek statues in our textbooks. I was accused of having a filthy book: a First Aid manual with diagrams.

On reaching Middle 6B and later Upper 6, I found the staff more human and approachable. Of course we were now 'top of the heap' and had some responsibilities. Mr Rotherham was no longer the furious avenger but a warm, likeable Yorkshireman who told us of another world up North where they played cricket but also mined coal, where back-to-back houses piled on top of each other up steep terraces in textiles towns, and rivers were stinking with chemicals. Geography was a dynamic subject where mountain ranges heaved up and storm flattened them: he would have enjoyed modern plate tectonics.

Mr Barnes, fresh from the Navy, had no respect for the old order: he widened our vocabulary more than our parents might have wished. He organised us to give talks and to produce a magazine using our own researched material. I had read a little book about spiders, which included the nugget of information that a spider weighing two pounds had been found by men working on the roof of Milan Cathedral. After giving my talk I was asked where the largest spiders in the world were to be found, and I replied without hesitation: 'In Milan Cathedral'. I never lived that one down.

Mr Wathen (Dub) we thought slightly mad, but he commanded authority as Headmaster. The strange rigmaroles in his French lessons only served to reinforce prejudices against the French, obviously a crazy race who went round greeting each other with 'On-y-en', screwing up their throats into impossible positions in the process. By teaching French as if it were like Latin, a network of tenses and parts of speech to be fitted together like a jigsaw, the sense of a living language was lost. Only with Mr Potts right at the start was French a means of communication, limited in scope, perhaps, but credible.

Mr Fyson (Billy) seemed as old as the Greeks and Romans he taught about. Latin and Greek were word games, not languages: we learnt the English equivalents of Latin words, but did not learn what those English words meant. We plodded through texts so slowly that we never found out what happened. A term never allowed us to finish *Alcestis* or *Medea*, nor to find out what Aeneas was supposed to be doing all the time. It was amazing to read the plays in translation in later life and discover how short they were: an hour or two on the stage, perhaps. In English as well, we tended to miss the ending of anything that was read in class: three acts of *As You Like It*, four of *Julius Caesar* – poor old Shakespeare never had a chance!

Mr Maclagan (Claggy) had the dual role of history master and Scoutmaster, and I can picture him better on parade than in class, trying to explain the Scout Law. While I was too immature for history and did not do very well at the time, he must have stimulated some interest in me. I could hang the facts on my mental calendar, but that was the only structure I could grasp, not the agonies of political decision-making, the enigmas of good and evil in the same personage, the problem of power. While the artist of the frieze around the hall had no doubts that history was propaganda, and the message was that Britain was a great nation peopled by heroes, and it was up to us chaps to keep it so, Mr Maclagan was perhaps sensitive that there was room for other points of view.

Of Mr Bathurst (Batty) I remember the distinguished beard rather like a Spanish portrait, and a quiet gentleman. The other staff, such as Mr Barron, I had less dealings with.

Having said that I missed out on science, art, school music, and other subjects which were not provided, I was also unaware of some of the facilities that were there, in particular the school library. In retrospect I would have welcomed more positive moves to encourage us to read widely, and to use public libraries. Some people learn about these things at home, but others need a bit of prodding.

* * *

The best educators were my friends, some of whom, coming from very cultured backgrounds, conveyed their enthusiasms and introduced me to different family settings.

Roger Whale was the younger son of the headmaster of Mill Hill School, and had the run of the place in the holidays. We explored the grounds and the swimming baths and had rather a wild time.

Nicholas Hawkes was the only son of Christopher and Jacquetta Hawkes, who lived in a fine house in a shabby street in Chalk Farm. Nicholas was looked after by Nanny, which made him the butt of teasing when he innocently divulged the fact, but as his parents were so often on site, excavating or writing, he was very much left to himself. He had a marvellous nursery, full of dartboards and bagatelle and other equipment I had not met before, and he knew all about archaeology. Later his parents separated and I once had tea in the Albany with J B Priestley, of whom I had never heard (such is life!).

Richard Gombrich arrived in the last year or so, bringing a living world of European culture, and appreciation of art and architecture. With a father like Professor Ernst Gombrich, director of the Warburg Institute, it would be difficult to be otherwise. Their home in Briardale Gardens was full of works of art, and I felt very gauche meeting them. I was offered sweetcorn as a starter at my first meal there, and told to begin; having no idea how to tackle it I prodded it with a fork – they laughed and used their fingers. I am not surprised to see Richard a professor of Sanskrit at Oxford, and taking a lead against the offering of honorary degrees to unsuitable recipients.

James Woodford lived in Hammersmith and was a boarder. His father was the sculptor of 'The Queen's Beasts' at the coronation and had a studio attached to the house. I remember James as a witty actor and mimic, rather shy but very kindly.

Michael Bacharach's father was the music critic, A L Bacharach, and Jasper Ungoed-Thomas's father was a Welsh Labour MP who became Solicitor-General.

Richard Rowlatt was another boy who was fairly unhappy about private education. He was asked which school he went to. He blushed. 'Eton, I'm afraid', he confessed. He was miserable about this, while his sisters went to the secondary modern.

I sometimes wonder how I would have coped in a broader and less specialised school. Was state education so bad at the time that all the expense was justified? Is it necessary to pressurize children by making them compete rather than co-operate in learning? Perhaps I seem to complain about problems that I would never have overcome anyway. And is it still like this, or is it all progressive, full of electronic gadgetry, science labs, socially aware and outward looking? Perhaps that is of no concern of mine now. But I wonder: did the fire damage that frieze? Do they still sing 'Stink in Altiora'?

Yes, Mr Ross, it did damage the frieze, and could you have seen it, or the sad last remnant of it, you would not have regretted its loss. And no, they don't sing 'Stink' – or even 'Hinc' – and I don't imagine you would regret that either. And would you begrudge your successors the science and technology which is now so familiar in schools?

A very personal picture from this period comes from another Hall scholar, the historian, Christopher Tyerman, Fellow of Exeter College, Oxford, who describes his debt to the school's teaching:

In retrospect, I realise we were exposed to an enormous amount of simple information – and retained some of it. The system was very rigorous, although I suppose we didn't notice it. In all things except sport (which may have pained some members of staff) it was an amazingly good school and the grounding I received there has served me in good stead ever since.

However one memory stands out because, in a sense, it is not a memory at all but remains part of me: the teaching and humane, worldly and wise personality of Ralph Bathurst. The physical picture of him is still clear; the pear-shape, the beard, the beret, the piece of saliva which always seemed to stick to the lip, the spectacles encrusted with chalk, the voice russet in tone, gentle yet emphatic. The world of the past was opened up and illuminated by 'Batty' not only through his seemingly effortless and endless stream of erudition, but by his approach, witty, slightly cynical, with an eye for the important and the colourful. He treated pupils, even in the Fours, as equals engaged in a pleasurable exercise of discovery.

Some, I expect, grew weary of the flow of facts, but even these were somehow charmed by his humanity. Keeping order was not his forte but, unlike others with the same problem, he had few difficulties because he radiated a feeling that he didn't really care too much for that side of the job and so he was difficult to rouse (which was usually the whole point of the operation as far as we were concerned). Above all, perhaps, he respected individuals and handled his pupils almost as adults, explaining not ordering, and holding what could be a fine temper as a potent last resort. What he taught me about how to look at the past, how to regard the world and myself, was immeasurable; he brought out much more than the mountains of information we were expected to know. His typed sheets of facts and interpretation on various central themes are remarkably good and a competition he ran including questions of fact and identification of quotations is positively shaming in showing how much I have forgotten in the last eighteen years. I suppose he was rather lazy, but that was the school's great good fortune, a sophisticate in a world of *ingénus*. He must have influenced many. The last time I met him was the term he retired. The elder Sanderson and I took him out to dinner in Hampstead. In the bus going up Haverstock Hill a strange man stood up and came across the bus: 'Forgive my interrupting', he said, 'but you are Mr Bathurst, aren't you? I must shake your hand and thank you for what you have done for ...'. A true story and a fitting one. In a selfish way, I was glad that I could get to his funeral in Wimbledon. He was important to me, probably more than he – or I at the time – appreciated. 'Batty' made history stimulating, entertaining, demanding yet satisfying. As a history don now, I am surprised

> how often I find myself saluting his shade, but I can hear him saying 'Ah, but you did a lot of reading by yourself; it wasn't me'. A quietly very remarkable man, unsentimental, generous in spirit and, for me, a revelation and an inspiration. 'Batty,' alone, made my days at The Hall memorable.

It was at this point that Thomas Chitty returned to the 'family' school. We have already learned of his father's briefly held position as Gladstone's partner in the early 1920s.

> Some twenty-six years later, I in my turn arrived to join my uncle GAW, as the most junior of assistant masters, and was given an attic room which must have been one of my father's. It was the spring term of 1947, although there was no spring to be seen. With the pavements of Hampstead trodden deep in grey snow, it wasn't till the following term that I discovered the playing fields. Indoors, however, there was quite enough to interest, indeed to astonish me. GAW was the only schoolmaster I have entirely admired. The Hall was his school and no one else's. He was always ready to find what was happening amusing, bringing with it a sense of incipient chaos and a sense that this was right and proper. The family tradition that he was the model for the character of Fielding in E M Forster's *A Passage to India* may not be the precise truth. 'Modelled on a Bombay schoolmaster, name forgotten', was Forster's answer when I wrote to ask him. But Forster knew Gerard Wathen in India and I suspect borrowed many of his qualities for the character. I can never read the book without imagining Fielding as a younger Gerard Wathen.

Two boys joined The Hall in 1947, close friends then possibly because their fathers were both distinguished doctors. Robert Boyd, son of a professor of medicine comments:

> I have been asked whether I have memories of The Hall. How ridiculous; that period of my life is my natural habitat. Somewhere, I am always a nine to twelve year-old. My main memories centre round the masters and boys, but I recall also marvellous assemblies; like the man who lectured to us on rebuilding the war-damaged Germany. 'It will take twenty years to clear the rubble alone from the streets.' Everything was surrounded by GAW's benign influence. But he could be angry, as when the funeral urn of Miss Large was broken in the sixth form yard! He could appear to have favourites, or 'ADCs', boys who were allowed to walk up forbidden stairs carrying his suitcase.
>
> Teaching was generally well prepared, exciting, demanding and excellent. There abounded poetry, plays, novels, boys' speeches –

> the one I prepared on the birth of a baby was considered to be not quite suitable! And the poetry competition, in the final of which I was beaten by Alec Guinness's son, I regarded as not altogether fair. Among the boys, friendship and alert friendliness, much fighting, occasional sexual explorations: it is a patch of my life which leaves me with much warmer memories than my public school. I think its success was compounded of a warm and relaxed chairmanship laid down by GAW, ('Neither cajolery, threats nor punishment have any effect on Robert's laziness', he once wrote) and the contributions of the boys themselves, many of whose families were refugees from Hitler.

As a professor of paediatrics Robert Boyd was destined in his turn for academic distinction. So was his close friend, Michael Barcroft, who became Headmaster of King's School, Peterborough.

> My early years had been spent in Northern Ireland, where my father was Professor of Physiology at Queen's University. I joined The Hall in 1947. Kindly and well-disposed, Mr Wathen dominates my memories. He used to visit my home: he had once been a 'flame' of my grandmother!
>
> He showed his Indian background by calling boys 'wallahs' and those doing especially well, 'pukka wallahs'. He would show his affinity for the French language by reading not from *The Bible*, but from *La Sainte Bible* at assemblies.
>
> The Hall seemed steeped in tradition. Typical of this was the Reading Over, with parents looking on over the balcony. Many a time I looked almost in envy at the mural of General Gordon being speared to death as the moment for my name to be read approached. I never shone academically. I learnt to say the Greek alphabet – backwards – faster than anyone else in Middle Six, and having struggled to Upper Six, was judiciously transferred to Middle Six A, with its two outstanding good teachers. One was 'Rozzy' Rotherham, entirely pragmatic, wholly intelligible and able to instil the fear of God into everyone through his 'Rozzy haircuts': approaching from the back he would seize the unsuspecting victim's hair above the scruff of the neck and turn it over in his clenched fist. The other was 'Batty' Bathurst, who made history come alive.
>
> There was a small 'museum' in a cupboard at the back of Middle Six A. The human appendix in alcohol always struck me as more interesting than the fossils which surrounded it. The furnishing of the form-rooms was rudimentary. We still used dip-pens which, as a left-hander, I found an almost impossible challenge to my attempts at literacy. Mr Roberts, the caretaker, used to fill the

ink-wells. The desk-tops were deeply scored and, when one's mind wandered, one could create a whole world similar to the Nile delta along which to run one's pencil.

Pencil-cases and fountain-pens were prized possessions, as were knives, particularly the Swiss Army type. Rationing was still universal and the diet meagre but, I suppose, adequate. It certainly did not lack variety. I can remember whale-meat, reindeer, sheep's brain and even horse. Usually such a menu was only served once and we had to depend on macaroni cheese or my favourite dish which was macaroni milk-pudding which had the edge on sago and tapioca. Food for the boarders did leave us hungry in the evening. We would hang about in school hall for the staff to finish their dinner. Occasionally, GAW would appear on the balcony and shout 'Chips, chips, chips!' There would be a mad rush for the staff stairs. The lucky boy there first would be rewarded with two or three chips from the dish.

Apart from in the form-rooms, recreation was in the playground, but we were allowed into the staff-room at a quarter to seven to listen to *Dick Barton, Special Agent* on the wireless and we sat on the table, swinging our legs. When I first arrived the main artefacts used for play were old car and lorry tyres used as hoops: the bigger the tyre, the more important its guardian. I recall Tom Kempinski, later to become a noted author and playwright, always seemed to land up with the largest and ruled the roost. Other games included 'chain-he', ending with a great line of boys chasing the last victim; it was often stopped for being too dangerous. In September and October, there was conkers, with bubble reputations quickly born. (Sinclair had a 'sixteener') and secret patent recipes. I thought age was a plus factor. My bucketful merely sprouted! Cigarette card games were another favourite occupation. Usually played indoors for fear the cards might be blown away, 'dropsies' or 'longsies' or 'knockdownsies' were the orders of the day. It was not unknown for as many as a hundred cards to change hands in a single game. So prized were the cards I remember a crisis after Mr Sleigh had confiscated about two hundred which were then stolen from his desk: a crime surpassing even the theft of the Crown Jewels. As boys, we were not angels. It became the fashion to fray the end of one's tie so that one could flick it at those who disturbed the peace. The more frayed the tie, the greater one's pride.

Memories of two sadder events: the first was the death of Gerald Wintour, knocked off his bicycle in Avenue Road. This stopped me racing; I once overtook Mr Roberts driving the school 'taxi' in Fitzjohn's Avenue. Then there was the memorable occasion when GAW called us all into the hall and told us of the death of King

George VI. We were very upset and shocked, and lunch was subdued. Strong exception was taken to the boy who admitted he was not altogether displeased as it would mean new stamps and coins, both of which he collected.

Those were the years of the real pea-souper 'smogs', years of my mongrel dog called 'Hinc' after the school motto and of the arrival at The Hall of Mr Earle or 'Early' as we called him. I was in his form, Upper Five, when he took his first lesson in an attic form-room. He took as his text the Winchester motto *Manners makyth Man* and told us it should be our guiding principle. I'm afraid it did not always weigh with me as much as it should at the time, but the message and the man are as vivid today as they were then.

Michael Graham had in common with Barcroft both that his father was a doctor and the family had migrated from the outposts of the British Isles to north London.

My father became doctor to The Hall and the Wathen family. We had spent the war in Aberdeenshire and on our return to London my brother (now a Major-General) and I were taken to the school for an interview. We learnt to speak the local dialect of our part of Scotland, largely unintelligible to Scotsmen let alone the English. I remember GAW asking my mother if we could read and being given the indignant reply 'Of course they can!' We were both given a paragraph to read which we rattled off, but only to elicit the comment from GAW: 'I suppose it's all right but I haven't understood a word.' We duly started in the Junior School in 1945. It was very different from Fyvie Village School. I was surprised how far ahead I was compared with these English boys. They were learning their two-times tables whereas I had learnt long division. Needless to say I rested on my laurels, allowing them to catch up and in due course overtake me, a situation I have never been able to rectify!

I can recall the playtimes in the yard and the rival gangs which spent most of the time fighting each other. Lunch was taken in some sort of restaurant in Belsize Park: the food was very nasty. Then in the Senior School, we started new subjects, notably Latin, with Miss Harbord, whose brother later taught me at St Paul's. Once, we were learning Latin words. She left the room and returned swinging an oriental club round her head. We thought she was quite mad. The club had been taken from the Headmaster's study. I still cannot remember the Latin for a club. Rugger was resumed, in Regent's Park, in the early 1950s and dancing lessons with girls from South Hampstead High School. The motive behind this innovation in what was then not a very musical school was that it would improve our football.

> Above all, one remembers GAW, a remarkable and much respected man, viewed by the boys with a mixture of veneration and affection. His behaviour was somewhat eccentric. His false teeth were liable to shoot out and when this happened during his speech thanking the organisers at the swimming sports, they fell into the water, amid hoots of laughter. Quite unabashed and with a wide grin he calmly asked Colin Frizzell, the school diving champion, to dive in and retrieve them. The teeth were replaced and the speech was continued.
>
> The Hall gave us a desire to learn and it was always a happy school with a great deal of freedom. It has been my privilege and pleasure to serve it as a governor for over ten years and it makes me happy to know that its traditions are being maintained.

Graham entered the world of insurance with his contemporary from The Hall, Colin Frizzell. A sometime Sheriff and an Alderman of the City of London, he has been, like GAW himself and Graham's fellow Old Boy, Julian Wathen, the Master of the Mercers' Company.

The 1950s was a period rich with boys of talent. Peter Buckman was yet another. He was to become a professional writer and novelist, which makes his recollection the more graphic, not least for the faintly unconventional, even irreverent attitude that he obviously has always adopted.

> 'If you're going to kill a man, Buckman, make sure it isn't a policeman.' Mr Wathen's advice has stuck in my mind more firmly than all the gerunds and subjunctives my parents paid to have crammed into me. The occasion was a French lesson on the morning when the 18-year-old Derek Bentley was to be hanged for an offence he didn't commit (his friend Ian Craig shot the policeman, but was too young to be executed). As the hour of execution approached, our class became restive, not in the sense of baying for blood but stirred, in good schoolboy fashion, by the injustice meted out to someone only five years our senior. Mr Wathen must have understood this feeling, for instead of dealing with us like fractious natives (he had become Headmaster after retiring from serving the Raj), he relaxed, made his joke, and in so doing defined the system for us – a thing that could be implacably vengeful if you broke the wrong rules. The trick was knowing which these were.
>
> No one impersonated the system better than the awesome Mr Rotherham. A small, fiery, grey-fringed Yorkshireman, fond of boasting that his native county contained more acres than there were words in the Bible, he was given to sudden explosions of inexplicable rage, and to hair-pulling that brought tears to the eyes.

He demonstrated both these forms of violence one lunch-time, when he was in charge of the school and his wife happened to be present. There was something in the look she gave him – the kind of look one's mother gave one's father when he had gone too far – whose unspoken disapproval consoled his victim with the secret triumph of right over might, something memorable because of its rarity.

I have to confess to one incident involving Mr Rotherham about which I still feel shame. Playing in the Memorial Garden with my friend Reichwald, a large vase got broken. Naturally we didn't report the matter, nor thought of it till word came from Mr Rotherham that the whole school would be punished unless the culprit came forward. Without thinking, I shopped my friend Reichwald, only realising the extent of my folly when I saw the terror on his face as he was called out for punishment. My friends sent me to Coventry, but I was more concerned about persuading Reichwald that my action was not based on malice, but on thoughtless impulse (a defence I have had to fall back on several times since). He forgave me, which I suppose taught me more about which rules are really important than any action by Mr Rotherham.

The school held a mock election to parallel the real thing in, I think, 1950 or '51. I stood as the Labour candidate, and seem to remember making impressive speeches about equality and justice which were received about as well as a lecture on the Punic Wars. However I was inspired to offer, if elected, an end to sweet-rationing (as it happened, my grandmother owned a sweet-shop). This was not exacly part of Labour's official policy, but I ensured my promise had substance by offering sweets to my supporters – not as a bribe, you understand, but to prove that, unlike other politicians, I meant what I said. My instinct for what an audience wanted, and my ability to deliver, proved as unerring then as now, and I got two votes.

I smarted over this defeat for many days, and since I valued being liked above political integrity, I decided (once and once only) to become a Conservative. I announced this conversion to my history teacher, Miss Walker, who remarked soothingly that 'it was such a comfort to belong to the majority'. I have to admit that the delicious feeling of bearing the same label and displaying the same prejudices as most of my fellows quickly wore off: I have since found that disagreeing with the majority is much more fun than nodding off in its company.

I kept a list while at the school of the Great Events I had lived through, though the only things I recorded were deaths – Stalin's, and to show I was even-handed, those of Field-Marshal Smuts and

Gandhi. The book in which these obituaries were inscribed became notorious when Paul Robeson wrote in it, on a visit to my parents' house. His action caused me some anguish, not because of the sentiments expressed by the great man (this wasn't during my brief Conservative period), but because we had all been warned of dire penalties if we scribbled on our covers. I made my father come to school and explain how the book had been used in this fashion – another lesson in how to breach the regulations if you have a good enough alibi.

I earn my living as a writer, but all my stories were rejected by the school magazine – until, that is, I became a member of its editorial board. That was when Mr Sleigh was in charge, who used to maintain that his initials stood for Lucifer Beelzebub (he later wrote a splendid book about names). Thanks to him I won my only prize (I don't count my Junior School triumph of coming second in spelling), a copy of *Pears Cyclopaedia* I still consult, mainly to discover which present is appropriate for wedding anniversaries. Looking at the bookplate, with its *Hinc Librum Honoris Diligentiaeque Causa*, I see they missed out not only one of my initials but also the reason for the award. Modestly pencilled in, in my finest italics, is *Michael Jackson Prize for the most work on the School Magazine*.

I remember Mr Prideaux, racked by coughing fits caused by mustard gas in the First World War; Miss Harbord, who looked every inch the old-fashioned schoolmarm, with round steel spectacles and hair in a bun; Mr Drury-Lowe, a pale young man in check shirts and cavalry twill, whom we all thought was a deb's delight since he always looked tired in the mornings and was often late for prayers. He nearly put me off writing altogether when he tossed my stories back at me with the crushing remark, 'They're only about money!' Perhaps that was the time when my friends and I were all ashamed of what our parents earned – whether it was too little or too much was irrelevant, it was the status it conferred.

There was Mr Earle, our Scoutmaster, a man of extraordinary patience and forbearance, even when I practically dislocated his thumbs trying for my knots badge. I must have been one of the least successful Scouts in the school's history, since I don't remember gaining any badges whatever: nevertheless he encouraged me to go to Scout camp, which I remember chiefly for pot-scouring, constipation (the cows kept blundering into the latrines we dug), and not cleaning my teeth for a week.

I was never exactly sporty, either: I once won the egg-and-spoon race, but when put in for the quarter-mile, I stopped to speak to my father on a bend rather than plod round the exhausting course. Of

> cricket I remember little except scoring; of swimming only that I was shouted at and learned how to hold my breath under water. It was to the school that I owe the worst report I ever had, the sort that holds out a dismal future of decadence and dissipation unless socks are pulled up and so forth. I don't remember much sock-pulling, but I became a model citizen, husband and father, as well as governor of two state schools, so the report must have been unduly alarmist. I have forgotten most of the things I was supposed to learn, in common, I imagine, with most people, but there are two things I'm proud of. One is when Mr Wathen, in his farewell report on me, described me as 'irrepressible', which I had to look up but which I have always regarded as a high compliment. The other is when Mr Cooper, who was after my time at the school, courteously refused my offer to donate a copy of my first novel to the library. Called *Playground*, it began with the junior pupils imprisoning the headmaster and worked its way up from there. Can't think why he refused – but I decided I must have got something right.

By way of a rather pallid excuse for the seeming discourtesy just described, perhaps it may be mentioned that The Hall library had at the date in question not expanded its shelves to accommodate literature that might be thought to hold faintly more progressive or 'dangerous' views. Since William Golding's *Lord of the Flies* achieved the accolade of respectability that arises from being a GCE set book, schools have grown less cautious.

We have reached the point in the story of The Hall through the eyes of its Old Boys when GAW was determining to hand over to The Hall School Trust. He had invited established friends to see the task through, when he quite unexpectedly developed serious cold feet about the whole operation. This explains the long hiatus that accompanied the process. GAW's instincts were right, but perhaps he was reluctant to contemplate the implications of an ultimate surrender of the reins. A rather sad element of doubt and suspicion surrounded the negotiations which were smoothed out by the tireless efforts of Miss Gladstone, who more than anyone else was responsible for seeing the matter through. L M Miall, an Old Boy, had by this time become a parent: he soon found himself a governor!

> I became closely associated with The Hall again in 1948, by which time my son David was at the Junior School. With no previous warning I was co-opted onto the committee of the Parents' Association to attend a meeting at which were described the outlines of a scheme to convert the school from private ownership to a charitable trust. Later that year I became one of the committee of potential governors charged with the negotiations of the scheme.

For no very good reason that I ever discovered this went into limbo for three years until 13th November 1951, when six of us met Wathen with his solicitor and accountant to be presented with the details. The meeting began with a bombshell: Wathen stated that he no longer approved. It later transpired that this was because he was as much in the dark as the rest of us. His solicitor had entirely failed to explain it to him or indeed to keep him in touch. The committee at first considered that, having been appointed by Wathen, it would have to resign, but I finally agreed to draft a letter putting the committee's viewpoint, which was in favour of the scheme in principle. I subsequently discovered that Miss Gladstone strongly supported us and poured oil on troubled waters. Anyhow, at two further meetings in January 1952, the scheme was agreed and after several more meetings to approve all the documentation, it was put into effect in July. Most of the committee stayed on to form the nucleus of the new governing body.

GAW remained Headmaster for a further three years while the governing body found its feet. It was strengthened by co-opting several public school headmasters and with Professor Paish, the economist as Chairman and with other legal and financial experts, soon constituted a strong team. Its first major job was to appoint the new headmaster, Mr R A Cooper. I stayed on until I left London in 1960 and recall a number of interesting and some difficult problems. The meeting I remember best was a company AGM which had to be held in a particular calendar year. It was finally convened, on the evening of 31st December, by a quorum of governors, by telephone, which adjourned for a further week. We were assured that this procedure was within the Companies Act! However, my most difficult job was that of delivering the valedictory address at the final presentation to GAW in March 1955.

Harold Preiskel, one of two brothers and the father of three sons at The Hall, tells of an episode during the last days of GAW. Such anecdotes are all part of the unforgettable tradition of any school. Lunch in his time was served both in the main hall and in the billiard room immediately above the kitchens, a room now used by the staff.

Perhaps the most amusing episode concerned lunches in the billiard room which was above the kitchen. Dishes were passed up and down by a primitive type of lift, known as a dumb-waiter. The container for the dishes resembled an open bookcase and there was a small counterweight that was nothing like a match for the fully loaded container. A separate cable operated a brake so that the cage could be gently lowered down to the kitchen. This descent had to be carried out with great care and it was difficult to judge the moment

> of landing the cargo, which was somewhat delicate, to put it mildly. Unknown to the master in charge the boys organised a competition that was monitored by a neutral observer armed with a stopwatch who timed the moment of departure to the time of landing. I held the record for some time as I had secretly marked the cable so that while nonchalantly counting aloud I knew exactly when to apply the brake. The attempt on my record was anxiously awaited. The cage was desperately overloaded. While the master in charge was, unsuspectingly, finishing his dessert, plates were piled high on top of the actual cage before the brake was released. The overloaded cage accelerated far quicker than expected, indeed the brake operator was still calmly counting when a considerable portion of the school's crockery arrived in the kitchen like an express train hitting a greenhouse. The effect was devastating. There was a thud followed by a never-ending crash of breaking crockery, splintering wood, yells from the kitchen followed by still more crashes as plates rolled and smashed in all directions. Nobody spoke for at least two minutes and I think cook had to go to hospital, shocked. Needless to say, the lift was not used again.

Preiskel subsequently became a pilot in the RAF and a consultant dental surgeon. The dumb-waiter was not used thereafter and the cupboard that housed it eventually accommodated the school's alarm systems.

More than one Old Boy recalls the last days of GAW. Two young malefactors were Peter Harris and Tom Hawksley. Their recollections follow:

> Every master at The Hall was a little eccentric, enough to show that the pursuit of excellence should not end in bookishness and it is, after all, the individual who is important. Most of them had their off-days and tantrums, sometimes amusing, sometimes terrifying, but, on the whole, I remember them as kindly people.
>
> I was only beaten once. I remember waiting for the punishment, like a condemned man, and then, to my enormous surprise and relief, discovered that there was no physical pain at all. Possibly I was lucky because Mr Wathen was about to retire and was well into his seventies.

★ ★ ★

> I can perhaps claim to be the last boy to be beaten by Mr Wathen before his retirement. I had hit another boy (I think one of the Summerson triplets) rather hard with my cricket bat, and this incident caught the attention of one of the staff. I was sent straight across to the Heamaster's house and beaten with a short leather strap. The Headmaster was furious and fierce until he stopped

thrashing, whereupon he became friendly and charming, and admired my bat!

And so to the reign of Cooper and somehow, it all seems to be so much less a matter of history. Perhaps for this reason, the flood of reminiscences from which this selection of accounts has been drawn rapidly dries up. Colin Sheaf left in 1965 when things were still much more akin to the ways of the Wathen than of the Heazell era.

I remember hundreds of 'day-bugs' playing in the yard against the boarders. I remember the prefects' table in assembly. I have hazy recollections of handing out rugby caps to the First XV when I was the captain (was I *really*?). Rugger on Primrose Hill was an uphill struggle; there was never a pitch (which we had to stake out) that was anything like flat and often there were some doggy obstructions to circumvent. The most enjoyable part was immersing oneself in a huge yellow-tiled communal bath back at school, where everything smelt of steam and mud – my first experience of this inimitable life-style.

The education was clearly outstanding, although, funnily, the academic side is not something which comes back in much detail. I can recall the hallowed precinct of the staff-room, venturing in to be greeted by the intelligently sardonic smile of Richard Dawson, or the beetling eyebrow raised by the Headmaster. I remember Mr Barron introducing every French lesson with the Lord's Prayer, in French, which would no doubt have the ILEA up in arms nowadays, on several grounds. There was 'Bob' Imlay giving us mind-bending chunks of Socratic dialogue to study; Jim Holden in the new and excellently equipped science laboratories. I suppose leaving home should have been a traumatic experience. I seem to remember enjoying it.

Things really have changed over the subsequent twenty years. There are no longer any boarders and all boys are 'day-bugs'. There is no rugger elite and the après-rugger bath has gone too. So have all prefects, apart from a head boy.

And now, by way of a postscript to the chapter, the recollections of someone who came to know The Hall well from a few fleeting visits in the 1970s. The fact that he was not a product of the school, but a teacher of its products, may perhaps give his judgement both of it and them just an edge of valuable objectivity. Mr Patrick Peacey writes:

It was at the suggestion of Arthur Harrison that I was first called to help at The Hall. Paddy Heazell had just arrived and his deputy, Tim Thornton, had been appointed to be Headmaster of Dean Close Junior. My first challenge was to be form-master of a scholarly but unruly Upper Sixth, containing a number of budding journalists, politicians and leaders of industry. I was given the choice of history or geography. I took the latter, saying that I could at least make environmental issues alive – I had been an observer at the 1974 UN conference in Nairobi, and had taught in Africa for fifteen years. My first difficulty was correcting a trial Common Entrance paper. I knew next to nothing about oilfields so I had to mark them on the authority with which the boy wrote. I neither returned the papers nor went through them in class!

I had never worked in a day school before, and could hardly accept the idea of a 4.30 pm evacuation of the school. A party I escorted in the midst of the 1976 heatwave to the Commonwealth Institute returned *very* late to their resignedly patient parents. Like everyone who has had any connection with The Hall, I retain vivid memories of that long walk down the Finchley Road to games. At the time, we had the Tikkoo boys, both material for kidnapping, and we were joined by their personal escorts. Some boys would always race ahead and others drag behind, bringing to mind A P Herbert's poem *The Poodle and the Pug*. It was a particularly hot and dusty summer and at the parched cricket ground would be leaky hosepipes with fine jets spraying up into the air. My children would strip off and dance dervish-like in the arching water. My sympathy was with them.

A year later I had the privilege of taking on 'Jimmy' Earle's role as form-master of boys who had just moved up from the Junior School, all really nervous about this entry into the wider world! What a delightful crowd they were in their eyrie in the attics. I still hear news of some of them and regularly use a book of prayers inscribed 'To Mr P C from the horrors themselves', signed by two boys whose fathers had also been to The Hall – Paget Dare Bryan and Jan Wise. This reminds me of the extreme generosity of Hall parents who felt their sons had been given extra help, of the sort that is quite the norm in a boarding school.

Other memories – a weekly session with the sea of young faces when taking Junior School prayers; the grandstand view from the staff room of traffic congestion and double parking in Crossfield Road; introducing Eco-politics and rejoicing at the Ecological Party candidate coming runner-up in the school's mock General Election; those Dizer walks; school services and assemblies; and a newly-emerged lime hawk moth on one of the trees opposite. Yes, even if there are some difficulties, life continues fresh and good, and now I come to think, they were happy days and the boys were excellent company. I must visit again; I usually get thrown into a classroom when I do!

APPENDIX 1

'Carmina Aulariensia'

Very possibly it was the pageantry of the Coronation of King George VI in 1937 that inspired the creation the same year of a formal Hall School Song. The writer of the words was Mr Millard, who regularly wrote poems which found a place in the magazine – and one presumes, elsewhere. The music was by the director of music, Mr Norman Collie, and the resulting 'carmen' was accorded the dignity of a formal publication by Novello's. It was given its first performances in both parts of the school in 1937. *Hinc in Altiora* emerges as a curious example of its genre, but over the years, sentiments have changed sharply, and it never fully survived even the war. It was 'killed' even in GAW's own time by the staff (both Millard and Collie were no longer on the strength by then) when, in 1950, the words were cruelly 'sent up' in a staff pantomime, to the extent that it was resolved to write new words to the tune of the Rossall School song, the old school of the author, Mr Fyson. *Hinc in Altiora* was given a last semi-serious airing, as an admittedly quaint curiosity, in 1977, when a group of Upper VI leavers performed the entire song before a somewhat bewildered and uncomprehending Junior School – and then, for good measure, repeated it to the Senior School, who clearly had no idea what their response was expected to be! For the sake of the historical record, the words of Millard's early song, the staff's 'spoof' and Fyson's new version are given below. The singing of a school song is no longer a part of the routine of The Hall.

2

HINC IN ALTIORA

Words by
Eric Millard

Music by
Norman Collie

16487

2. There are things to be learnt and you learn them at school,
By playing the game and not the fool.
There are 'stars' to be won, there are 'crosses' to bear:
In after-life you'll get your share.
These lessons learnt you'll then re-call:–
Hinc in Altiora – Up, The Hall!

3. There are 'overs' and 'unders' in life all through,
And a Head who is watching all you do.
There's a goal at the end of the long, long road;
You must shoulder your burden and bear your load.
Don't turn a deaf ear but heed the call:–
Hinc in Altiora – Up, The Hall!

4. 'Be Prepared', as in scouting, and follow the trail;
There's a hill at the other side of the vale.
If you stick to your purpose, nor fail, nor stop,
At the last 'Reading Over' you'll reach the top,
And there again you'll hear the call:–
Hinc in Altiora – Up, The Hall!

The Staff 'Spoof'

Now a story we've told for whoever will hear;
It's exciting, revealing and certainly queer;
You can take it from us that it's true, what's more

* * *

So now can be heard the inspiring call,
Help! It's Cinderellus! Watch the ball!

There are things to be learnt – you can take it from us,
You can whisper the truth to your friends in the bus.
We have plied you with learning and wherefore and why,
And you know never once have we told you a lie.
So be sure you can trust us and stir to the call,
Help! It's Cinderellus! Watch the ball!

There are crosses and twos in your life all through,
Whichever the football pool you do.
But nobody told you – we're quite sure of this –
Cinderellus played football, a footballing miss.
So that's why we sing you the fearful call –
Help! It's Cinderellus! Watch the ball!

Be prepared, as in scouting, for any surprise.
Don't always believe what you're told if you're wise.
For now you know something that no one else knows:
You've been fooled all your life at these pantomime shows.
Cinderella's a BOY, not a female at all.
Help! It's Cinderellus! Watch the ball!

* * * *A line is lost here: no record of it survives!*

Fyson set about writing another school song.

The Hall School

Children we of many a nation,
Let us sing in admiration
Praise of you, our own Hall School;
You our father and our mother,
You our kindly elder brother,
Nowhere shall we find another
Like to you, our own Hall School.

Here we learn true friendship's measure,
How to work, and use our leisure,
Thanks to you, our own Hall School;
Cubbing on the Heath and scouting,
Games and swimming, many an outing,
Weariness or boredom routing,
'Neath your smile, our own Hall School.

See old England's pictured story,
Famous schools' emblazoned glory
Shining round this our Hall School;
In the gallery names recorded
Tell how work has been rewarded,
Others on the Stone are hoarded
In the heart of this our Hall School.

When we in our turn are wending,
Hinc in altiora tending,
We'll still love our Old Hall School;
'Mid new toils and pleasures ever
There will crown each fresh endeavour
This old thought – forgotten never –
Life and health to our own Hall School!

APPENDIX 2

The Hall War Memorial

Sadly, no list survives – if indeed one ever existed – of the casualties suffered by Old Boys during World War 1. This may have been because the reports of them were clearly very painful to the teachers who were reluctant to record them. It is true that the headmastership of The Hall changed just at the moment when a formal memorial might have been erected.

Things were very different during and after the Second World War. A Roll of Honour was established and very shortly after the end of hostilities a plan was launched to establish a fitting Garden of Remembrance, containing a memorial stone with the names of The Hall's sixty-one dead. This number was significantly high for a school without any marked military tradition. It represented almost two years of admissions into the school. The names of those that fell are reproduced here:

		Date of Entry to The Hall
A Abels	RAF	1927
H J Adler	Rifle Brigade	1922
P S Adler	RAMC	1922
G B Armstrong	RAC	1931
A C Q Aspinall	King's African Rifles	1931
D K Atkinson	RAF	1923
J L Atkinson	RAF	1921
R F Barham	RA	1918
M Barnby, DFC	RAF	1926
O de la Poer Beresford	RAF	1926
J M Bewley	Glider Pilot	1927
T D B Blake	RAF	1925
M G Boggon	RAFVR	1929
B E Bonham-Carter	Black Watch	1930
M C B Bonham-Carter	London Irish Rifles	1928
N H Bowack	RAF	1921
O O Breakwell	Coldstream Guards	1928
J Charley	RAF	1933
M W Colledge	RAF	1926
O P Croom-Johnson	RAF	1922
A Debroy Somers	RNVR	1929
J R Dight	RN	1925
J N Eagleston	RASC	1920
T J Earle	RNVR	1926

P C Franklin	Highland Division RA	1927
M B Freeman	RA	1928
A L Green	Burma Commandos	1927
D J Herbert	RAF	1929
J Horne	Black Watch	1928
R A Jackson	RAF	1924
R L Knight	RAF	1924
J N Kennedy	RNVR	1926
J R Kennedy	RE	1913
J Landale (Landauer)	HAC	1926
G D A Langner	RAF	1926
J E S MacAlister	RAF	1925
P D MacAlister	RAF	1926
D S Macleod	HAC	1924
G C Miall	RAFVR	1924
G O Nares	12th Royal Lancers	1924
J Nicholls	Commandos	1928
J R Peacock	RA	1922
I M Rees	RN	1925
W H Reeve	RHA	1924
C L Rosenheim, MC	Welsh Regiment	1922
J D Rubinstein	RAF	1932
P D Rumsam	RAFVR	1928
M Scott	Commandos	1926
P M Shearman	RASC	1926
M J Steadman	Royal Sussex Regiment	1929
G H Strauss	Queen Victoria Rifles and Manchester Regiment	1924
A J C Stuart	RAF	1920
R L Temple	RAF	1924
A D van Gelder	The Buffs	1929
J G Vaughan	RN	1926
P P Vernon	RAFVR	1928
J F Wilford	RNVR	1929
S F J Wood	RN, Fleet Air Arm	1928
S K Woolf	Merchant Service	1928
J Wordman	Royal Tank Regiment	1931

The moves that the school and the parents took to create the Memorial Garden have been described earlier in this book. The dedication of the War Memorial Stone and the Memorial Garden in which it stood took place on 19th July 1949. The guests included the current parents and relatives of every one of the Old Boys whose names appeared on the Roll of Honour. The clergy who took part in a short and simple service represented the local churches and synagogue. They were led by the Very Reverend Dr W R Matthews, KCVO, Dean of St Paul's, who reminded his listeners that this garden and its adjoining playground provided a perpetual memory of the sacrifice of these men for as long as the school endured. The garden was in fact not completely fitted out, but the flowers and shrubs that adorned it for the occasion were established to make this a notable and well-remembered, if not always fully respected feature of The Hall for just forty years. The Memorial Garden itself became a victim of that acute pressure on space which has been so often recorded in these pages. Its valuable site, earmarked for incorporation into the Centenary Building, was excavated for the Activity Hall in 1987. The War Memorial stone, with its precious names, was carefully dismantled for subsequent re-assembly as a part of the centenary celebrations.

For the record, the architect's original scheme for the Memorial Garden is reproduced below, although, in the event, the wrought-iron gates were erected at the eastern end to lead into the existing playground.

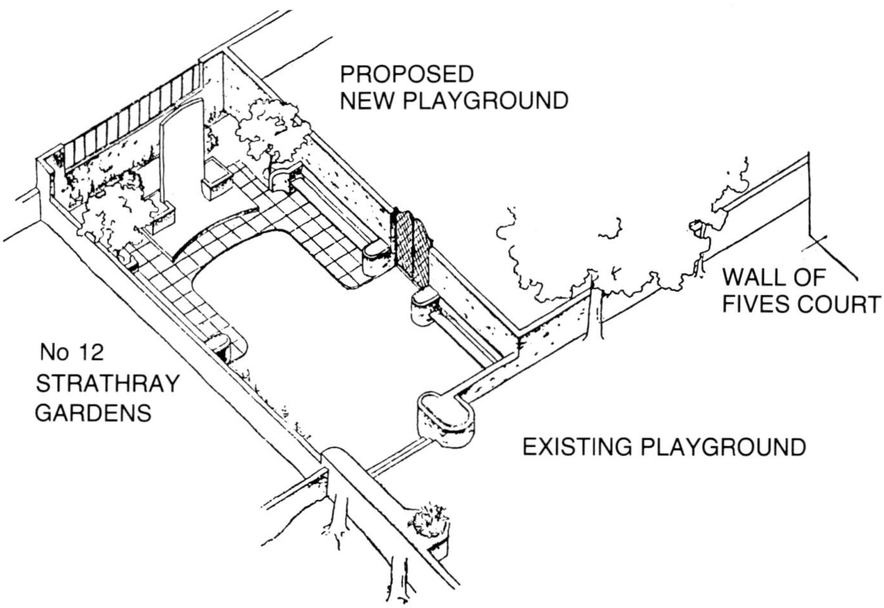

THE HALL · CROSSFIELD RD NW3
PROPOSED WAR MEMORIAL & EXTENSION OF PLAYING FACILITIES

APPENDIX 3

Scouting and Cubbing at The Hall

The first reference to scouting at the school is in an article in the magazine for the Easter term, 1913, which was just six years after the Scout Movement itself had been founded by Lord Baden-Powell. This article was written by a senior boy, Dick Hart.

Mention has already been made of Hart, since it was his portrait of his headmaster, Montauban, which appeared in the 75th anniversary history of the school, part of which is quoted earlier in this volume. Hart was a very remarkable person, deserving a brief comment in his own right. Although such a passionate advocate of scouting, he was never a scout himself; he was physically incapable of being one in an age less well equipped to provide for the severely handicapped than in more recent times. Hart was an acute spastic. He could not walk until he was seven. He was sent to live with an uncle and aunt in Hampstead to have treatment in London, and by the time he was ten he was considered strong enough to manage a prep school education. He was a musical boy and he had a flair for reading and writing. He subsequently went to UCS and to Cambridge, where he read law and in due course, became the law correspondent of *The Times*. Not the least of his triumphs was the award of a Defence Medal for his bravery in the ARP during the war. His courage and success in overcoming his handicap inspired the British Council for the Welfare of Spastics to commission him to write his life story, *A Spastic Wins Through*. As a young boy, one of his earliest excitements was reading the works of Kipling, and in particular, *The Jungle Book*. He also read, and in his own words, 'practically learned by heart', the first edition of *Scouting for Boys*, which had appeared in 1908. By 1910, when he joined The Hall, Hart had already become intrigued with the ideas put forward in it.

Hart's article was written just before the outbreak of war and perhaps with a not altogether perfect understanding of the basic philosophy of scouting. While no one should imagine that it is a mere 'playing at soldiers', he saw one of its principal benefits as helping boys to be of use 'if England was suddenly attacked'. He was not far from the mark in defining its aim and object: 'By a course of training, to make boys honest, useful and loyal citizens, so that they may 'be prepared' for anything and everything.'

There are no more references to scouting at the school for ten years. By then, a new Headmaster was installed, one highly sympathetic to scouting. On 16th May 1923, Mr E V Millard, Scoutmaster of the 25th Hampstead, came to The Hall to talk to the boys on scouting. About thirty boys attended, and Gladstone readily agreed that Hall Patrols should be formed, to be attached to the 25th. Since the four Houses were fairly equally represented, it was decided to constitute them by Houses. Each House was then asked to elect two members for training for promotion to the rank of Patrol Leader and Second. These boys were the pioneers of scouting at The Hall, and within the year, this was to become the first purely school Scout Troop in London.

Training began promptly, and by 4th June the first scouts were ready for investiture. There were initially some 25 boys, in four Patrols, led by J N Eagleston, 'Dutchy' Stuart (both destined to be killed in the war), G U Salvi and G E G Brown. By 16th June they were ready for the Troop's first week-end camp.

From January, The Hall scouts were registered as a Troop, the 8th Hampstead, and its scarf in the school colours – pink with a narrow black border and a black 'Maltese' cross in the apex – became part of the uniform, as did the school badge on the right breast of the jersey. The early summer camps were held at Chesham, Kenwood or Pulborough in Sussex, and the favourite spots for week-end camping were Preston Road and Carpender's Park. Tents were often pitched on the green at the corner of Eton Avenue and Strathray Gardens (long since built over). Since it was much easier to reach open country in those days, a trek-cart was considered an essential part of a troop's equipment and it figured prominently in the annual displays which Scouts and Cubs were to give to the school.

Alan Bedford-Smith was the first Scout to gain the King's Scout Certificate at The Hall, a rare achievement for a thirteen year-old. By April 1925, less than two years after the launching, some 85 boys had become Scouts and nearly 150 badges had been gained. The Troop's first Colour was shortly to be presented, by Sir Westcott Abell. It was a highly elaborate flag – a St George's cross superimposed by a Maltese cross – used for almost 40 years, being finally laid up in 1964. The Hall Troop took just three years to become the largest prep school Troop in England, when it received an official inspection from a representative from Imperial Headquarters.

Just as B-P had found out eight years earlier, the younger boys were now clamouring for training along scout lines, so the Cubs came into being in 1924. The first Cubmaster* was Miss Mason who started a Pack in the Junior School. Like their elders, the Cub Sixes were grouped initially by Houses. Demand for cubbing was so great that less than two years later, a Pack in the Senior School was formed, and

* Such was her title in the age unaffected by the Equal Opportunities Commission.

eventually there had to be four Packs, two in each part of the school. Meetings were held at school each week, while activities on the Heath took place every Saturday.

When the war broke out the numbers of Scouts and Cubs decreased sharply, and all activity was suspended until 1945, when scouting and cubbing came back into their own. Steadily thereafter, the scope of events widened and the style of scouting became 'modernised'. An important decision was taken to separate scouting from the school: meetings were held away from the school and outside school hours. This was in part because of a gradual evaporation in teaching staff willing or able to share in the responsibilities of running scouting. Mr Barron was followed by Mr Earle, and with the cubs, Miss Bearman, Mrs Thallon and Miss Harbord were stalwarts. From the 1960s, it was the parents who increasingly recognised the enormous value of scouting to their boys and who willingly took over running the Group. Chief, but by no means alone among these, were the members of the Frais family.

The relevance of scouting over the years has in no way declined. In earlier days, it was perhaps softer and more leisurely. The first summer camps were on a lavish scale, with the Patrols sleeping on palliasses in white bell-tents and Mr Roberts, the school handyman, was there to cook for them. Not so in more recent years. Tents have shrunk, boys must cook and fend for themselves. The value of scouting and cubbing for bringing somewhat sheltered Hall boys into close contact with boys from other sectors of the community is not to be forgotten. Hall Patrols and Packs have over the years taken part in a host of district and national sporting and other activities, often distinguishing themselves against boys much older than themselves; age boundaries in the 8th Hampstead tend to be arranged to suit school convenience, so that 12 year-olds may well find themselves up against 14s.

Social and community service has always been an important element in 'doing the good turn'. In 1953, Hall Scouts were on official duty on the route of the Coronation Procession. Scouts in particular, and Cubs as well, have helped in hospitals, old peoples' homes and elsewhere, to raise money, bring good cheer, entertain and generally lend a helping hand.

In the 1960s, scouting seemed to be facing a major challenge. The climate of the age was changing and the Scout Movement had to review its style, its methods and its very appeal to the young. Changes were introduced, and The Hall Group of course responded. Some of these changes were regretted. In a world that was in danger of leaving B-P's ideas and ideals behind so that boys might no longer have the time or the inclination to enjoy his creation it was significant to note the response from the boys in Hampstead. London boys can be very unforgiving of the boring or the pedestrian. Equally, their need for open-air activities and physical challenges is perhaps greater than that of their country cousins. The response of the 8th Hampstead through the crisis period of the 1970s was instructive. Boys did not drift off to more exotic attractions. Indeed, the chief problem was a swelling demand which could not be satisfied. The explanations for this happy state of affairs were various. The role of a senior member of staff to act as Group Leader and a Headmaster entirely sympathetic to the contribution scouting was making to the welfare of the boys were valuable. This meant that staff helped out in greater or lesser ways, especially with camps. The formalising of the Group Parents' Committee brought the parents even more prominently into touch with the extraordinarily enterprising programme which from the mid-'70s was being offered to the boys. Above all, however, it was the personnel involved which explains the surging popularity of scouting and cubbing at The Hall.

Mr Earle's contribution to scouting in Hampstead was always far greater than he would ever admit. His award of the movement's *Order of Merit* was a just tribute to him for all that he had done for it. The measure of the calibre of the scouters that have given so much to Hall boys may be judged by the list of awards given to the three members of the Frais family for their work. Tony, Ian and Barbara have all three gained the *Medal of Merit*. In addition, Barbara and Tony have the coveted *Silver Wolf*. Under the tireless and utterly professional leadership of this trio, backed by a regular brigade of friends, parents and Old Boys, each year a truly formidable programme of drills, training, expeditions and camps has been arranged. Scouting and cubbing at The Hall have never been more active, more valuable or more appreciated, and all just at a time when counter-attractions might have undermined them. How GAW would have rejoiced to see this happen.

One footnote: the annual summer camp in 1973 took place in Holland. As a result of the contacts made and friendships established, an official twinning between the 8th Hampstead and the 9th Den Haag was effected. Thereafter, joint camps and exchanges have taken place, all part of the routine of major summer expeditions to the Continent, the Scillies or the Channel Islands.

APPENDIX 4

Governors of The Hall

The Governing Body of The Hall was initially an Advisory Council, invited by the Headmaster to assist him, in particular over the selection of his successor. By long tradition, the headmasters of the London public schools which The Hall supplied in greatest numbers have been invited, almost ex officio, together with Old Boys, parents and local figures interested in the continuing prosperity of The Hall.

The Inaugural Council – 1935

J Bell, MA, *High Master of St Paul's*
Rev H Costley-White, DD, *Headmaster of Westminster*
Dr J A H Johnston, MA, DSC, *Headmaster of Highgate*
B S Townroe, MA, JP, *Mayor of Hampstead*

Council 1940

J T Christie, MA, *Headmaster of Westminster*
C F Bell, MA, *Headmaster of Highgate*
W F Oakeshott, MA, *High Master of St Paul's*
Dr T K Devvy, MA, *Headmaster of Mill Hill*
B S Townroe, MA, JP
Sir I MacAlister, MA★

The Inaugural Governing Body – 1952

A J F Wrottesley† *(Chairman)*
C W Myring★
D Robertson★†
L M Miall★†
C D Hamilton★
Miss K H Gladstone
G A Wathen, MA★
W Hamilton, *Headmaster of Westminster*
Dr R E James, *High Master of St Paul's*
Professor F W Paish★
W R Hornby-Steer

★ parent † Old Boy

Governing Body – 1972

J P G Wathen★† (*Chairman*)
Hon D Astor★
Miss D Burchell, *Headmistress of Camden School for Girls*
J D Carleton, MA, *formerly Headmaster of Westminster*
A J F Doulton, OBE, TD, MA, *Headmaster of Highgate*
Miss K H Gladstone
T E B Howarth, MC, MA, *High Master of St Paul's*
Dr R C James, MA, *formerly High Master of St Paul's*
C W Myring, MA★
Mrs C Nicholson
D M Peattie★
J Rae, MA, PhD, *Headmaster of Westminster*
S V B Van de Weyer, MA, FRICS★
B T Wigoder, MA, QC★

Governing Body – June 1988

J P G Wathen, *(Chairman)*★†
W L Banks, MA★
I D S Beer, MA, JP, *Headmaster of Harrow*
D D C Belchamber, MA, *Bursar, King's College School, Wimbledon*
Mrs M I Gee★
R C Giles, MA, *Headmaster of Highgate*
N Gill, MA, *Director of Education, Barnet*
Alderman A M Graham, JP†
Dr A Hearnden, MA, *General Secretary, ISJC*
W H Moseley, MA, *Hawtrey House, Eton*
Rev Canon P Pilkington, MA, *High Master, St Paul's*
Sir Mark Potter, QC★
Lady Ridley
J H Ritblat *(Vice Chairman)*★†
Professor H B Rose, *London Business School*★
D M Summerscale, MA, *Headmaster of Westminster*
V E Treves, MA, *(Clerk)*★†

★ parent † Old Boy

APPENDIX 5

Open Awards

Scholarships, exhibitions, competitive bursaries, and awards in music and art, gained by Hall boys

1900	H L Geare	*Westminster*
1902	D Nathan	*Clifton*
	D Davison	*Fettes*
1903	E S Wood	*Westminster*
1904	K Davison	*Dover*
	G V Brewer	*Highgate*
1906	J B Calkin	*Westminster*
1907	B W Wilson	*Aldenham*
	P H Barringer	*U C S*
	W D Churcher	*Cheltenham*
	E T Hippesley	*Westminster*
	E H Wood	*Westminster*
1908	W E Klein	*Epsom*
	D Hartley	*U C S*
	B Wearne	*Bromsgrove*
	C Meadmore	*Highgate*
1909	A P Wornum	*Aldenham*
	R H Tipper	*Highgate*
1912	R F Halford	*Clifton*
1913	R A P Bevan	*Westminster*
	R S Cahn	*Westminster*
1914	C M Cahn	*Westminster*
1915	R F Bennet	*Felsted*
	F E Ballin	*Felsted*
	J E Brock	*St Paul's*
	A G Churcher	*Aldenham*
	J R Gomme	*Giggleswick*
	W G Howard	*St Edward's, Oxford*
	R M Rattenbury	*Westminster*
1916	P Lacey	*St Edward's, Oxford*
	R A Manclark	*St Edward's, Oxford*
1917	B E Malek	*Charterhouse*
	W J B Hirsch	*U C S*
	C H Hindley	*Blundell's*
	M H V Fleming	*Mill Hill*
1918	A W Franklin	*Mill Hill and Epsom*
	E N Neave	*Mill Hill*
1919	L S Falk	*Uppingham and Charterhouse*
	D R Malden	*King's, Bruton*
1920	A B Steinheim	*St Paul's*
1922	M L Rosenheim	*Shrewsbury*
	P May	*Westminster*
	A F Heim	*Mill Hill*
	T V Anthony	*Sedbergh*
	D J Loebl	*St Paul's*

1923	W S Hyde	*Stowe*
	G A Hummel	*St Paul's*
1924	A Bedford-Smith	*King's, Canterbury*
	F J B Friedeberg	*St Paul's*
1925	A Bedford-Smith	*Aldenham*
	A F L Bagley	*St Paul's*
	D E Harker	*Cheltenham and St Paul's*
1926	F N Steiner	*St Paul's*
	C L Rosenheim	*Bromsgrove*
	J O Trilling	*St Paul's*
	N J Klugman	*Cheltenham*
	P Bradley	*Highgate*
1927	N M Gordon	*Repton*
	W H Reeve	*Mill Hill*
1928	J G Allan	*Charterhouse*
	H R L Del Mar	*Marlborough*
	S J Adler	*Mill Hill*
	C Oppenheimer	*St Paul's*
	C Englander	*St Paul's*
	J R G Trenchman	*R N C, Dartmouth*
	R A Henderson	*Merchant Taylors*
1929	J S Neel	*Lancing*
	C E Feather	*Eton*
	W P G Thompson	*Glenalmond*
	S J Picciotto	*St Paul's*
	J A Scott	*St Paul's*
1930	D M Hawke	*Charterhouse*
	A C Lloyd	*Shrewsbury*
	D F Hubback	*Cheltenham*
	A D S Swenson	*Westminster*
	A Lourie	*Highgate*
	R F Mayer	*Highgate*
	D Orlik	*St Paul's*
	P R Latchman	*Highgate*
	A G F Watts	*Brighton*
	J G Dight	*R N C, Dartmouth*
	F W Wilkinson	*Dover*
	J D K Lauber	*St Paul's*
1931	H G Vevers	*St Paul's*
	D Latifi	*Rugby*
	L F Pearson	*St Paul's*
	E G Sita	*Kingswood*
	P I Bretzfelder	*St Paul's*
	C O L Coburn	*Rugby*
	M Bonham-Carter	*Clifton*
1932	L S Shultz	*St Paul's*
	P J Markbreiter	*Bedford*

	J D W Geare	*Westminster*
	J G Vaughan	*R N C, Dartmouth*
1933	O O Breakwell	*Harrow*
	P E Jarrett	*Highgate*
	P H K Kuenstler	*Rugby*
	R D Keynes	*Oundle*
	J F Wilford	*Bedford*
	J M Powell-Davies	*Wycliffe*
	D J Maisel	*Highgate*
	H S C Darke	*St Paul's*
	A K Dodds	*R N C, Dartmouth*
1934	J E Martin	*Highgate*
	H C Booth	*Highgate*
	C J C Bradshaw	*St Paul's*
	J Lister	*St Paul's*
1935	S E Toulmin	*Oundle*
	T L Zinn	*Charterhouse*
	A E Andrade	*St Paul's*
1936	J P Johnstone	*Westminster*
	D Hadfield	*Charterhouse & Eton*
	F J Bradshaw	*St Paul's*
	K F Chappel	*U C S*
	S G Waley	*St Paul's*
	O P Trubshawe	*Bedales*
	A Bowen	*St Paul's*
1937	J P G Wathen	*Harrow*
	H G Woods	*Highgate*
	R E D Harvey-Samuel	*St Paul's*
	C S Hirschman	*St Paul's*
	J L Spanyol	*Bedford*
	J Lister	*St Paul's*
1938	C C B Braune	*Gresham's*
	A D Marks	*Malvern*
	E A Faulkner	*St Paul's*
	J R Fischel	*Cheltenham*
	J C Marris	*Bryanston*
1939	J J Woodcock	*Felsted*
	P H Ramsey	*Mill Hill*
	O S Waley	*St Paul's*
	J A Hunter	*Rugby*
	K G Allison	*Westminster*
	A T S Sampson	*Westminster*
	R C Martin	*R N C, Dartmouth*
1940	A D Bradshaw	*St Paul's*
	H J D Cole	*Winchester*
	J R Gilbert	*St Paul's*
	P H Marris	*Bryanston*
1941	C H L Goodman	*Harrow*
	S Goldblatt	*Eton*
	G N Locke	*Aldenham*
	J B Visser	*Mill Hill*
	B S Read	*Framlingham*
1942	D M Shaw	*St Paul's*
1943	D B Bower	*Winchester and Oundle*
1944	N F Lewis	*Epsom*
1945	P Kovacs	*St Paul's*
	C M Moss	*St Paul's*
	A G C Paish	*St Paul's*
	M C Jaffe	*St Paul's*
	B Mindell	*St Paul's*
	C B Filmer	*R N C, Dartmouth*
	P Beckman	*St Paul's*
	B J Cryer	*St Paul's*
	O W Sacks	*St Paul's*
	A Young	*St Paul's*
1946	R C Penney	*R N C, Dartmouth*
	M E Korn	*St Paul's*
	T C Dann	*St Paul's*
	R P Harben	*Winchester*
	D L Sussman	*Clifton*
	A D G Jones	*St Paul's*
1947	G Nathan	*Mill Hill*
	M R C Lovell	*St Paul's*
	D Gilbert	*St Paul's*
1948	M Whitby	*St Paul's*
	D J Whale	*Winchester*
	S J Harris	*Rugby*
1949	M A Jackson	*Harrow*
	D L Wingate	*Harrow*
	J R W Christie-Brown	*Harrow*
	G Pincherle	*Malvern*
	R J Cryer	*St Paul's*
	E Lyons	*St Paul's*
	J D Boyd	*Westminster*
	M O L Bacharach	*St Paul's*
1950	N C Deakin	*Westminster*
	M A Marshall	*Westminster*
	G J S Ross	*Westminster*
	R F Gombrich	*St Paul's*
	J J Harris	*Rugby*
	J E Lehrer	*City of London*
1951	J M Goldman	*Westminster*
	A N Seal	*King's, Canterbury*
	C Greening	*Highgate*
1952	J Gutenstein	*St Paul's*
	H Burlingham-Rose	*Bradfield*
	L R Clayton	*Mercer's*
	B C Hurst	*Oundle*
1953	W R Dunham	*St Paul's*
	J F McCleary	*Westminster*
	D M Miall	*Stowe*
	P G W Simmonds	*Harrow*
	P F Merry	*St Benedict's*
	J N Chapple	*Rugby*
	R B de Sousa Pernes	*Bryanston*
1954	P L P Humpage	*Brighton*
	T S Lyon	*U C S*
	T M Neurath	*Charterhouse*

	D A Newton	*St Paul's*
	V T Treves	*St Paul's*
1955	M D Stern	*City of London*
	H A W Pilkington	*Rugby*
	D G Bainbridge	*Monkton Combe*
	A M Devine	*St Edward's, Oxford*
	R S Elkeles	*Highgate*
	G G Lewis	*Westminster*
	D R Myring	*Westminster*
	P R Slesser	*Ampleforth*
1956	D C Rose	*Highgate*
	A E M Fine	*St Paul's*
	W N Oulton	*Uppingham*
	M C R Paul	*Rossall*
	R F W Ungoed-Thomas	*Eton*
1957	P G Browne	*Lancing*
	J C Howard	*Westminster*
	C Irvine	*Gordonstoun*
	A P E Nathan	*St Paul's*
	G Pooley	*Westminster*
	G M Ross	*Mill Hill*
1958	J B M Roberson	*Highgate*
	D A F Gifford	*Westminster*
	F E T Sanders	*Ampleforth*
	R A Jackman	*Aldenham*
	A W Floyd	*Leighton Park*
	P Detre	*Ampleforth*
1959	A R Tresidder	*Uppingham*
	R D Fine	*St Paul's*
	J D Seres	*St Paul's*
	D Goreham	*Highgate*
	N F Simpson	*Lancing*
	A P M Dent	*Uppingham*
	N St J Hutchinson	*Bryanston*
	R J Dickinson	*Mill Hill*
	P G Levy	*Clifton*
1960	A E Durham	*Westminster*
	K M Kafetz	*Eton*
	K C Houston	*Westminster*
	S J Barber	*Uppingham*
	D J Macintyre	*Bradfield*
	J V Gifford	*Bradfield*
	R G A M Sayer	*Cranleigh*
	C F M Twigge-Molecy	*Blundell's*
	C R J Hubback	*Bryanston*
	J R B Cooper	*Bryanston*
	D L Ivory	*Frensham Heights*
1961	S A Nathan	*Cranleigh*
	S Burridge	*St Lawrence, Ramsgate*
	J W Scadding	*Bryanston*
1962	J Ashmore	*Westminster*
	R D Bainbridge	*Monkton Combe*
	A C W Beaumont	*Bryanston*
	O M J Carsten	*St Paul's*
	J W T Gairdner	*Sedbergh*
	F M Jacobs	*St Paul's*
	J Minton	*Highgate*
	J P Morton	*St Paul's*
	D Nabarro	*Clifton*
	J L E A Ravet	*Bryanston*
	H R Richmond	*Aldenham*
	T J W Scott	*Westminster*
1963	T P Besterman	*Stowe*
	N Finer	*Mill Hill*
	N Gaulk-Roger	*Westminster*
	M Henrion	*Bryanston*
	G J H Low	*Westminster*
	J C Miller-Jones	*Leighton Park*
	J H B Poole	*King's, Canterbury*
	D E H Thistlethwaite	*Lancing*
	S J Winner	*St Paul's*
	D J Zeitlin	*Highgate*
1964	J E Deanfield	*Westminster*
	H P J Karsten	*Eton*
	M C Kulukundis	*Harrow*
	R S A Lubett	*Westminster*
	A J Neuberger	*Westminster*
	R H Tyerman	*Harrow*
1965	S R Kirkham	*King William's, IOM*
	M J Lewison	*St Paul's*
	A C Mills	*Brighton*
	H E Poole	*Grenville*
	N P Warren	*Epsom*
1966	J J N Campbell	*Westminster*
	J Hermele	*City of London*
	N J Hersov	*Bryanston*
	P G D Kaufmann	*St Paul's*
	A J P Korner	*Eton*
	N J Lidwell	*Mill Hill*
	F N Morton	*St Paul's*
1967	T C Evans	*St Paul's*
	R J P Godlee	*Marlborough*
	J P Lavecky	*Eton*
	A J Rawlings	*Bloxham*
	Q A Rigby	*Cheltenham*
	J F W Sanderson	*Westminster*
	R L A Saxton	*Bryanston*
	M H Spottiswoode	*Bryanston*
	C J Tyerman	*Harrow*
1968	N V Brotherton	*Harrow*
	P Gilyard Beer	*Bloxham*
	J W Hamilton	*Bryanston*
	G M Hermele	*Eton*
	J S Joseph	*Harrow*
	R L M Schlee	*Ampleforth*
	R W Unite	*St Paul's*
	P E O Williams	*Mill Hill*
1969	A C Evans	*Uppingham*
	G A Hersov	*Bryanston*
	P Hodgson	*Westminster*

	N J A Littlewood	*Westminster*
	M A Pappeneim	*St Paul's*
	A J Reizenstein	*St Paul's*
1970	T J English	*Highgate*
	W J Hamilton	*Bryanston*
	J L Rawlinson	*Eton*
	M L Speyer	*Bloxham*
	T J Vulliamy	*U C S*
1971	R B Cattell	*Marlborough*
	J A Crowcroft	*Bedales*
	A M Dodd	*Bloxham*
	M R Gottlieb	*Eton*
	D C Owen	*Marlborough*
	J M Wood	*Monkton Combe*
1972	P L H Brooke	*Westminster*
	N B Dillon	*Eton*
1973	J H Arnott	*Oundle*
	T W Bailey	*Westminster*
	D W S Black	*U C S*
	S W S Chatterton	*Leighton Park*
	R M Durbin	*Highgate*
	J A Erskine	*U C S*
	T M Gladstone	*Highgate*
	A J Lowe	*Bloxham*
	A C Maroudas	*St Paul's*
	J A Moody	*Westminster*
1974	E J Bishop	*King's, Canterbury*
	J O Goldblatt	*Eton*
	D A Kampfner	*St Paul's*
	P Marshall	*Westminster*
	G J Mulgan	*Westminster*
1975	D Freedman	*Westminster*
	R J F Lemkin	*Westminster*
	L M Lyons	*Highgate*
	O J Moore	*Bryanston*
	R C Peters	*Marlborough*
	M A S Poole	*Marlborough*
	D J Reid	*Oundle*
1976	A J Durbin	*Highgate*
	M V R Lightbown	*Westminster*
	M C S Lloyd	*Bryanston*
	F I Maroudas	*St Paul's*
	R D Simon	*Clifton*
1977	W R Brandon	*Winchester*
	G D Gampell	*Charterhouse*
	S L Pearce	*U C S*
	W J P Wrathall	*Westminster*
1978	C W Potter	*Westminster*
	G W B Smith	*Clifton*
	H J B Smith	*Eton*
1979	D C Little	*Tonbridge*
1980	T H Bingham	*Winchester*
	A J Dale	*Westminster*
	T D Gee	*Marlborough*
	M C Jefferson	*Felsted*
	D W Runciman	*Eton*
1981	O W A Rock	*Eton*
	A N Rosenthal	*U C S*
	A S Williams	*Westminster*
1982	F Davis	*City of London*
	J S Lambert	*Westminster*
	G N Pugh	*Marlborough*
	B J B Smith	*Clifton*
	L P R Tennant	*Eton*
1983	H J Baring	*Eton*
	G H Crown	*St Paul's*
	E G W Keene	*Westminster*
	J H Read	*Westminster*
	M J Blau	*St Paul's*
1984	J M H Harris	*City of London*
	C T Lambert	*Eton*
	D M Rosenthal	*U C S*
	I St P Slatter	*Marlborough*
	N C Warner	*Harrow*
1985	O N J Blackburn	*Westminster*
	S D Levene	*St Paul's*
	J G Polonsky	*St Paul's*
	M J T Preston	*St Paul's*
	G A Rook	*The Leys*
1986	A D Blau	*St Paul's*
	E A Cargill Thompson	*Harrow*
	N B Coates	*Highgate*
	M R Fara	*Westminster*
	L F Gillam	*Westminster*
	M B Godfrey	*St Paul's*
	A J Warner	*Harrow*
1987	W A Kirk-Wilson	*Marlborough*
	M M Lavy	*Winchester*
	T P G Le Quesne	*Marlborough*
	A E Osmond	*Eton*
1988	E F Bell	*Harrow*
	A C M Davenport	*Highgate*
	N R Jackson	*U C S*
	M R A Mocatta	*Highgate*
	R T N Preston	*St Paul's*

APPENDIX 6

The Sixth Form Society

The Hall Sixth Form Society was created by R A Cooper and instantly became an institution that may scarcely be matched in any other prep school. For this reason alone, it merits a special mention in this history.

An august minute-book contains on its title page the following brief exposition of the constitution:

> The Society was inaugurated at a meeting in the Billiard Room on 1st February 1957. There were present: the Headmaster, Linwood Sleigh Esq, and twenty-seven boys. The Headmaster made the following points.
>
> 1. The purpose of the Society was to bring members of the VIth Forms in contact with interesting people and subjects not normally part of the school curriculum.
> 2. It would meet normally three times a term; one meeting occasionally to be a debate.
> 3. Meetings to be on Fridays or Tuesdays, during Prep time.
> 4. Members were to be elected by age or seniority, not to exceed 27 in number.
> 5. The Headmaster would be President; L Sleigh Esq, Vice-President and the Staff Honorary members.
> 6. A committee should consist of President, Vice-President, Chairman and Secretary.
> 7. A Senior Prefect, normally the Captain of School, should be Chairman.

It should be remarked that since this was reported some significant modifications have occurred:

The Billiard Room has become the Staff Common-room, and meetings are held in the main hall.

Meetings take place at the possibly rather less popular times after full school.

The numbers have grown to match the increase in the sixth form. Up to 40 boys are now elected.

Over the following thirty years, some 280 meetings were held. In the summer of 1987, the anniversary was celebrated with a special programme which included a visit to Lord's as the guest of the Treasurer, Hubert Doggart, during the bicentenary celebrations of the MCC; a debate with the girls of South Hampstead High School on the same motion, the merits of co-education, as had been held on the very second meeting in 1957; and a special all-day expedition to Greenwich as guests of the Maritime Museum to see, among other things, the reserve collection at Kidbrooke, not normally shown to the public. The Society's very first guest speaker, David Davis, (Uncle David of BBC *Children's Hour*) was invited to return, but pleaded understandable 'seniority' in asking to be excused.

Over the ninety terms of its existence, a long string of very distinguished, interesting and important names have appeared in the Society's Minute Book. A selection of these follows:
Dame Peggy Ashcroft, Hon David Astor, Sir Douglas Bader, Lord Balneil, Raymond Baxter, James Blades, Edward Blishen, Ray Buckton, James Cameron, Admiral Sir Desmond Cassidi, Col Spencer Chapman, Sir Colin Davis, Clement Freud, Martin Gilbert, Lord Home, Lady Howe, Lord Jay, Brian Johnstone, Sir Keith Joseph, John le Carré, Marghanita Laski, Sir Richard Marsh, Professor PB Medawar, Lady Medawar, Bernard Miles, Lord Norwich, John Pardoe, Professor Nickolas Pevsner, Dilys Powell, Lord Roskill, Anthony Sampson, Professor Keith Simpson, Geoffrey Smith, General Sir John Stanier, Sir John Summerson, E W Swanton, John Tusa, Reverend Chad Varah, Wynford Vaughan-Thomas and Kenneth Williams.
(Titles as at the time of the visit).

APPENDIX 7

The Early Magazines

It was in the spring of 1904 that the first formal printed magazine appeared. The editor, in its opening page, implied that a lively literary tradition existed, although he did not refer to any specific school journal which might claim to have anticipated this production. He referred, rather extravagantly, to the evident mountains of contributions from eager 'budding journalists'. He went on to explain, perhaps a shade pretentiously: 'This entirely non-political journal will appear twice a year, and is designed to be an abstract and brief chronicle of the times, as well as to elicit the latent literary talent of Belsizians, present and past.' The rather grand style attached to what was, by standards of later years, a modest production, rarely as many as twenty pages in length, extended even to its manufacture. Printed by Priory Press, of St John's Street, London EC, it aspired to the dignity of a publisher, in the form of Sydney C Mayle, of 70 High Street, Hampstead. Its cost was one shilling.*

The Hall was not the first preparatory school to boast a formal termly or annual magazine. A few schools had such productions at least a decade earlier than the first Belsize School Magazine of 1904. The Hall is lucky to possess such an early record. The editor was justly proud of this new venture.

A single collected volume of the 10 issues of what we must, for reasons shortly to be explained, refer to as Volume 0 of the Magazine has survived. It was the editor's personal copy, which came to an Old Boy, H W Dallas, a pupil throughout the years these magazines cover. Dallas presented it to The Hall at the time of the 75th Anniversary celebration, in October 1964.

The editor was Mr W W Osborn. He was undoubtedly a man of many parts, the type of prep school all-rounder that the more specialised curriculum of later years has made impossible. His marriage in September 1908 is reported on the final page of the 10th and last issue of this series, immediately above a notice of Dallas's appointment as a prefect. Whether it was the editor's new domestic responsibilities or the departure shortly afterwards of the Headmaster we can only guess, but from 1909 sadly no further issues seem to have appeared. If they did, no copy has survived in the school's collection. Osborn left The Hall for Ovingdean School, Sussex, to be with

*Eighty years later, the cost per copy had risen 200-fold!

Marshall, who took over the headship there that same year. A new regime at The Hall under the energetic Montauban began.

In due course, a new format of magazine was devised and launched, in 1913. The most curious thing about this new venture was the seeming lack of any awareness of its precursor. The series which continues unbroken to the present day, apart from the Winter term of 1939, begins again at issue No 1 of what was regarded as Volume I.

The earliest numbers of the magazine came from the Belsize School. The transfer to Crossfield Road occurred in time for a somewhat cursory reference in the fourth issue. But the title of the magazine remained unaltered for a further 28 issues: it remained the Belsize School. A curious uncertainty seems to permeate its pages. Belsize and Hall seem interchangeable, and the boys themselves clearly felt the tradition of being members of the first quite as strongly as of the second.

It was however the combined effects of major wartime expansion and the enforced division of the school with the partial evacuation to Berkshire which resolved the issue. The retirement of Montauban from the Senior School in 1920 clinched the matter. Gladstone and his partner came to The Hall and forgot the Belsize heritage and from their first term, with Vol III no 5, the magazine abruptly switches its name to The Hall Magazine.

Back in 1904, when the first editor explained the function of the magazine, there is a significant lack of obvious official backing for the venture: approval and encouragement, doubtless, but no formal school support in the key area of finance. Hence, an appeal to Old Boys for subscriptions and news follows the cry, in the opening page of issue No 1, to readers within the school for literary contributions. When in 1913, Montauban saw the re-launch of the 'new' magazine, the same explicit financial restraints were in force.

The figures make quaint reading with the passage of time. In 1917, in issue 15, the accounts are published. Subscription income was £23 5 7½d (£23.28), representing about 450 sales at 1/– (5p) each. One must suppose that the value of this vehicle for school publicity gradually became more recognised as a school responsibility, for the references to financial constraints disappear.

The magazine can provide an interesting indicator of priorities attached to the various areas of school activity. By the mid-'20s, the picture is in fact faintly surprising, for the proportion devoted to sport implies that it ruled the minds of all – when clearly, at The Hall, it didn't. Issue 44, of September 1927 was 45 pages in length. Sport in all its manifestations is given 25 pages, and the literary contributions scarcely occupy a single page.

This lack of boys' writing is the more surprising because the school was no less articulate or full of ideas and opinions than sixty years later. Furthermore, it was powerfully encouraged in its English work by Wathen, a passionate advocate of the subject. Sadly, all too little flair in original writing is evident in the pages of the magazines in the third and fourth decades of the school's history. One item deserves quotation, not because of its particular merit, but because of the identity of its author. The young Stephen Spender*, at his Public School in Hampstead, bequeathed this doubtless forgotten piece as a leaving present; quite why it is included in the 1927 issue is unclear, since he left The Hall in 1923!

The Poet in Spring: *A Triolet*

I must not write about the spring,
    However much I long.
It would be such a hackeneyed *(sic)* thing;
I must not write about the spring.
I'd like it much to rhyme with 'sing',
    And 'heard' and 'bird' aren't wrong –
I must not write about the spring!
    However much I long . . .

Forty years on from the school's foundation, its magazine was an established feature. As a vehicle for Old Boys' reports, as a journal of record and as a means of recording school news and views term by term with, by now, regular illustrations, either of leavers who had distinguished themselves or groups of boys or staff, The Hall magazine was on its way to becoming what it has developed into by the 1980s, an essential annual publicity document, heavily subsidised by school funds and produced with quality of content and presentation as a prime consideration.

*Later knighted, and quoted as a contender for the Poet Laureateship

APPENDIX 8

The Aims of The Hall School

Partly in response to a national mood of educational reform and revaluation, the Headmaster was instructed by the Governors in June 1984 to draw up a policy statement which indicated the philosophy of The Hall for the 1980s. It was observed at the time that such a document could easily appear both trite and smug. What follows is something of a personal expression of the views of the current Headmaster, as approved by his two deputies, Robert Chambers and Julia Allen. It amplifies what was then stated in the prospectus. It became the informal statement of the philosophy of The Hall which the Governors were thereafter pleased to disseminate publicly, and it is therefore an historic document worthy of record in these pages.

The Hall cannot escape being affected by its history and its location. The parents of its boys have a quite distinctive attitude and bring to bear positive influences on the boys. The school would be imprudent to ignore this fact in assessing its aims. Hence it has taken a more progressive view than most Preparatory Schools over content of curriculum and over the relationship between teacher and taught. Today, these trends have grown more widespread, and The Hall has kept pace with them. The curriculum has to take into account the requirements of the examinations boys sit at 13 but every effort is taken to keep the content as wide as possible, to allocate time to non-examined activities and to implement the ideal that exams are a means to an end and not ends in themselves. Boy/staff relationships today are less formal than in many schools. The ideal is that a balance is struck between the two sides, of mutual affection and respect. Formalised rules and regulations are kept to a bare minimum.

This is not to say that the school is indifferent to ill-discipline or bad manners and the school does attempt to establish clearly the boundaries beyond which poor personal and social behaviour becomes unacceptable. The prefectorial hierarchy (as normally understood) doesn't exist. The hope is that boys will work if they are encouraged to adopt self-discipline rather than by an imposed discipline: that true satisfaction over every aspect of school life arises when a boy is properly motivated to want to achieve, and such motivation can occur in a free and openly stimulating community.

This approach is designed to achieve long term and lasting educational success. It is less 'efficient', it permits occasional short term 'failures' and it is certainly far harder work for the staff than a more structured regulated, regimented system. And it doesn't always suit every boy. However, it is in character with the traditions of The Hall and it does create generally a mature, self-assured and genuinely independent-minded boy, which is what I have no doubt the Public Schools welcome.

In applying all the above, the dangers of arrogance, elitism and precocity and of apparent liberalism degenerating into licence are, I believe, constantly in the minds of us all.

I firmly believe, and remind all prospective parents, that a Preparatory School is meant to prepare and not perfect. We are not here to turn out a finished article. To over-laud the 13 year old, giving him illusions of greatness of achievement and magnitude of authority, often the result of intensive drilling and driving, leads to premature 'peaking' and the onset of severe disillusionment. Such boys may never again in their lives sense in themselves such feelings of grandeur. It is rather sad if you reach your apogee before puberty! Furthermore, results gained by strait-jacket methods of externally applied pressures, however skilfully or humanely done cannot be in the best long-term interest of the young. Their faculties, stretched to the break point as the result of the whips being out, inevitably slacken the moment the whips are withdrawn. Limbs, used to operating only with the support of a scaffolding of directed instruction, atrophy the moment the scaffold is removed. Such methods gain spectacular results in the short term. The Hall however remains far more concerned with the medium and long term. While never indifferent to examination results or the marks scored, it prefers to be judged by the progress its boys make after they have left rather than by the glitter of their performance as they leave.

I am absolutely satisfied that the majority of Hall boys are indeed thoroughly well prepared not so much in accumulated knowledge as in attitude of mind to do better and better at their Public Schools. I cannot provide statistical proof and the disappointments and failures are perhaps discreetly kept from my notice; but that the vast majority do thus progress I am totally confident.

R P H

APPENDIX 9

Selected Class Lists

(Note: There follow three complete class lists of The Hall, chosen to represent evenly distanced and significant points in the school's history: Easter 1924, Easter 1954 and Autumn 1988. These show the school at the moment when GAW joined, when he departed, and when the school reached its centenary year. It may be observed that the first two appear as a final class order of merit, while the third is purely an alphabetical order. This change in policy was made in the late 1950s, one of Cooper's innovations.)

Final Order, March 1924

Senior School

VIa	VIb	C.E.	V
Salvi	Orlik	MacLulich	Klugman
Grumbar i	Furth	Rae	Klauber
Bagley i	Price	Bowack	Gordon
Rees	Payne	Winter i	Peacock
Weiss	May	Paton	Miall
Levison	Edwards	Vashkoff	Bradley
Harker	Stuart	de Smith	Carton
Bedford-Smith	Abell	Giesecke	Brown
Steiner	Nathan		Rosenheim
Griffith Jones			Kunstler
Friedeberg			Welford
Eagleston			Macdonald
			Soutar
			Pearce
			Atkinson
			Marriott

IV	III	II	I
Whitney-Smith	Swyers	Stern	Bruce
Maisel	Jolowicz	Grumbar ii	Neter
Wathen ii	Austin	Mason	Holland
Trilling	Salamon	Lotinga i	Marquand
Bagley ii	Rowe i	Solomon	Winter ii
Drummond-Hay	Densham	Scholl	Wykes
Neroslavsky	Wertheimer	Raffety	Ward
Worobieff	Gardiner	Maddocks	Stansbury
Yarrow	de Laszlo	Plimmer	Rowe ii
Wathen i	Lourie	Lotinga ii	Allan
Sarkies	Berger	Vernon	Dodd
Woolf i	Bayes	Pycroft	
Earle	Franks	Morriss	
Kennedy	Davis	Shearman	
Del Mar	Stockford		
Croom-Johnson	Woolf ii		

Junior School

A	B.I	B.II
Neroslavsky	Jordan	Wertheim
Oppenheimer	Martin	Berger
Stride	Allan	Harbury
Atkinson	Neel	Clarke ii
Steiner	Blake	Cobourn
Salamon	Seymour	Hubbard i
Erroll	Adler iii	Rappaport
Speelman	Farman	Mc Gregor
Lyons	Englander	Adler ii
Joseph	McLeod	Gilchrest
Barnett	Abrahams	Coppel i
Croom-Johnson	Goldschmidt	Whiley
Del Mar	Shann i	Adler i
	Strauss	Scott i
	Clark-Wilson i	Nares
	Campbell	Kisch
	Lawson	Gosschalk
	Lang	Clark i
	Monico	Salamon
	Levy	

C.I	C.II
Gee	Wilson i
Feather	Friedberg
Scholl	Wilson ii
Cohen i	Hubbard ii
Scott ii	Johnson
Miall	Orlik
Bedford-Smith	Greaves
Cranston	Luker
Fraser ii	Hill
Kunstler	Ehrmann
Zimbler	Smith
Coppel ii	Stanford
Sokal	Clarke iii
Fraser i	Musman
Cohen ii	Bertish
Charig	Veale
Druiff	Salamon ii
Tyser	

Minimi

Div I	Div IIA	Div IIB	Div III
Melford	George	Vevers	Rhodes ii
Coburn	Lourie	Stephany	Morton
Landauer	Franklin ii	Bleasby	Canti
Gardiner	Frankau	Cheeswright	Clark-Wilson ii
Klauber	Drage	Walker	Ward
Theodor	Shann ii	Gilbey	Lee
Yavchick	Barnett ii	Friedberg ii	Soref
Rhodes i	Kennedy		Gray
Picciotto			
Franklin i			
Staal			
Edwards			

Final Order, March 1954

Senior School

UVI	MVIA	MVIB	LVI
Pilkington	Helby	Elkeles	Allen
Neurath	Epstein	Mackenzie, M	Jacobs, H
Devine	Berger	Bainbridge	Tweddell
Palairet	Reichwald	Lewis, W G	Trist
Lyon	Macalpine	Ungoed-Thomas, R	Stansbury
Myring	Kensit	Whyte	Jacobs, T
Lewis, G	Blennerhassett	Colvin	Young
Thompson	Humpage	Slesser	Jenkins
Gordon	Gibbs, R	Kolb	Lewis, M L
Sonabend	Starling	Fine	Rainer
Wingate	Wood,	Hill	Rob
Cole	Marks	Brough	Curry
Sedgwick	Lowenstein	Oulton	Leach
Buckman	Mackie	Robertson, H	Baxter
Stern	Rushton	Bennett, N	Barrett
	Greayer	Rado	Robertson, J
	Stoneman	Medawar	Edward
	Smith	Gilbert	Chester
	Stowe	Lidwell	Whittuck
	Diamond	Nathan	Koby
		de Wardener	Lee
			Herbertson

UV	MVA	MVB
Holmes, J	Hamilton, M	Cooper
Hawkins, M	Pollard	Dixon
Kane	Freeman	Harvey
Lockwood	Goss	Groves
Rose	Davey	Harley
Yoffey	Kearsey	Irvine
Dicks	Layton, J	Harford
Rigby-Jones	Bieber	Eisen
Eskdale	Payne	Dunbar
Jackson	Uhlman	Winkler
Howard	Hillman	Spence
Neel	Lee Clarke	Stewart
Ralph	Rumble	Hayward
Soskice	Bowlby	Woolf
Stone	Cameron	Viklund
Helby	Wilson	Shaine
		Barnett
		Lossos
		Williams
		Harris, P

UIV	MIV	LIV
Karsten	Villeneuve	Seres, J
Leach, D	Gee	Pollard
Humphreys	Garvin	Scott
Bonehill	Sumner	Wood, K
Greenstone	Manderson	Floyd
Seres	Lewis, B E	Hughes, J
Miller Jones	Hawkins, R	Hyman
Ader	Rowen	Renton
Edler	Dickinson	de Lotbiniere
Ross	Dow, A R	Ronson
Hamilton, A	Greayer, A	Worledge
Brown	Paul	Hartley
Asher	Snowman	Wellings
Curtis	Horder	Cohn
Purcell Manser	Bundy	Mackenzie
McDowall	Posner	Hughes, O
Holmes, J T	Sonabend	Paterson
de Sousa Pernes	Cansino	Mason
Roberson	Cartmell	Marsh
Selwyn	Nesbitt	
Lawson	Hamilton, N	
	Pincombe	

Junior School

Upper 3	Middle 3A	Middle 3B
Gifford, P	Cameron, B	Sanders
Lucia	Rose, L	Bennett, C H
Bender	Ward, M V	Gordon, H
Hale, A	Nicholls	Meredith
Tresidder	Whittuck, A	Maitland
Jessup	Neel, A	Cunningham
Melville	Rosner	Hitchman
Harris	Wichmann, O	Kahn
Layton, M	Wilson	Shane
Arnold	de Wynter	Winterbottom, N
Prideaux	Low	Gardiner
Thomas	Richards, A	Levin
Saphir	Lewis, E	Cole, B M
Ramsey		Spender
Cockburn, A		McCormick, B
Nares		Marin, C A
Manwaring		Dent
Garrett		Goreham
		Cooper, C S

Upper 2	Middle 2	Lower 2
Christian	Campbell Johnson	Winterbottom, T
Lewis, M Q	Summerson, E	Woolf, I
Curtis Clarke	Shepperd	Karmel
Enthoven	Kent	Gifford, J
McDowall, D	Summerson, R	Gaster
Hawksley	Ravenscroft	Berger
Fine, R	Hamilton, N D	Brough, C L
Schieldrop	Phillips	Summerson, T
Ward, J P	Bird	Hayward, F H
Winkleman	Wynbourne, S A	Braithwaite, A
Gant	Buchholz	Wrottesley
Gumb	Simpson	McCormick, M
Callow	Ritterman	Barrett, J
Lee Clarke, D	Goldsmith	
Kearsey, T	Goss, T	
Burchard	Patten	
Rumble, N		
Wynbourne, A S		
Griffiths		

Upper 1	Middle 1	Lower 1
Elliott	Gross	Cameron, E
Rob, P	Finer	Woolf, C
Levy	Chitty	MacDonald
Rigby Jones, N	Wickmann, F	Harraway
Marin, S G	Twigge Molecey	Martin
Harvey, H	Fountain	Buckley Sharp
Kleiner	Searle	Bennett, J M
Fitzgerald	Bainbridge, P	Vaughan
Kay	Braithwaite, H	Cocking
Chapman	Reichwald, P	Garvin, D
Lossos	Hamilton, J	
Renton, A		
Woodhouse		
MacPhee		

Final Order, Centenary Year September 1988

Senior School

Upper VIC	Upper VIF	Upper VIM	Middle VIA
Agnew	Boyd	Brendel	Birksted
Beer	Brass	Brostoff	Buckley
Cole	Cannon	Copeland P	Cartwright J
Dellinger	Clayton	Crocker	Claassen
Glyn	Cooke	Dixon	Conway-Gordon
Haines F	Firebrace	Fisher W	Danos
Howard S	Flesch	Holden S	Florentin-Lee Y
Kirk-Wilson	Karger	Howard N	Forsyth M
Shapiro J	Mosley	Jackson	Francis
Strelitz	Sandler A	Jacobs B	Hameed H
Vanhegan H	Sherwood	Mulder	Holden J
Wilson N	Willison	Osborne	Hunt
Wright T	Woolman	Preiskel	Jacobs J
		Roth	Lerner
		Scott	Meek
		Singer	Oldroyd
		Strathdene	Roberts J
			Wicks

Middle VIH	V I	V V	V W
Baughan J	Blee	Berger	Blank
Brough	Dives	Coltart	Bloom
Brunner	Goldsmith	Durban P	Cecil
Davis	Green J	Eley	Durham
Eppel J	Jackling O	Eppel M	Gee
Fisher T	Lambert	Fox	Hay B
Gibberd M	Lawrie R	Franks	Hegde
Green I	McEwen D	Fry	Jacobs A
Gripari	Monro	Goldman	Kwok
Gross	Paul	Hayter W	Milligan
Haines R	Powell	Lascelles	Morgan W
Humphrey X	Prevezer	Lawrie W	Paleocrassas N
Trup S	Pryce	Rice	Roberts J
Ward	Ratzer	Sussman	Sanderson
Webb J	Schram	Welsford	Shapiro J
Wilton	Stern O	Wilson B	Thomas
Zeki	Webb A	Wyand	Williams

IVA	IV N	IV W
Archibald	Atherton	Baughan N
Felix	Bean A	Berry
Forwood	Boucher M	Betney
Gibberd D	Jacobs T	Boot
Hinton T	Johnston-Wood	Hornak
Holden B	Karimjee	Humphrey A
Los	Kerr-Dineen	Law
Maule	King C	Lipka
Potter	Latner N	Lorimer J
Sallon	McEwen D	MacLennan
Sandler J	McIvor	Melvin
Silverstone	McKinnon	Offenbach
Smadja	Michaels	Ross
Trup J	Mocatta	Waltham
Watkins R	Roskill M	Youngstein
Wise	Rushdie	
Wober	Shelley	
Zalocosta	Slatter	

Junior School

IIIC	IIIM	IIIW
Abrahams	Beecroft	Clark
Beards	Bradley A	Copeland M
Boulderstone E	Cartwright S	Eppel G
Camber	Chadwick	Farmiloe
Eziefula	Clegg	Gripari L
Glass	Cox	Hall
Gray	Crystal David	Hinton D
Jenkins T	David	Levin T
Knight	Leader N	Lorimer W
Lee	Metliss	Nedas
Livanos	Morton	Omond M
Nabarro L	Ormerod	Paleocrassas A
Odgers	Pantucci R	Payman
Paisner N	Royalton-Kisch M	Phillips
Ponniah D	Smith	Sinclair
Rankin	Stern W	Skeaping
Sinden	Webb W	Sofer
Van Allan	Wilson B	Spinney
Watts	Xylander-Swannell	Steinfeld M

IIDP	IIL	IIW	IH
Bamberger C	Ainger	Alaghband	Boulderstone T
Brearley	Aiyela A	Chappell	Camrass
Fry R	Arnold	Forsyth J	Cherniavsky
Futter	Bean T	Georgi	Cunningham
Garton	Boucher R	Hameed I	Farthing
Harrison	Charlton	Hayter G	Jenkins E
McFadden W	Crane	Hicks	Leader M
Naftalin	Durban D	Hurndall	Lewison
Palmer	Farren	Hurst	Morgan H
Roskill O	Florentin-Lee B	Jackling T	O'Kelly
Salem	Goodkind	Lawrence	Rainer
Sellers	Hay F	Luthy	Reicher
Tilberis	Hickox	Neicho	Shuckburgh
Vanhegan I	Pryce A	Omond A	Sommer
Wilcox	Rose	Reid	Sorrell
Wood	Rosen	Stone	Steinfeld S
Wyand	Thompson	Vanhegan T	Wilson S
		Wright C	

Kindergarten

IKW	IPW	01	02
Beaton	Allsop	Aiyela T	Brunner N
Churchill B J	Carvalho A	Bamberger	Carvalho
Dives J	Dana	Braune	Dissanyake
Hazell	Englehart	Brough N	Goldman
King J	Eppel L	Churchill T	Guy
Latner R	Lockett	Forwood A	Levy
Levin A J	Pantucci N	Goldsmith	Littlejohn
Long	Peek	Kohli	Nabarro A
Sebag-Montefiore	Pritchard	McFadden S	Sallon J
Shaw	Robson	Norris	Wadhwani
Vicefield	Rodopoulous	Paisner S	Wilson T
Watkins H	Siddle	Ponniah S	Yorke
	Simpson	Reizenstein	
	Stacey	Rook	
	Sternberg	Royalton-Kisch D	
	Walt	Sadie	
		Silver	
		Stern A	

HALL SCHOOL STAFF

September 1988

Headmaster: R P Heazell, MA, Dip Ed
Principal of Junior School: Miss C J Allen, Cert Ed
Deputy Headmaster: P C Cheeseman, BA, Dip d'Et Fr

Senior School Staff

Miss E R Aitken, BA, PGCE, (D&T, science)
Miss K Anderson, BA, (General subjects)
C J M Cutcliffe, MA, BSc, (Physics & chemistry)
M J FitzMaurice, A C P, Cert Ed, (Maths & computing)
C A Gilbey-Mackenzie, MA, (English & drama)
G J Heazell, MA, Cert Ed, (Geography)
C J Hely, BA, (Maths & PE)
P R Ilott, BA, (History)
A T Kyan, BA, PGCE, (French)
E J Newton, BA, PGCE, (Classics)
Mrs A B Smith, BA, (Classics, French: Academic Tutor)
J A Southall, BA, (Biology)
Rev M D Vine, MA, (Maths)
T Wincott, T Dip, (English & Librarian)
Mme N Woodin, Bac. Fr., (French)

Junior School Staff

Miss K M Crew, B Ed
Miss S M Douglas-Pennant, B Ed
Miss N J Fletcher, B Ed
Mrs C Hurley, B Ed
Mrs J Le Moine, B Ed
Mrs J Mance, Cert Ed
Miss L Timmis
Mrs A Webb, B Ed
Miss S L Wedd, B Ed
Miss P Weld, Cert Ed
Miss S L Wesson, B Ed
Miss K D Whitelaw, B Ed
Miss G E Wilson, B Ed

Music Department

Director of music: R V Pipes, LTCL, A Cert CM
Music master, Junior School: R Wilkins, BMus, LRAM
Head of strings: Miss K Sweeney, LRAM
Director of Group string classes: Mrs W Max

A G C Adams, LTCL ('cello & bass)
Miss T Brain, GRSM, LRAM (brass)
M A Burke, Dip. RCM, (guitar)
Miss H Goode, G Mus RNCM, (oboe & clarinet)
Mrs K Gordon, LRAM, (piano)
A Hampton, BA, (clarinet & saxophone)
Miss L McLarin, BA, Dip RAM, (flute)
Miss M Polasek, LRSM, ARCM, (piano)

Art Department

Head of art: Miss P Trent, BA, PGCE
Mrs R de Lacey
Mrs M McGowan (pottery)

Administrative and support staff

Bursar: Mrs F H Rollason
School Secretary: Mrs I M Davies
Principal of Junior School's assistant secretary: Mrs K Gordon
School Medical Officer: Dr N Elliott Burrows
Senior Matron: Mrs H Justice
Junior school matron: Mrs S A Morgan
Caterer and senior cook: Mrs B J Lazenby
Assistant cook: Mrs G Watson
School caretaker: Mr Stan Bond
Building maintenance: Mr Chris Coltman
Repair maintenance: Mr Pat Murphy
Principal cleaning staff: Mrs Elaine Longinotti
Mrs Maureen Wilson